Russia
and the
Commonwealth

Regional Studies Series

The Regional Studies Series

Africa
China
Europe
The Subcontinent of India
Japan and Korea
Latin America
The Middle East and North Africa
Russia and the Commonwealth

Russia
and the
Commonwealth

Regional Studies Series

Consultant

Michael Kort

GLOBE BOOK COMPANY
A Division of Simon & Schuster
Paramus, New Jersey

Michael Kort

Michael Kort holds a doctoral degree in Russian history from New York University. He is associate professor of social science at the College of General Studies of Boston University. He has written several books, including *The Soviet Colossus: A History of the USSR* and has written biographies of Mikhail Gorbachev and Nikita Khrushchev. He is also a consultant of the volume on China in Globe Book's Regional Studies Series.

Area Specialist: Allen Lynch, former assistant director, W. Averell Harriman Institute at Columbia University; associate professor of Government and Foreign Affairs at the University of Virginia

Reviewer: Bruce Rosen, social studies teacher, Edison Technical High School, Rochester, New York

Executive Editor: Stephen Lewin
Project Editor: Helene Avraham
Art Director: Nancy Sharkey
Cover Designer: Armando Baez
Photo Research: Jenifer Hixson
Production Manager: Winston Sukhnanand
Manufacturing Coordinator: Lisa Cowart
Marketing Manager: Elmer Ildefonso

Cover Image: After the coup of August 1991, the people of the former Soviet Union began openly to express feelings of nationalism. This photo shows the citizens of Moscow unfurling a gigantic Russian flag in front of St. Basil's Cathedral on Red Square.

Maps: Mapping Specialists, Ltd.
Graphs, Diagrams, and Charts: Keithley & Associates

Photograph acknowledgments appear on page 274

ISBN 835-90428-8

Printed in the United States of America   7 8 9 10

CONTENTS

Graphs, Charts, and Diagrams

Introduction:
The Fall of a Superpower

For more than 350 years, from the early 1600s until the late 1900s, one gigantic country stretched from Eastern Europe across Asia to the Pacific shore. For most of the period before 1917 that country's name was Russia, or the Russian Empire, and was ruled by the Russian czar (ZAHR). In 1917, Russia collapsed and its czar was overthrown. After several years of turmoil and civil war, the country was reunified under a Communist dictatorship. In 1922, it was renamed the Union of Soviet Socialist Republics, or Soviet Union.

The Russian Empire, and later the Soviet Union, was the largest country in the world. At its peak size in the 1800s and 1900s, it had an area of more than 8.6 million square miles (22.3 million square kilometers). More than 100 different national groups lived within its vast borders. It had abundant resources, including large quantities of timber and oil and much rich farmland. The Soviet Union was larger than two of the world's continents — Australia and South America, and almost as large as North America. Both its nextdoor neighbors and distant nations were in awe of its size and feared its power.

Despite its size and resources, Russia suffered many hardships during its history. Most of Russia's people were poor farmers who were serfs. Until 1861, these peasants could not move from the estates they worked on, but could be sold by the owner of the land. Often there was famine and several times there were violent rebellions of serfs against their owners. Russia fought long and bitter wars with many of its neighbors during the 1600s, 1700s, and 1800s. During the first half of the 1900s, when Russia became the Soviet Union, its people were battered by war, revolution, civil war, invasions, famines, and terror under a Communist dictatorship.

Continued Growth. Despite its many problems, this enormous country managed to survive and continue growing. During the 1800s, Russia conquered additional territory in both central and eastern Asia, as well as in Europe. In the years immediately after 1917, the Soviet Union lost a little of its territory in Europe. It later regained some of that land and added new European territory to its possessions.

By the mid-1900s, the Soviet Union, along with the United States, was one of the world's two superpowers. While the United States was the leader of the world's capitalist nations, the Soviet Union was the world's leading communist nation. Each superpower had a huge arsenal of nuclear weapons capable of wiping out life on earth.

The Soviet Union also had other impressive strengths. Until the 1980s, only the United States produced more goods and services than it did. Beyond its own borders, the Soviet Union controlled a bloc of countries in Eastern Europe. It had allies all over the world. It was one of only five nations with a permanent seat on the United Nations Security Council. With almost 290 million people, the Soviet Union trailed only China and India in population.

The Beginnings of Collapse. Although by the 1980s the Soviet Union faced major problems, few people thought these problems were serious enough to threaten the country's survival. Yet that is exactly what happened. In 1985, a new leader named Mikhail Gorbachev came to power in the Soviet Union. He began a reform program, attempting to solve the country's serious economic, social, and political problems. Gorbachev introduced free elections and tried to reform the Soviet Union's inefficient planned economy. As you will read in Chapter 6, Gorbachev's policies did not solve the Soviet Union's problems. Rather, his reforms were followed by radical political, social, and economic changes that Gorbachev himself was unable to control.

Most dangerous for the Soviet Union, the non-Russian nationalities within the Soviet Union began to demand more freedom. Some even demanded complete independence. They rejected the argument that officially the Soviet Union was a voluntary union of 15 republics, each representing one of the major nationalities in the country. To them, the Soviet Union was nothing but the Russian Empire in a new form. Its largest republic belonged to the Russian people and contained half the population and three quarters of the territory of the Soviet Union. In addition, Russians held most of the important positions in the Communist party and the Soviet government. In other words, the 14 non-Russian republics believed they were little more than territories controlled by the Russian-dominated Soviet government.

The End of a Nation. In 1991, after six tumultuous years of reform and radical change, the Soviet Union, like the Russian Empire before it, collapsed. Unlike the 1917 collapse, there were no forces powerful enough to restore unity. Instead, the country broke apart.

The blow that shattered the Soviet Union was a coup, or uprising, in August 1991 by old-line Communists opposed to Gorbachev's reforms. The plotters held Gorbachev under house arrest for three days, but their coup collapsed, and Gorbachev was restored to power.

However, Gorbachev no longer had the power to hold the Soviet Union together. In September, the Soviet government recognized the independence of Latvia, Lithuania, and Estonia, three republics that had been trying to break away from the Soviet Union for several years. The final collapse came in December 1991, when leaders from 11 of the remaining 12 republics met and together proclaimed the end of the Soviet Union. They created a new organization which they called the Commonwealth of Independent States.

The Commonwealth of Independent States was not a unified nation like the former Russian Empire or the Soviet Union. It was made up of 11 independent nations. Each of these nations had a seat in the United Nations. Each was recognized as an independent country by the United States. However, the Commonwealth members maintained some ties with one another. For example, they worked to establish a joint defense policy concerning control of nuclear weapons.

All these newly independent nations must rebuild their economies and governments after 70 years of Communist mismanagement. All face the problem of finding a way for the different ethnic groups within their borders to live together in peace.

A New Beginning. An enormous change has taken place in a vast and important part of our world. Where for centuries there was one powerful state, there now are 15. Several of these states are large and powerful, particularly Russia and Ukraine. Others are small and weak. Several are hostile to one another because of old ethnic hatreds. This means that in large parts of both Europe and Asia, where for hundreds of years there was unity and stability, suddenly there is disunity and uncertainty. The collapse of the Soviet Union therefore is one of the most important events of the 20th century. However, events are still in flux. The final chapter regarding what will take its place has not yet been written.

The aim of this book is to provide an understanding of the history and traditions of Russia and the other newly independent nations of Eurasia. You will learn how the Russian Empire developed and eventually collapsed before your parents were born, and how the Soviet Union met the same fate in your lifetime. You will see how Russians and non-Russians lived for centuries in a powerful state under Russian control. You also will learn how Russia and its neighbors must now solve new and complex problems as they begin a new era as independent states at the dawn of the 21st century.

I love my country, but that love is odd:
My reason has no part in it at all! . . .

Ask me not why I love, but love I must
Her fields' cold silences,
Her sombre forests swaying in a gust,
Her rivers at the flood-like seas. . . .

—Mikhail Lermontov

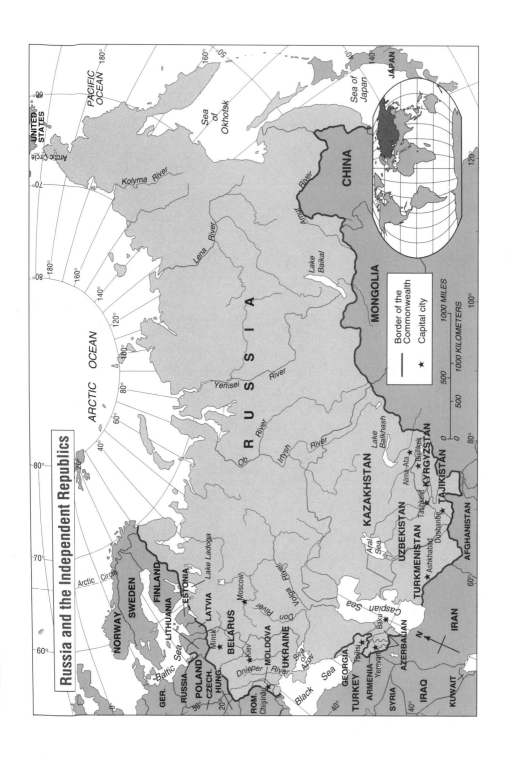

Russia and the Independent Republics

1 The Land and Its Peoples

Russia and the other newly independent republics occupy an enormous area with a great diversity of geographic features, climates, and natural resources. It is an area that is home to a wide variety of people. Knowledge of these factors will help you understand the history of this important part of the world.

SIZE AND LOCATION

The Commonwealth of Independent States (CIS) covers an area of approximately 8.6 million square miles (22.2 million square kilometers). More than three-quarters of that area—over 6.6 million square miles (17 million square kilometers)—belongs to Russia. The second largest state is Kazakhstan (kah-ZAHK-stahn) in Central Asia, with an area of just over 1 million square miles (2.6 million square kilometers). Ukraine (yoo-KRAYN), with an area of about 230,000 square miles (595,700 square kilometers), is the largest Commonwealth state that lies entirely within Europe. Of the eight remaining states, four are in Europe: Belarus, Moldova, Armenia, and Azerbaijan (ahz-uhr-beye-JAHN). The four other Asian states are Uzbekistan (ooz-BEK-ih-stahn), Turkmenistan (terk-MEN-ih-stahn), Kyrgyzstan (kir-GEEZ-tahn), and Tajikistan (tah-JIK-ih-stahn). The vast territory of the Commonwealth covers about half of Europe and almost two fifths of Asia. It is nearly seven times the size of India and larger than the United States and Canada combined. Russia alone is almost the size of all of South America.

The three most western states of the CIS are Belarus, Ukraine, and Moldova. Russia stretches eastward from Belarus and Ukraine like a gigantic ribbon across eastern Europe and Asia. South of Russia, in the Caucasus Mountain region between the Black and Caspian seas, are Armenia and Azerbaijan. In western Asia, Kazakhstan lies directly south

1

COUNTRY	CAPITAL	AREA (square miles)	POPU-LATION (in millions)	PER CAPITA GNP	URBAN POPU-LATION	LIFE EXPEC-TANCY (at birth, in years)	FERTILITY RATE *
Armenia	Yerevan	11,500	3.5	$4,710	68%	69 M 75 F	2.9
Azerbaijan	Baku	33,400	7.1	3,750	53	67 M 74 F	2.7
Belarus	Minsk	80,200	10.3	5,960	67	67 M 76 F	1.9
Georgia	Tbilisi	26,900	5.5	4,410	56	68 M 76 F	2.2
Kazakhstan	Alma-Ata	1,049,200	16.9	3,720	58	64 M 73 F	2.7
Kyrgyzstan	Bishkek	76,600	4.5	3,030	38	64 M 72 F	3.7
Moldova	Chisinău	13,000	4.4	3,830	48	66 M 72 F	2.3
Russia	Moscow	6,592,800	149.3	5,810	74	64 M 75 F	1.9
Tajikistan	Dushanbe	55,300	5.5	2,340	31	67 M 72 F	5.0
Turkmen-istan	Ashkhabad	188,500	3.9	3,370	45	62 M 68 F	4.2
Ukraine	Kiev	233,100	52.1	4,700	68	66 M 75 F	1.9
Uzbekistan	Tashkent	172,700	21.3	2,750	40	66 M 72 F	4.0

Russia and the Independent Republics: Population Statistics

* Average number of children born to a woman during her lifetime.

Source: 1992 World Population Data Sheet of the Population Reference Bureau, Inc. and *Time Magazine,* September 9,1991

of Russia. South of Kazakhstan are Turkmenistan, Uzbekistan, Kyrgyzstan, and Tajikistan.

When you travel from the Pacific coast across the United States to the Atlantic Ocean, you pass through four time zones. This means that when it is noon in San Francisco, it is 3 P.M. in New York. Between the Commonwealth's western and eastern borders, you move through 11 time zones! For example, when it is 6 P.M. in Moscow, it is 5 A.M. of the next day in the Pacific-coast city of Vladivostok (vluh-dee-vahs-TAWK).

From north to south, the Commonwealth stretches from the Arctic Ocean to the Black Sea and the mountains of Afghanistan's borders. From west to east, the region extends from the Baltic Sea in Europe to the Pacific shore, about 6,000 miles (9,654 kilometers) away. (See map on pages 4–5.) The western part of the CIS is part of the continent of Europe. The eastern part is part of the continent of Asia. At its easternmost point, the Siberian region of Russia almost borders the United States. Only 50 miles (80.5 kilometers) of water at the Bering Strait separates Siberia from Alaska.

The Commonwealth of Independent States is very much a northern territory. Its most southern point is 36° north latitude, and most of its territory is north of 50° north latitude, one degree farther north than the United States-Canadian border. Moscow, the capital of Russia, is at the same latitude as Sitka, Alaska. Yalta, a resort on the Black Sea in Ukraine, is at 45° north, the same latitude as Portland, Oregon.

TOPOGRAPHY

The topography, or physical geography, of the CIS is expansive. The CIS contains vast plains, a number of mountain ranges, and hundreds of thousands of lakes and rivers. The geography of the region has helped to shape its history, economy, and culture.

The Eurasian Plain. Over one half of the CIS is a great plain with gentle, rolling land. This large area is similar to, but larger than, the western plains of the United States and Canada. It begins in Europe and extends east to the Yenisei (yeh-nih-SAY) River in Siberia, halfway across Asia. (See map on pages 4–5.) This huge area is divided by the Ural Mountains, which run north to south. West of the Urals, the plain is called the Russian Plain. East of the Urals, the plain is called the West Siberian Plain. Most of Russia lies within the Eurasian Plain, as does all of Ukraine, Belarus, and Moldova.

Transportation over much of the Eurasian Plain is relatively easy because there is no great natural barrier except distance to hinder the traveler. The lack of mountains has made it easy for Russia to expand its territory during its long history. However, the lack of natural barriers also has disadvantages. One of these is that nothing prevents arctic winds from bringing severe weather across the plains. Another disadvantage is that there are no high mountains (except in the south) to block invasions.

3

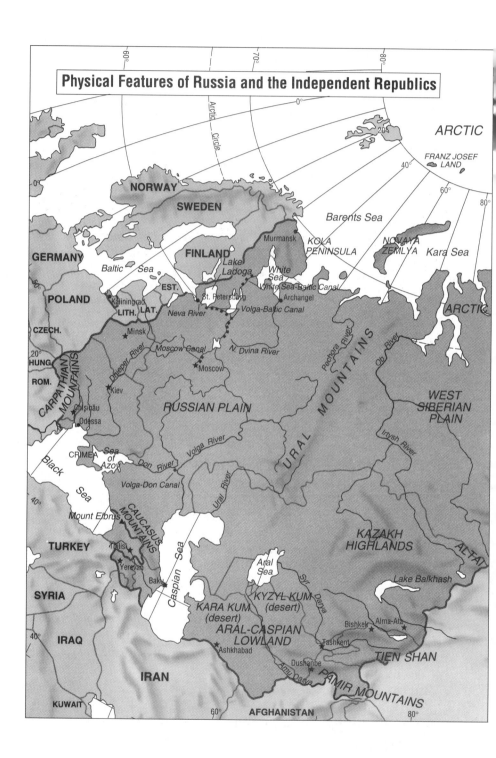

Physical Features of Russia and the Independent Republics

ARCTIC

FRANZ JOSEF LAND

NORWAY

SWEDEN

Barents Sea

Murmansk

KOLA PENINSULA

NOVAYA ZEMLYA

Kara Sea

GERMANY

Baltic Sea

FINLAND

Lake Ladoga

White Sea

White Sea-Baltic Canal

EST.

ARCTIC

POLAND

Kaliningrad

St. Petersburg

Archangel

LITH. LAT.

Neva River

Volga-Baltic Canal

CZECH.

Minsk

Moscow Canal

N. Dvina River

Pechora River

Ob River

HUNG

CARPATHIAN MOUNTAINS

Dnieper River

Moscow

URAL MOUNTAINS

WEST SIBERIAN PLAIN

ROM.

Kiev

RUSSIAN PLAIN

Chişinău

Odessa

CRIMEA

Sea of Azov

Volga River

Irtysh River

Black

Sea

Don River

Volga-Don Canal

Ural River

KAZAKH HIGHLANDS

ALTAI

Mount Elbrus

CAUCASUS MOUNTAINS

TURKEY

Tbilisi

Yerevan

Caspian Sea

Aral Sea

Syr Darya

Lake Balkhash

SYRIA

Baku

KYZYL KUM (desert)

Bishkek

Alma-Ata

KARA KUM (desert)

IRAQ

ARAL-CASPIAN LOWLAND

Tashkent

TIEN SHAN

Ashkhabad

Dushanbe

IRAN

Amu Darya

PAMIR MOUNTAINS

KUWAIT

AFGHANISTAN

4

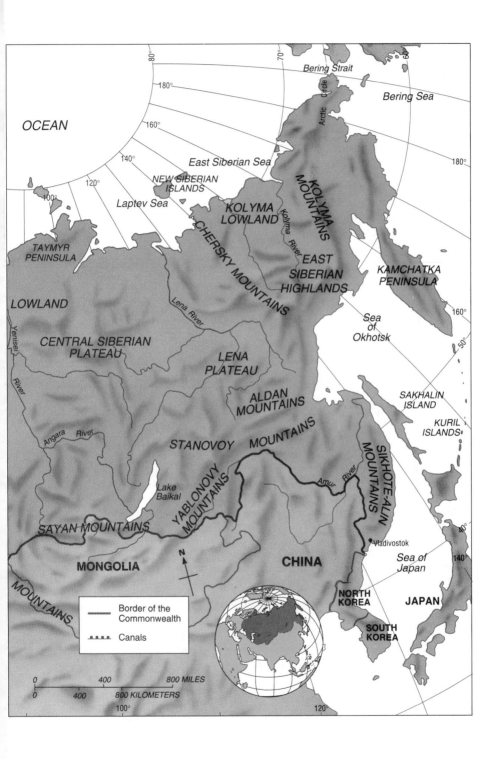

OCEAN

Bering Strait

Bering Sea

Arctic Circle

80°
70°
60°
180°
160°
140°
120°
100°

East Siberian Sea

NEW SIBERIAN
ISLANDS

Laptev Sea

KOLYMA
MOUNTAINS

180°

KOLYMA
LOWLAND

Kolyma River

TAYMYR
PENINSULA

CHERSKY MOUNTAINS

EAST
SIBERIAN
HIGHLANDS

KAMCHATKA
PENINSULA

LOWLAND

Lena River

Yenisei

CENTRAL SIBERIAN
PLATEAU

Sea
of
Okhotsk

160°

50°

LENA
PLATEAU

River

ALDAN
MOUNTAINS

SAKHALIN
ISLAND

KURIL
ISLANDS

Angara River

STANOVOY   MOUNTAINS

Lake
Baikal

YABLONOVY
MOUNTAINS

Amur River

SIKHOTE-ALIN
MOUNTAINS

SAYAN MOUNTAINS

40°

•Vladivostok

MOUNTAINS

MONGOLIA

N

CHINA

Sea of
Japan

140°

NORTH
KOREA

JAPAN

Border of the
Commonwealth

Canals

SOUTH
KOREA

0   400   800 MILES
0   400   800 KILOMETERS

100°

120°

Mountains. The Ural Mountains in Russia divide the Eurasian Plain between the continents of Asia and Europe. However, the Urals are not very high, averaging only 3,000 to 4,000 feet (900 to 1,200 meters), with no peak higher than 6,500 feet (1,980 meters). The Carpathian (kahr-PAY-thee-uhn) Mountains, another relatively low range, separates Ukraine and Moldova. In the Asian section of Russia, the Eurasian Plain gives way to more mountainous territory as one travels eastward. Northeastern Siberia has several high mountain ranges such as the Chersky (CHER-skee) Mountains, whose highest peak is over 10,000 feet (3,048 meters).

The highest mountains in the CIS are found in its southern regions. (See map on pages 4–5.) The Caucasus (KAW-kuh-suhs) Mountains form a spine that runs between the Black and Caspian seas. This chain contains some peaks over 16,000 feet (4,877 meters) high, including Mount Elbrus (el-BRUZ), at about 18,500 feet (5,639 meters), the highest peak in Europe. The Pamir Mountains separate the CIS from China and Afghanistan. In southern Siberia are the Tien Shan (TYEN SHAHN) and Altai (AL-teye) mountains. They separate Russia from Mongolia and China. The high southern mountains prevent moist, warm air from the south from reaching most of the CIS countries of Central Asia. Just to the north of the high mountains in Central Asia is the Aral-Caspian Lowland. This area is mostly desert and plateau.

Coastline and Ports. The republics of the CIS have a coastline that is almost 27,000 miles (43,451 kilometers) long. Almost all of it belongs to Russia, the only exception being the Ukrainian coastline along the Black Sea. The other CIS states are landlocked or border seas that do not have access to oceans. Both Russia and Ukraine border the Black Sea, which is connected to the Aegean (ee-JEE-uhn) and then the Mediterranean Sea by two narrow straits, the Bosporous and the Dardanelles. The rest of Russia's coastline touches the Baltic Sea in the northwest, the Arctic Ocean in the north, and the Pacific Ocean in the east.

In spite of its length, only a small part of this coastline is useful for trade. The reason is that most of the coast is icebound for much of the year. This is the situation at St. Petersburg, Russia's major port on the Baltic Sea, and at Vladivostok, its major Pacific port. Ukraine has a similar problem—its port of Odessa is frozen over for one month of the year. Ironically, Russia's port of Murmansk (muhr-MANSK) on the Arctic Ocean is ice-free because it is grazed by part of the Atlantic Gulf Stream and North Atlantic Drift known as the Norwegian Current. This current brings warm air to the region. However, Murmansk is too

Icebreakers keep shipping lanes open in the frozen Arctic waters off the Russian coast. Except for Murmansk, all other Arctic cities are icebound much of the year.

remote to be a major trading port. In addition, Russia's major ports, including St. Petersburg, Vladivostok, and the ice-free ports on the Black Sea, have their access to the open sea controlled by foreign powers. For example, ships leaving ports on the Black Sea must pass through the Bosporus Straits, the Sea of Marmara, and the Dardanelles, all controlled by Turkey.

The Russians have managed to increase the usefulness of their ports by using icebreakers, including atomic-powered ships. Still, the lack of a major warm water port open all year with unobstructed access to the open sea is a problem. Throughout Russian and later Soviet history, acquiring such a port was a key objective.

After World War II, the Soviet government annexed some former German territory on the Baltic Sea that included the ice-free port of Königsburg, which Soviets renamed Kaliningrad. However, like St. Petersburg, ships leaving Kaliningrad must pass through waters controlled by Sweden and Denmark before reaching the open sea. In addition, since the break-up of the Soviet Union, Kaliningrad, which belongs to Russia, is separated from Russian territory by the independent state of Lithuania. (See map on pages 4–5.)

Inland Waterways: Rivers and Lakes. There are over 150,000 rivers in the CIS. These rivers, along with the lakes, have long formed a water highway for communication and trade. However, two factors have limited the usefulness of these rivers. The severe winters cause the rivers to freeze over, often for six months or longer and sometimes as far south as the Black Sea. Also, many of the rivers flow north to the Arctic Ocean rather than east-west, which is the traditional flow of trade and commerce.

In the European part of Russia, the Northern Dvina (dvee-NAH) and the Pechora (pee-CHAW-ruh) flow north into the Arctic Ocean. (See map on pages 4–5.) The Western Dvina flows west into Belarus, and from there into Latvia before emptying into the Baltic Sea. Among the major trade routes are three rivers that flow generally southward. The 1,420-mile-long (1,984-kilometer) Dnieper (DNYEPR) rises in Russia and flows mainly through Belarus and Ukraine before reaching the Black Sea. The Don (DAHN) flows through Russia for 1,224 miles (1,958 kilometers) before emptying into the Sea of Azov (AY-zawf), which is connected to the Black Sea. Russia's mighty 2,194-mile-long (3,669-kilometer) Volga, the longest river in Europe, begins near Moscow and flows first eastward and then south into the Caspian Sea.

Of the four longest Siberian rivers, three—the Ob (AWB) and its tributary the Irtysh (eer-TISH), 3,362 miles (5,410 kilometers) long, the Yenisei, 2,543 miles (4,092 kilometers) long, and the Lena (LEE-nuh), 2,734 miles (4,400 kilometers) long—flow north into the Arctic Ocean. Despite their limited usefulness as highways, they possess tremendous potential for hydroelectric power. The fourth major Siberian river, the Amur (ah-MUHR), 2,744 miles (4,416 kilometers) long, initially flows east and southeast and then northeast before emptying into the Pacific Ocean.

The CIS has at least 250,000 lakes, including some of the largest in the world. The Caspian Sea, 143,244 square miles (371,000 square kilometers), is the world's largest inland sea. (See map on pages 4–5.) Russia, Azerbaijan, Kazakhstan, and Turkmenistan have coastlines along this huge lake. Russia's beautiful Lake Baikal (by-KAHL), which fills 12,162 square miles (31,500 square kilometers), is the world's deepest lake and the largest single source of fresh water. Other large lakes are Kazakhstan's Lake Balkhash (bahl-KAHSH), with 7,115 square miles (18,428 square kilometers), and Russia's Lake Ladoga (lah-DAW-guh), with 6,835 square miles (17,703 square kilometers).

During the Soviet era, the government constructed canals to link up the major rivers and seas and provide a continuous flow of water traffic throughout a large part of the country. A 63-mile (101-kilometer) canal joins the Don and Volga rivers. This and other canals have helped create a network that links the region's "five seas": the Baltic, White, Caspian, Azov, and Black seas. The region's 80,000 miles (128,744 kilometers) of inland waterways link major cities with these seas, even though many of the cities are inland. Thus, Moscow, hundreds of miles from any sea, is sometimes called the "Port of Five Seas."

CLIMATE AND VEGETATION ZONES

It is important not to confuse climate with weather. **Weather** is a term that refers to how cold or hot and how wet or dry it is somewhere at a given time. **Climate** is the type of weather a place has over a period of time. Climate is influenced by many factors, such as altitude, latitude, rainfall, and large bodies of water.

A vital fact about Russia and the other republics is that ocean breezes, which make winters less cold and summers less hot, do not reach most of the region. Therefore, much of the CIS has brutally cold, long winters and hot summers. The severe climate, especially the terrible winters, has affected every aspect of life in the countries that are located on the Eurasian Plain. The climate affects how people find amusement, how they build their houses, and, with backbreaking effort, grow and gather enough food to survive in their often harsh homeland.

Because of the region's large size, it contains a great variety of climate zones. They range from the frigid regions around the Arctic Circle in Russia to the searing deserts in the Central Asian states around the Caspian and Aral seas. The climate zones correspond closely to vegetation zones and may be divided into six different kinds: the polar (tundra), the subarctic (*taiga*), the humid-continental, the steppe, the desert, and the Mediterranean climate and vegetation zones. (See map on pages 10–11.)

The Tundra. The **tundra** (TUN-druh), lying in Russia mainly in and around the Arctic Circle, is the most northern of the Commonwealth's vegetation zones. The climate is usually called a **polar climate**. For eight months or more each year, the temperature averages below freezing. In northeastern Siberia, winter temperatures can drop to -90° Fahrenheit. The frozen ground, called **permafrost**, thaws only as far as 2 feet (0.6 meters) below the surface for a short time in the summer. During summer much of the permafrost region becomes swampy. Mosses, lichens, and small shrubs grow. Some flowers and berries also appear during the summer months. However, there are no tall trees, and the tundra is not

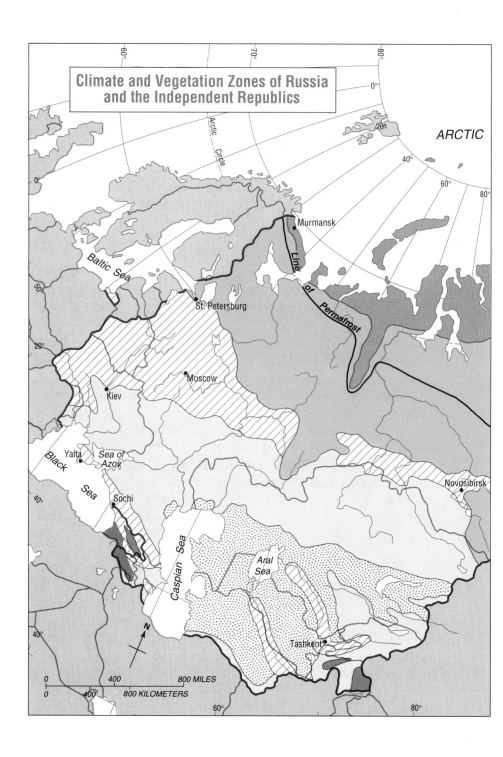

Climate and Vegetation Zones of Russia
and the Independent Republics

ARCTIC

Murmansk

Baltic Sea

Line of Permafrost

St. Petersburg

Moscow

Kiev

Yalta   Sea of
         Azov

Black

Novosibirsk

Sea

Sochi

Caspian Sea

Aral
Sea

N

Tashkent

0   400   800 MILES
0   400   800 KILOMETERS

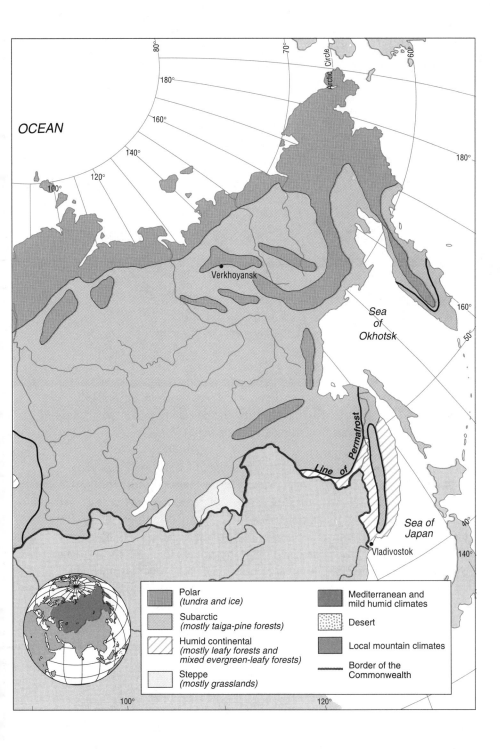

OCEAN

Verkhoyansk

Sea
of
Okhotsk

Line of Permafrost

Arctic Circle

Sea of
Japan

Vladivostok

	Polar (tundra and ice)		Mediterranean and mild humid climates
	Subarctic (mostly taiga-pine forests)		Desert
	Humid continental (mostly leafy forests and mixed evergreen-leafy forests)		Local mountain climates
	Steppe (mostly grasslands)		Border of the Commonwealth

A reindeer breeder tends his flock on the tundra of the Kamchatka Peninsula. Locate this peninsula on the map on pages 4–5.

suitable for agriculture. South of the Arctic Circle, small bushes and trees provide cover for reindeer, lynx, arctic foxes, bears, squirrels, and rabbits. The few people who have settled in the region make their living by herding reindeer and by fishing and hunting.

The *Taiga*. South of the tundra is the *taiga* (TEYE-guh). *Taiga* means "thick forest" in Russian. The *taiga* stretches across almost the entire Russian nation. The firs, spruces, and other trees that cover this vast zone provide about a quarter of the world's supply of timber along with wood for other commercial purposes. The *taiga* also has many rivers, ponds, and lakes. There are large marshy areas in parts of the West Siberian Plain. Most of the *taiga* region has a **subarctic climate**. The subarctic climate is severe: a temperature of 40° below zero is not unusual in the winter. In this zone, there is permafrost for at least part of the year. The forest soil is poorly suited for agriculture. However, where the trees have been cut down, farmers raise rye, oats, and potatoes.

The Humid-Continental Zone. The **humid-continental** zone is located south of the *taiga*. The winters here are long and cold, the summers, short and warm. The temperatures are similar to, but a bit colder than, those of the northeastern United States and the northern Great Lakes region and the Central Plains of the United States and Canada. The

12

humid-continental climate can be found in the western part of the CIS, along the Baltic coast, and eastward for almost 3,000 miles (4,827 kilometers). Usually there is moderate precipitation suitable for growing wheat and corn. Forests are made up of leafy trees or have mixed leafy trees and pine trees. This climate zone covers part of both Russia and Ukraine and all of Belarus and Moldova. Another humid-continental area of Russia is in the eastern part of the country, north of North Korea. The climate here is affected by seasonal moisture-laden winds blowing off the Sea of Okhotsk (ah-KOHTSK).

The Steppe. The **steppe** (STEP), the Russian term for plains, is south of the humid-continental and *taiga* zones. The steppe is grassland extending from Ukraine and Russia in Europe through Kazakhstan in Asia to the borders of China. Although the steppe makes up only about 12 percent of the CIS's area, it contains about 44 percent of the population and about two thirds of the country's **arable** lands, those suited to farming. The steppe's deep, fertile soil, especially the black earth of Ukraine and Russia called *chernozem* (chair-nah-ZYEM), is among the world's best farmland. Farmers of this fertile region raise large amounts of wheat, barley, oats, rye, and flax. The main difficulty they face is a

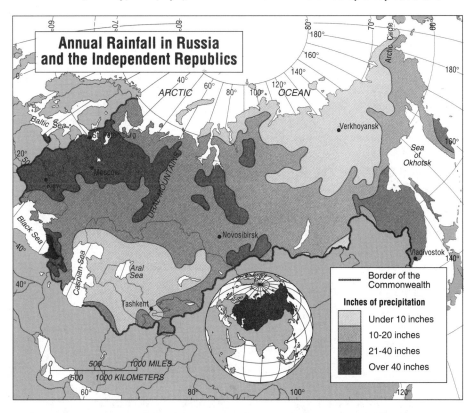

CASE STUDY:

The Russian Steppe

Anton Chekhov (1860–1904), a major Russian playwright, is also considered one of the world's greatest short-story writers. Here is his 1888 description of the Russian steppe as seen through the eyes of one of his short-story characters, Yegorushka. Yegorushka is a young boy traveling in a horse-drawn carriage to attend a school far from home.

Meanwhile, a wide boundless [endless] plain encircled by a chain of low hills lay stretched before the travelers' eyes. Huddling together and peeping out from behind one another, these hills melted together into rising ground, which stretched right to the very horizon and disappeared into the lilac distance; one drives on and on and cannot discern [see clearly] where it begins or where it ends....

The cut rye, the coarse steppe grass . . . all withered from the sultry [hot, damp] heat, turned brown and half dead, now washed by the dew and caressed by the sun, revived, to fade again. Arctic petrels [birds] flew across the road with joyful cries.... In the grass crickets, locusts, and grasshoppers kept up their churring, monotonous music.

But a little time passed, the dew evaporated, the air grew stagnant [not fresh] and the disillusioned [disappointed] steppe began to wear its jaded [worn out] July aspect. The grass drooped, everything living was hushed. The sun-baked hills, brownish-green and lilac in the distance, with their quiet shadowy tones, the plain with the misty distance and, arched above them, the sky, which seems terribly deep and transparent in the steppes, where there are no woods or high hills, seemed now endless....

How stifling and oppressive it was! The chaise [carriage] raced along, while Yegorushka saw always the same—the sky, the plain, the low hills....

But now the wheat, too, had flashed by; again the parched plain, the sunburnt hills, the sultry sky stretched before them; again a hawk hovered over the earth.

Anton Chekhov, "The Steppe, " In *The Tales of Chekhov, Vol. 7, The Bishop and Other Stories*, translated by Constance Garnett. New York: The Ecco Press, 1985, pp. 165-166, 169. Copyright © 1919, 1972. Reprinted by permission.

1. From Chekhov's description, what can you learn about the climate and the physical features of the Russian steppe?

2. Chekhov mentions two crops grown on the steppe. What are they?

lack of rain. Most of the steppe gets between 10 and 20 inches (25 to 50 centimeters) of rain per year (less as one moves eastward). Sometimes the erratic rainfall gives way to severe droughts and hot, dry winds. In the southwest, tobacco, corn, and sugar beets are grown as well. The Asian part of the steppe supports both beef and dairy cattle. The short grasses are also suitable for sheep, goats, and horses. But the lack of rain makes agriculture a very risky business.

The Deserts.   Deserts and semideserts extend east from the Caspian Sea south of the grassland of the steppes. Some of the soils of this region are fertile when watered. During the Soviet era, the government used irrigation to turn millions of acres into good farmland producing a variety of crops, including cotton and fodder crops. Kazakhstan, Uzbekistan, and Turkmenistan all include large desert regions.

The Mediterranean Zone.   Certain sheltered parts of the Black and Caspian seacoasts are similar to the shores of southern California. These areas enjoy a Mediterranean climate, with relatively short, mild winters, abundant rainfall, and hot, dry summers. The southern shore of the Crimean Peninsula around the town of Yalta in Ukraine produces grapes and other fruits. But it is primarily known as the region's most desirable vacation spot because of its warm sun, beautiful beaches, and sparkling waters.

Its warm climate and mineral springs have made the Black Sea city of Sochi a popular holiday and health resort.

ECONOMICS

The success of a region relies, in part, on its supply of natural resources, both mineral and nonmineral. The CIS is fortunate to have large reserves of many of the world's most valuable natural resources.

Natural Resources. In the industrial age, a nation's strength and power depend, in part, upon its supply of coal, iron, oil, aluminum, and other raw materials, as well as its food supply. The CIS as a whole probably has the greatest overall quantity and variety of natural resources in the world. However, much of this natural wealth is found in remote regions. It has therefore been very difficult to reach and make use of. Since the collapse of the Soviet Union, this wealth also has been divided among 15 countries.

Most of the valuable natural resources are in Russia and Ukraine. No state in the CIS can match the natural resources of Russia. In fact, the United States is the only nation in the world with natural resources comparable to those of Russia. But the United States has been drawing upon its resources more intensively and over a longer period of time. For this reason, Russia's supply of vital natural resources can be expected to last longer. This is true of oil and natural gas. It is even more true of several rare metals with important industrial and military uses, such as chromium, manganese, platinum, cobalt, and vanadium. Russia is a major producer of these metals, while the United States must rely on imports to help meet its needs.

Timber, Mineral, and Fuel Resources. Russia has the largest timber resources in the world. Its mineral deposits of iron ore, manganese, and coal are also among the largest in the world. Russia has had difficulty taking advantage of this wealth because much of it is found in remote parts of Siberia, where climate and rough terrain inhibit development. Siberia's wealth includes deposits of copper, diamonds, and gold, as well as major reserves of oil and natural gas. Ukraine and Kazakhstan also have significant resources. Ukraine is rich in iron, while Kazakhstan has large deposits of copper, lead, zinc and oil.

Until after World War II, the states that today make up the CIS, depended upon coal as their major source of power. By the 1960s and 1970s, the Soviet Union, along with the other major industrial states, increased its use of oil and natural gas. Prior to World War II, its major oil fields were in the northern Caucasus, in what is today the nation of Azerbaijan. During the 1950s and 1960s the Volga-Ural fields, in what is

World's Leading Mineral and Industrial Producers

ALUMINUM	U.S. 23%	CIS* 14%	Canada 8%	Australia 5%	Others 50%
COAL	China 20%	U.S. 18%	CIS* 17%	Germany 11%	Others 34%
COPPER	Chile 17%	U.S. 14%	Canada 9%	CIS* 8%	Others 52%
IRON ORE	CIS* 28%	Brazil 17%	Australia 12%	China 8%	Others 35%
MANGANESE	CIS* 34%	South Africa 16%	Gabon 12%	Brazil 12%	Others 26%
PETROLEUM	CIS* 21%	U.S. 16%	Saudi A. 8%	China 5%	Others 50%
POTASH	CIS* 34%	Canada 24%	Germany 21%	U.S. 5%	Others 16%
RUBBER (synthetic)	U.S. 24%	CIS* 24%	Japan 13%	France 6%	Others 33%
TIN	Malaysia 19%	Brazil 13%	CIS* 12%	Indonesia 12%	Others 44%
TUNGSTEN	China 32%	CIS* 20%	Canada 6%	S. Korea 6%	Others 36%

CIS = Commonwealth of Independent States

*There is no data available for the states of the Commonwealth. These figures include all the republics of the former Soviet Union, including Georgia, Latvia, Lithuania, and Estonia.

Source: *Goode's World Atlas,* 18th Edition

today Russia, became the country's major producer. In the 1980s, the gigantic fields of western Siberia took over that role, with the Tyumen (TYOO-min) region accounting for some 60 percent of total oil output. Today, Russia is the largest oil producer in the world.

Russia has the largest natural gas reserves in the world. Production expanded rapidly during the Soviet era. Gas pipelines were built from the gas fields to major population and industrial centers in the former Soviet Union. Furthermore, the Soviets built the world's longest gas pipeline, in large part with the help of Western technology, to carry their gas to the energy-hungry countries of Eastern and Western Europe. Today, production and use of oil and natural gas far exceed that of coal in both the United States and Russia.

Water Power and Nuclear Power.   The former Soviet Union was a world leader in developing hydroelectric power. It built four of the world's ten largest hydroelectric plants. Although there are some hydroelectric projects in European Russia, the greatest potential for this source of power is in Russia's great Siberian wilderness. At Bratsk, on Siberia's Angara (ahn-gah-RAH) River, the Soviet government built a power plant with a generating capacity of 4,500,000 kilowatts. Siberia is clearly becoming the key source of energy and other vital resources needed by the population and industrial centers of Russia and the other European states of the CIS, especially Ukraine.

During the Soviet era, increasing the production of nuclear energy was a stated goal. However, a tragic nuclear accident at Chernobyl in 1986 released high amounts of radioactivity causing a number of deaths and many potentially fatal illnesses among thousands of people. This incident cast fear and doubt about the safety and reliability of nuclear energy. The future of nuclear power now lies with the governments of the newly independent republics. Many people in the CIS and neighboring countries are concerned about the safety of nuclear energy as well as its impact on the environment.

Agriculture.   Despite its size, much of the CIS is poorly suited to agriculture. Its greatest farming area is the **Fertile Triangle**, a belt of farmland that begins near the Black Sea. The western side of the triangle stretches across Ukraine and Russia, from the Black Sea in the south through Kiev (KEE-ev) to St. Petersburg in the north. The triangle extends east to the southern Ural Mountains and beyond to Novosibirsk (noh-voh-seh-BEERSK). (See map on pages 20–21.) The Fertile Triangle is the heartland of CIS farming. Located in the steppe, much of its soil is *chernozem*. The area is flat and suitable for the use of machinery. The major crop of the *chernozem* belt is wheat, most of which is grown in the western, rainier part of the triangle. In most years, the states of the CIS together have been among the world's top three producers of wheat.

The region's other chief farm products are rye, barley, potatoes, sugar beets, flax, cotton, and wool. Rye is second only to wheat as the important grain product. It can be grown north of the Fertile Triangle, where the climate is cooler. Many Russians eat black rye bread. Flax, oats, barley, and white potatoes grow in the cooler areas of the CIS.

During the Soviet era, the region became a world leader in cotton production. Nearly all of it is produced on irrigated land in the dry regions of Central Asia. Very fine cotton is grown in scattered oases in the dry lands east of the Caspian Sea. Textile mills are supplied with wool, too. Thousands of sheep graze along the border of the steppe and the southern Caucasus Mountains, the old grazing grounds of the Mongols. Only Australia produces more wool than the CIS does. In addition to sheep, farmers raise hogs and cattle in great numbers. Second only to China in the number of hogs, the CIS raises 10 percent of the world's cattle. (See graphs on page 38.)

Still, the agricultural potential of the CIS states combined is not as great as that of the United States. Only about 28 percent of the land is arable or pasture. Crops are sown on only about 10 percent of the total land area. In the north, where rain is moderate, the soil is thin and poor. Along the southern steppe, where the *chernozem* is most fertile, rainfall is unreliable at best and often inadequate. Almost everywhere in the CIS the long, cold winters leave the farmer with a short growing season. Thus, even when the weather is good, it is difficult for the CIS to feed itself. For centuries, Russia faced serious crop problems. By the 1970s, bad management and poor weather hurt the harvest and helped to turn the Soviet Union into the world's largest importer of grain.

Industry. Before the Revolution of 1917, which you will learn about in Chapter 4, Russia was largely a farming nation. While the countries of Western Europe were building many large factories, Russia, in comparison, had few. In 1928, the Soviet Union began a massive drive to industrialize. The Soviet Union changed from a farming nation to a land of mills and factories. In the mid-1960s, about one out of every three workers was employed in the agricultural sector of the economy. That included mainly farming, but also forestry, hunting, and fishing. By the 1980s, the agricultural sector accounted for only about one in seven workers. The other six filled industrial or service jobs. This meant a great migration of people away from the farms and into the cities.

There were several reasons for the Soviet Union's change to an industrial power. First, as you have learned, the Soviet Union had a greater variety of mineral resources than any other nation in the world, including the United States. Second, there were many sources of power to fuel industry. Third, the Soviet government owned the natural resources and factories in the nation and planned how they would be used. Planners decided how many houses, dams, or factories were to be built. Wherever possible, factories and cities were located in industrial regions near the sources of raw materials. Factories were built and run by the government, and the Soviet leaders decided how and where the goods were to be sold.

19

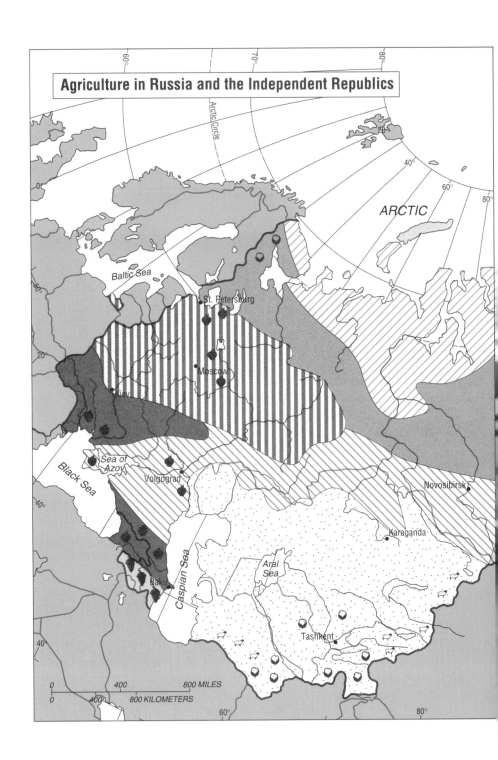

Agriculture in Russia and the Independent Republics

ARCTIC

Baltic Sea

St. Petersburg

Moscow

Kiev

Sea of Azov

Black Sea

Volgograd

Novosibirsk

Karaganda

Aral Sea

Caspian Sea

Baku

Tashkent

Arctic Circle

| 0 | 400 | 800 MILES |
| 0 | 400 | 800 KILOMETERS |

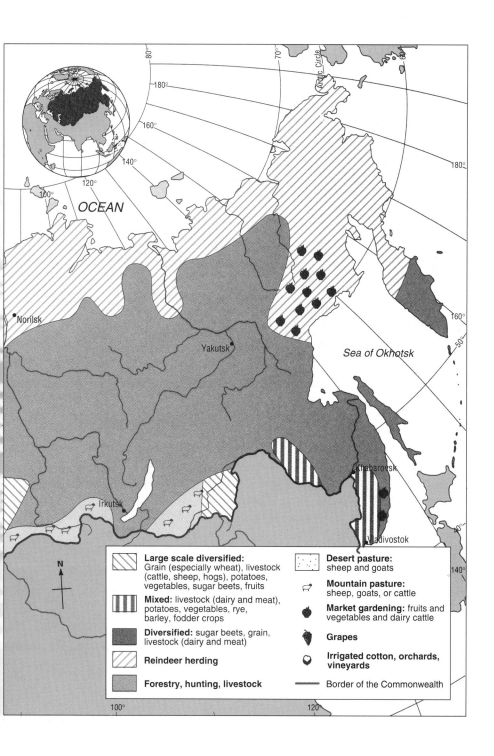

Large scale diversified: Grain (especially wheat), livestock (cattle, sheep, hogs), potatoes, vegetables, sugar beets, fruits

Mixed: livestock (dairy and meat), potatoes, vegetables, rye, barley, fodder crops

Diversified: sugar beets, grain, livestock (dairy and meat)

Reindeer herding

Forestry, hunting, livestock

Desert pasture: sheep and goats

Mountain pasture: sheep, goats, or cattle

Market gardening: fruits and vegetables and dairy cattle

Grapes

Irrigated cotton, orchards, vineyards

—— Border of the Commonwealth

N

OCEAN

Norilsk

Yakutsk

Sea of Okhotsk

Irkutsk

Khabarovsk

Vladivostok

Workers at a Russian oil installation. Russia and Kazakhstan have huge petroleum resources that remain to be tapped.

Largely as a result of Soviet era policies, there are several important industrial regions in what is today the CIS. (See map on pages 24–25.) The major European ones are the **Donbas** (dahn-BAS), or **Donets** (dah-NYETS) **Basin**, in southeastern Ukraine and Russia, the **Volga region** along the middle and lower Volga River, and the **Moscow-St. Petersburg** region in Russia. Three important Asian industrial regions are Russia's **Urals region** just east of the Ural Mountains, its **Kuzbas** (kooz-BAS), or **Kuznetsk** (kooz-NYETSK) **Basin**, in south-central Siberia, and the **Karaganda** (ka-ruh-GAN-dah) **region**.

The most important industrial region in the CIS is the Donbas, located mostly in Ukraine. Coal, iron ore, and manganese are mined here. The Donbas coal field supplies fuel for the steel mills. Dams on the Dnieper River provide electric power. The capital and chief city of Ukraine is Kiev.

The Volga industrial region grew up along the Volga River. It has important oil and natural gas resources. This region's important cities include Volgograd, Kazan, and Perm. The Volga River is a vital transportation route. In the south, it is connected by canal to the lower Don River and therefore to the Black Sea. In the north, the Volga is linked by a canal to Moscow, the capital of Russia.

The Moscow-St. Petersburg area is one of Russia's oldest industrial regions. It got its start as a populous transportation center, connected by railroad, river, and canal to the sources of needed raw materials. The Volga River's waterways link the Moscow region to all the seas surrounding the European part of the CIS. As a result, goods flow steadily in and out of the Moscow-St. Petersburg area. The region is known for both heavy industry, such as automobiles, machinery, and chemicals, and light industries, such as textiles and shoes.

The Soviet government began to develop the Urals as an industrial region before World War II, partly for military reasons. When the German armies overran the Ukraine (see page 125), they hardly touched the iron and steel production of the Urals. Rich in iron, copper, manganese, asbestos, and platinum, the mountains also contain oil and natural gas on the western and northeastern sides of the range. In addition, pipelines carry oil from fields located near the Caspian Sea directly to Black Sea ports. Coal is brought by rail from newly found deposits in Karaganda, about 600 miles (966 kilometers) to the east. Magnitogorsk (mug-nee-tah-GORSK) is the leading iron and steel city in this region.

The Kuzbas is about 1,200 miles (1,924 kilometers) east of the Ural Mountains. It is also very rich in coal. At first, Kuzbas coal was taken by rail to the Urals and iron ore was brought from the Urals. This two-way shipment of coal and iron between the two regions made both of them leading iron and steel centers. However, the steel was very expensive because of the long distance it was shipped. Iron ore has since been discovered near Kuzbas and coal discovered at Karaganda, a city much closer to the Urals. Today, Novosibirsk is the great steel city of the Kuznetsk Basin.

The Karaganda region is in the northern part of Kazakhstan, about 600 miles (966 kilometers) east of the Urals. After World War II, the Soviet government invested a great deal in its iron and steel industries and chemical plants. There are coal, copper, and other mineral resources in the region, as well as some iron ore. However, much of Karaganda's iron ore is transported from the Urals. Since the 1950s, this region's importance as a food-processing center has grown as local grain production increased.

There were handicaps in the development of industry during the Soviet era. (You will learn about some of these in Chapter 7.) One of the major problems was the transportation system. While the CIS as a

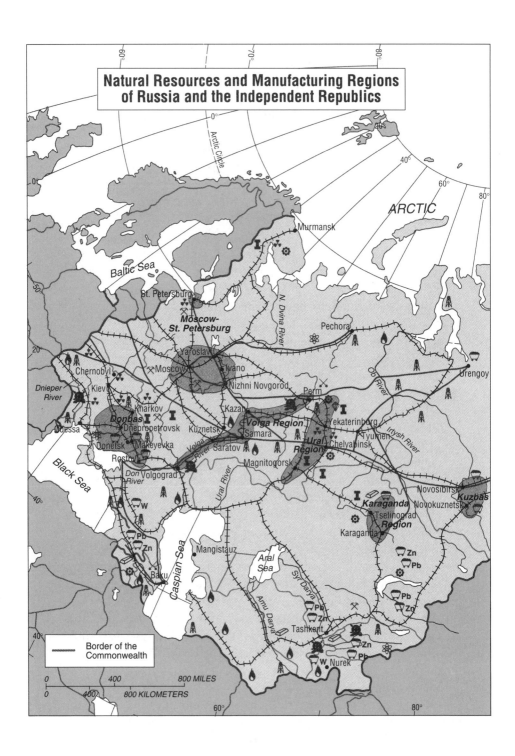

Natural Resources and Manufacturing Regions of Russia and the Independent Republics

ARCTIC

Murmansk

Baltic Sea

St. Petersburg

Moscow-St. Petersburg

Pechora

Yaroslav

Chernobyl

Moscow

Ivano

Kiev

Nizhni Novgorod

Perm

Urengoy

Dnieper River

Kharkov

Kazan

Donbas

Dnepropetrovsk

Kuznetsk

Volga Region

Yekaterinburg

Odessa

Donetsk

Makeyevka

Volga River

Samara

Ural Region

Tyumen

Chelyabinsk

Irtysh River

Rostov

Saratov

Magnitogorsk

Black Sea

Don River

Volgograd

Ural River

Novosibirsk

Kuzbas

W

Karaganda

Novokuznetsk

Pb

Tselinograd Region

Zn

Karaganda

Mangistauz

Aral Sea

Zn

Baku

Caspian Sea

Syr Darya

Pb

Amu Darya

Pb

Pb

Zn

Tashkent

Zn

Zn

Pb

W Nurek

| | Border of the Commonwealth |

| 0 | 400 | 800 MILES |
| 0 | 400 | 800 KILOMETERS |

24

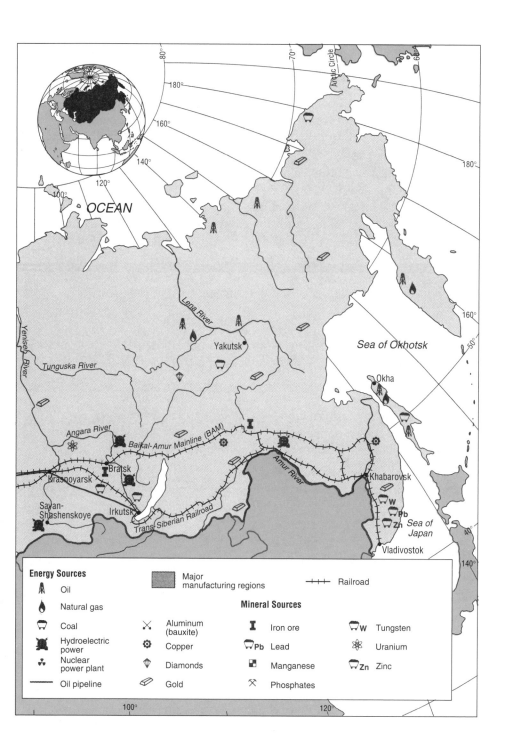

Energy Sources

🪏 Oil

🔥 Natural gas

⬡ Coal

⚒ Hydroelectric power

☢ Nuclear power plant

— Oil pipeline

⬛ Major manufacturing regions

+++ Railroad

Mineral Sources

✕ Aluminum (bauxite)

⚙ Copper

◈ Diamonds

⬗ Gold

I Iron ore

Pb Lead

▪ Manganese

✕ Phosphates

W Tungsten

❋ Uranium

Zn Zinc

OCEAN

Lena River

Yenisei River

Tunguska River

Angara River

Baikal-Amur Mainline (BAM)

Amur River

Trans-Siberian Railroad

Yakutsk

Sea of Okhotsk

Okha

Bratsk

Krasnoyarsk

Sayan-Shushenskoye

Irkutsk

Khabarovsk

Sea of Japan

Vladivostok

Arctic Circle

whole has the largest railroad system in the world, the region is vast and many places are far from railroad lines. Railroads carry much of the region's coal, ore, timber, steel, and grain. Most of the tracks are in the European and central parts of the CIS. However, the Trans-Siberian line connects eastern Siberia with the western part of the region. (See map on pages 24–25.) By the late 1980s, the newly built Baikal-Amur Mainline (BAM) connected many of the new industrial areas of eastern Siberia with the rest of the region. The BAM runs parallel to the Trans-Siberian line for about 2,000 miles (3,219 kilometers), but it runs about 200 miles (322 kilometers) to the north.

Air travel is very important for both freight transport (the carrying of goods) and passenger service. Only the United States leads the CIS in air transport. A look at a map can tell you why air travel is so popular. It is the fastest way to travel over the country's huge distances. This is especially important for the towns in northern and eastern Siberia.

Road transport is also important, especially in the European part of the CIS. Thousands of communities are served by bus routes and millions commute to work by bus. Not many people in the CIS own cars when compared with the number of car owners in Western European countries or in the United States. The repeated freezing and thawing of the thin layer of topsoil above the permafrost makes road building (and railroad building) very difficult in the cold northern and eastern regions.

As was discussed on pages 7–9, inland waterways are an important part of the total transportation system. Only the United States carries more inland freight than does the CIS. The river and canal networks are used to carry oil, timber, gravel, ores, coal, and grain. As you have learned, a major problem is that many rivers and canals freeze over for much of the year.

Finally, coal and iron deposits are not always found near each other. Because of the high cost of transporting these heavy materials by rail, the Soviet government tried to make each industrial region as self-supporting as possible. Each region was encouraged to produce as much as possible of what it needs.

CITIES

About two thirds of the CIS's population live in towns and cities. There are 22 cities of 1 million or more people. (See map on page 27.)

Moscow, the capital of Russia and largest city in the CIS, is home to over 8.8 million people. The offices and residence of the government,

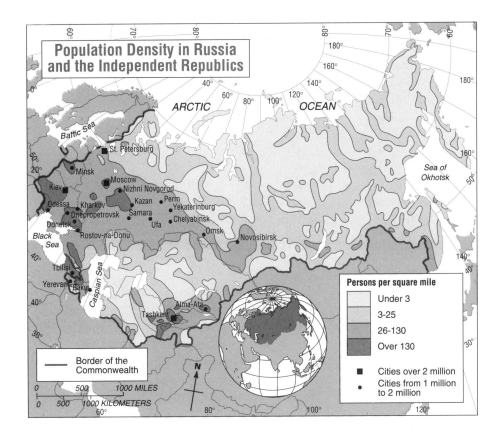

Population Density in Russia and the Independent Republics

Persons per square mile

- Under 3
- 3-25
- 26-130
- Over 130

■ Cities over 2 million
• Cities from 1 million to 2 million

Border of the Commonwealth

0   500   1000 MILES
0   500   1000 KILOMETERS

called the Kremlin, are located here. Red Square is among the city's many cultural and historical attractions. Moscow is also a major industrial center.

St. Petersburg, with nearly 5 million people, is the second largest city. It is an important shipping, commercial, and industrial center. St. Petersburg contains many museums and art galleries, such as the Hermitage, located in the former Winter Palace of the Russian czars. One of the most interesting is the Museum of the Revolution.

Kiev, the capital of Ukraine, has a population of over 2 million. Kiev is the industrial center of Ukraine, along with Kharkov (KAR-kohf), a major industrial and railroad center in the area.

Novosibirsk, in the Asian part of Russia, is a center of scientific research. During the Soviet era, the government made huge investments in developing cities in Asia such as Krasnoyarsk (kruhs-nuh-YARSK), Irkutsk (eer-KOOTSK), and Khabarovsk (khah-BAH-rufsk). (See map on pages 24–25.)

PEOPLES OF THE INDEPENDENT REPUBLICS

About 285 million people live in the Commonwealth of Independent States. Of the countries of the world, only China, with over 1.1 billion people, and India, with about 800 million people, have larger populations. The United States has about 253 million people.

Nationalities. A **nationality** is a group of people sharing a common origin, language, and traditions. The CIS is made up of many distinct nationalities. Many of the individual CIS states, especially Russia, include a variety of nationalities. For example, almost 20 percent of Russia is made up of non-Russian nationalities, including Ukrainians and Tatars (TAHT-ehrs). About 60 percent of Kazakhstan is comprised of non-Kazakhs. Official statistics covering the CIS as a whole list over 100 national groups and separate languages.

The former Soviet Union was divided into 15 large political units called **union republics.** The union republics corresponded to the largest national groups. The largest republic in the former Soviet Union was called the Russian Soviet Federated Socialist Republic, and included over three quarters of the Soviet Union's land area and over half its population. Soviet policy permitted the various nationalities to retain their languages and customs. However, there were many restrictions that limited and discouraged their development. For example, the Russian language and culture were promoted in the 14 non-Russian republics, and it was impossible to rise very high in Soviet society without a knowledge of Russian. While this was intended to promote unity, often it led to resentment among the Soviet Union's non-Russian population.

When the Soviet Union collapsed in 1991, it broke apart along the lines of the union republics. In fact, it was the leaders of the union republics, led by Russian President Boris Yeltsin, who made the final decision to abolish the Soviet Union and form a new Commonwealth of Independent States. Three of those republics—Latvia, Lithuania, and Estonia—had established their independence three months before the Soviet Union collapsed. When the CIS was founded, a fourth republic—Georgia—remained outside the new organization. That left the CIS with 11 member republics.

The East Slavs: Great Russians, Ukrainians, and Belorussians. About 70 percent of the population of the Commonwealth of Independent States is East Slav. The East Slavs originally were one people, but over time historical events divided them into three groups. (See Chapter 2.)

By far the largest group is the Great Russians, who normally are referred to simply as Russians. There are over 145 million Great Russians, comprising about 71 percent of the East Slav population. The Great Russians built the Russian Empire in the centuries after 1500 by gradually conquering territory from their neighbors or absorbing them altogether. They also were the group that dominated the Soviet Union. Over the centuries, the Great Russians migrated outward in several directions, so that today millions of them live outside the borders of Russia. (See map on pages 224–225.)

The Ukrainians number about 44 million. When the first Russian state was founded in the 800s, its center was in what today is Kiev, the capital of Ukraine. However, in the 1200s, Kievan Russia was conquered by the Mongols. From that time, Ukraine enjoyed only brief periods of independence. Usually, it was dominated by other powers, including the Mongols, the Lithuanians, and the Poles. During the 1600s and 1700s, Russia gradually conquered most of Ukraine. After a brief period of independence when the Russian Empire collapsed in 1917, Ukraine was overrun by Communist forces and absorbed into the Soviet Union in 1922. The Ukrainians speak a language closely related to but distinct from Russian.

The smallest group of East Slavs, numbering about 10 million, are called Belorussians or White Russians. Today their country is called Belarus. Prior to the collapse of the Soviet Union, the Belorussians had enjoyed only a brief period of independence. Their territory was fought over by more powerful neighbors for centuries. After the Mongol invasion, Lithuania, Poland, and Russia struggled to control the region. The Belorussian language, like Ukrainian, is closely related to Russian.

Peoples of the Caucasus. The Caucasus mountain region is home to a large variety of national and ethnic groups. Although they live close together and often share the same territory, ethnic and religious differences have divided them and have often led to bitter conflicts.

The Armenian people had their own republic in the former Soviet Union and today their state belongs to the CIS. The Armenians are an ancient nation who can trace their existence as a people back well over 2,000 years. They have a long Christian tradition that dates from their conversion around 300 A.D. The Armenian written language, which dates from about 400 A.D., has a longer history as a written language than does Russian. During their history, the Christian Armenians have had conflicts with and suffered severe persecution at the hands of their more numerous Muslim neighbors. The worst events occurred during

World War I, when over 1.5 million Armenians living southwest of the Caucasus in the Ottoman Empire were massacred by the ruling Turks. Many Armenians fled, some to Russia and the Middle East. A number immigrated to the United States at this time.

The Azerbaijanis, whose state borders Armenia to the east, are Muslims who are a mixture of Iranian, Turkic, and other peoples who have lived in the Caucasus region. The first great oil producing regions of pre-1917 Russia were in Azerbaijan. Baku, the country's capital and largest city, became the oil capital of the Russian Empire. Today one of the most bitter ethnic conflicts in the CIS is over a territory called Nagorno-Karabakh (nuh-GAWR-noh kahr-ah-BAHK), which is part of Azerbaijan but inhabited mainly by Armenians.

The Georgians are the other major nationality of the Caucasus. Like the Armenians, the Georgians are Christian and have a long history. Georgia became part of the Russian Empire in the 1700s and was part of the Soviet Union. However, because of political divisions and violence in Georgia after the Soviet Union collapsed, Georgia did not become part of the CIS.

Peoples of Central Asia. Five Muslim nationalities now have their own independent states in Central Asia that belong to the CIS: the Kazakhs (kah-ZAHK), Uzbeks (OOZ-bek), Turkmen, Kyrgyz (kir-GEEZ), and Tajiks (TAH-jihk). All make up a majority of the population within their republics, with the exception of the Kazakhs, who account for only about 40 percent of the population of Kazakhstan. As a group, the Muslim nationalities are the most rapidly growing segment of the population of the CIS.

The Kazakhs speak a Turkic language and trace their origin to nomads who have lived on the Asian part of the Eurasian Plain since the time of Genghis Khan in the 1200s. They are closely related to other peoples of Central Asia, particularly the Kyrgyz. During Joseph Stalin's dictatorship, the Soviet government brutally forced them to give up their nomadic ways and become farmers on Soviet-style collective farms. As many as 1 million Kazakhs, a quarter of the population, died during the violence and chaos that resulted.

The Uzbeks also are a Turkic people, although they have intermingled with Iranians and Mongols over the centuries. They are the single largest Muslim group in Central Asia. Unlike the nomadic Kazakhs, the Uzbeks have long been settled farmers.

The Turkmen are traditionally a nomadic people who speak a Turkic language. Their ancestors arrived in Central Asia between the

An Uzbek grandfather prepares a meal for his eager grandchildren. Uzbeks are among the many national groups in the CIS.

700s and 900s. Those who settled in mountainous regions mostly became farmers. Others lived semi-nomadic lives.

The Kyrgyz are of uncertain origin, although they seem to be a mixture of Turkic and Mongolian groups. They developed into a national group in the 1500s, although they still have strong loyalties to their local tribes and clans. The Kyrgyz traditionally have lived as nomads.

The Tajiks are the only major nationality in Central Asia who speak an Iranian rather than a Turkic language. They trace their ancestry to people who lived in Central Asia over 1,000 years before the first Turkic groups arrived in the region. Today the Tajiks are Muslims, like the vast majority of the peoples of Central Asia.

Other Groups.   Along the border of Romania is the republic of Moldova. Moldovans live on territory the Soviet Union annexed from Romania during World War II. In fact, the Moldovans are ethnic Romanians. The region they live in traditionally has been called Bessarabia, which was claimed by both Romania and the Russian Empire during the early 1800s. After 1815, Russia won control of it. Romania managed to seize control of Bessarabia in 1918 after the collapse of the Russian Empire, but the Soviet Union took it back as a result of World War II.

31

A large number of other nationalities and ethnic groups live in both the European and Asian parts of the CIS and do not have states of their own. Between 2 and 3 million Jews, most of whom live in Russia, Ukraine, and Belarus, are scattered throughout the CIS. However, their numbers have decreased in recent years due to emigration. There are almost 2 million people of German descent in Russia, who also have been emigrating in large numbers in recent years. Large parts of extreme northern Russia are inhabited by people who speak languages related to Finnish. People were living in these regions long before the arrival of the East Slavs.

The most numerous nationality without an independent republic in the CIS are the Tatars. There are over 6 million Tatars living mainly between the Volga River and the Ural Mountains. The Tatars are significant in Russian history far beyond their current numbers, for they are the most direct descendents of the Mongols who conquered and devastated Russia during the 1200s. The Tatars, who are Muslim, also live in Kazakhstan, Uzbekistan, and the Crimean Peninsula.

There are several other ethnic groups in the Caucasus region, who live as minorities within the various republics. They include the Ossetians (ah-SEE-shahns), Circassians (sehr-KASH-ens), Chechens, and Lezgins. Most of these peoples are Muslims, although some groups are Christians. Several communities of Jews who have lived in the region since ancient times also are scattered throughout the Caucasus.

A large variety of ethnic groups, none numbering more than a few hundred thousand, are scattered throughout Central Asia and Siberia. Some are Turkic, others are Mongolian in origin, and still others are related to the Eskimo peoples who live in Alaska and northern Canada.

Languages. The people of the CIS speak over 100 languages. During the Soviet era, a strong effort was made to promote Russian as the second language in the non-Russian speaking regions of the country. People found it important to speak Russian to get a first-rate education and get ahead in Soviet society. Since the collapse of the Soviet Union, it is likely that the study, use, and knowledge of Russian will decline in the newly independent states of the CIS.

Religion. Over 70 years of atheist Communist rule did not eliminate religion in the Soviet Union. During the Soviet era the government officially permitted freedom of worship but tried to discourage people from following a religion. The number of churches, mosques, and synagogues was strictly limited. In schools throughout the Soviet Union, students

Worshipers in a Russian Orthodox church. Religions have gained new followers since the collapse of the USSR.

were taught that religion is harmful superstition and a barrier to progress. Churches could not give religious instruction to anyone under the age of 18. People who practiced a religion were barred from serving in high positions in the Soviet government or the Communist party.

The largest religious denomination among the peoples of the CIS is the Russian Orthodox Church. Most Russians, Ukrainians, and Belorussians are Russian Orthodox by tradition, even though many abandoned religious practice under Soviet rule. Between 150 and 200 million people in the CIS trace their religious roots to Russian Orthodoxy. During the Soviet era, the Russian Orthodox Church was subordinate to the Communist state. Yet despite official opposition to religion, there were over 50 million active Orthodox in the Soviet Union by the 1980s, and their numbers were growing rapidly. With the collapse of the Soviet Union and the restoration of religious freedom, the Russian Orthodox Church has experienced a surge in interest and will probably grow in number and influence in Russia, Ukraine, and Belarus.

While all religions suffered from severe restrictions during the Soviet era, some religious minorities were singled out for harsh treatment, particularly the Jews and some Christian denominations that stood up for the right to worship freely.

By the 1980s, about 50 million Soviet citizens were Muslim. That made them the second largest religion in the former Soviet Union. With the collapse of the Soviet Union, it is expected that the influence of Islam will increase in Azerbaijan and the republics of Central Asia.

There are several other non-Orthodox Christian churches with followers in the CIS. The most influential of them is the Uniate church, which is a Catholic church that follows certain Orthodox rites. Its center is in Ukraine. Another important Christian denomination is the Armenian Catholic Church.

Small numbers of Hindus and Buddhists live in the eastern parts of Russia. Overall, it was estimated that 30 to 40 percent of the Soviet people practiced some form of religion despite several generations of antireligious propaganda. With the end of Soviet rule and its antireligious bias, the role of religion in the lives of people throughout the CIS is likely to increase.

As you study Russia and the other countries of the Commonwealth of Independent States, here are some important facts to remember:

1. The CIS has great extremes of weather—from tundra cold to desert heat. Much of the region is very far north.

2. The greater part of the CIS is at the center of a large land mass. It has tremendous diversity in its physical geography.

3. The mountains in the southwest keep out moisture-carrying winds from the Indian and Pacific oceans, thus creating large areas of desert or near-desert land.

4. The flat nature of the land permits cold winds from the Arctic to sweep as far south as the Black Sea without meeting any obstacles.

5. The CIS, in spite of its huge size, has a smaller proportion of land for agricultural use than does the United States.

6. The CIS has a tremendous supply of natural resources and is an important producer of agricultural and fiber products. Its resource-rich environment enabled the former Soviet Union to become a leading world power.

7. Oil, natural gas, and nuclear and hydroelectric power were developed rapidly during the Soviet era for industrial, commercial, and home use.

8. The CIS is a region of urban dwellers, with two thirds of the people living in cities and towns.

9. The people of the CIS have a variety of languages, customs, and religions. Russians make up about half of the population of the CIS and were the dominant nationality during the Soviet era.

REVIEWING THE CHAPTER

I. Building Your Vocabulary

In your notebook, write the numbers from 1 to 6. After each number, write the word that matches the definition.

permafrost   tundra   *chernozem*
taiga   nationality   steppe

1. most northern climate zone, partly in the Arctic Circle, with long, severe winters

2. extremely rich, black, fertile soil

3. a group of people who share a common origin, language, and traditions

4. vast, thickly forested subarctic region

5. grassy plains region

6. frozen ground of the tundra and *taiga* regions

II. Understanding The Facts

In your notebook, write the numbers from 1 to 5. Write the letter of the correct answer to each question next to its number.

1. Which of the following cities is located on Russia's Pacific coast?
   a. Moscow   b. Vladivostok   c. Odessa

2. Which of the following cities lies at the same latitude as Yalta, a resort on the Black Sea?
   a. Paris, France   b. Mexico City   c. Portland, Oregon

3. Large amounts of wheat, barley, oats, rye, and flax are grown
   a. on the steppes.   b. in the Mediterranean zone.
   c. along Russia's coastline.

4. Which of the following cities has the largest population?
   a. Kiev   b. St. Petersburg   c. Moscow

5. The largest national group in the CIS is made up of
   a. Armenians.   b. Great Russians.   c. Kazakhs.

III. Thinking It Through

In your notebook, write the numbers from 1 to 6. Write the letter of the correct answer to each question next to its number.

1. Because of the lack of natural barriers in the northern CIS
   a. many invaders from the north have swept across the region.
   b. trade moves easily along the rivers located there.
   c. there are many beautiful lakes in the region.
   d. severe weather sweeps across the plains.

2. One reason the rivers of the CIS have limited usefulness is that they
   a. are short and shallow.
   b. are frozen over for long periods.
   c. flow through sparsely populated regions.
   d. are too narrow for large ships.

3. Siberia is an important region of Russia because it
   a. is rich in raw materials.
   b. is very accessible to the West.
   c. has an excellent transportation system.
   d. has many popular vacation resorts.

4. Murmansk is an ice-free port most of the year because
   a. it is in the southern part of the country.
   b. atomic-powered ice-breakers keep it open.
   c. warm Atlantic currents flow nearby.
   d. it is located on the Caspian Sea.

5. One result of the breakup of the Soviet Union is that the role of religion in the CIS will probably
   a. increase.
   b. decrease.
   c. not change.
   d. be severely restricted.

6. Which of the following statements best describes the Commonwealth of Independent States?
   a. The main disadvantage of the CIS is its lack of natural resources.
   b. Most people in the CIS live in rural areas.
   c. The most common religion in the CIS is Islam.
   d. The population of the CIS includes more than 100 different nationalities.

DEVELOPING CRITICAL THINKING SKILLS

1. How has the lack of natural barriers affected transportation and climate on the Eurasian Plain?

2. Describe how the climate and soil affect the kinds of crops grown in the different parts of the CIS. How has this influenced population distribution? Give some examples.

3. Discuss the importance of rivers in trade and transportation. How have rivers in the western part of the CIS aided interaction with southeastern Europe? How does the direction of the flow of Siberian rivers present problems for commerce or trade?

4. People often alter the environment to make geographically harsh regions more productive. During the Soviet era, how did the government change the desert regions in Central Asia to make them more productive? What kinds of alterations were made to the Siberian region to extract the natural resources located there?

5. Discuss the advantages and disadvantages the former Soviet Union had in its drive to industrialize.

6. Explain why the Russian language was promoted in the non-Russian republics of the former Soviet Union. Discuss how the breakup of the Soviet Union might affect Russian language and culture in the non-Russian republics.

INTERPRETING A GRAPH

Study the bar graphs on pages 17 and 38. Then answer the following questions.

1. What percentage of aluminum do the republics of the CIS produce?

2. Which nation produces the largest percentage of cotton?

3. Who produces more barley, the United States or the CIS?

4. What percentages of coal and petroleum does the CIS produce?

5. Agree or disagree with the following statement. "The nations of the CIS lead the world in the production of many natural resources and may emerge as leaders among the industrialized nations of the world." Use information from the graphs to support your answer.

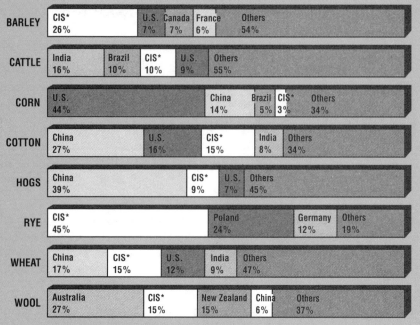

World's Leading Agricultural Producers

BARLEY	CIS* 26%	U.S. 7%	Canada 7%	France 6%	Others 54%	
CATTLE	India 16%	Brazil 10%	CIS* 10%	U.S. 9%	Others 55%	
CORN	U.S. 44%		China 14%	Brazil 5%	CIS* 3%	Others 34%
COTTON	China 27%	U.S. 16%	CIS* 15%	India 8%	Others 34%	
HOGS	China 39%		CIS* 9%	U.S. 7%	Others 45%	
RYE	CIS* 45%		Poland 24%	Germany 12%	Others 19%	
WHEAT	China 17%	CIS* 15%	U.S. 12%	India 9%	Others 47%	
WOOL	Australia 27%	CIS* 15%	New Zealand 15%	China 6%	Others 37%	

CIS = Commonwealth of Independent States
*There is no available data for the states of the Commonwealth. These figures include all the republics of the former Soviet Union, including Georgia, Latvia, Lithuania, and Estonia.

Source: *Goode's World Atlas,* 18th Edition

ENRICHMENT AND EXPLORATION

1. The Crimea has unique climate and physical features. Write a short essay describing the climate, agriculture, and economy of the Crimean region. Be sure to discuss how these features differ from the rest of the Commonwealth.

2. Select one nation of the Commonwealth of Independent States. Prepare an illustrated report on its history and culture. Include information on family life, food, music, language, education, and other traditions.

3. Using tracing paper, create a map of one of the Asian republics of the CIS. Use colored pencils to shade the country's climate and vegetation zones. Then use symbols to show which agricultural products are grown in the nation. Design a key for your map. Write a caption that explains how the climate of the country affects which agricultural products are found there.

2 *The History of Russia to 1917*

The ancestors of today's Russian people were the East Slavs. The origins of the East Slavs and the precise time they first settled on the Eurasian Plain are not known. These origins have been obscured by many waves of invasion and migration, and by the passage of more than a thousand years. But we do know that by the A.D. 800s the East Slavs had begun to develop their civilization there. During the 900s, the first Russian state grew along the rivers that form a natural waterway between the Baltic Sea and the Black Sea. The ruling dynasty of this state was a group of powerful merchant warriors from Scandinavia, the Vikings, who gradually merged with the native Slavs. The term *Rus* came to be used for this combination of Scandinavians and Slavs.

KIEVAN RUSSIA

The center of the first Russian state was Kiev, a city in what today is Ukraine on the lower reaches of the Dnieper River. (See map on page 41.) Kiev was not a unified nation like the Russian Empire or the Soviet Union. It was a loose federation of city-states, each one controlled by a prince of the ruling family. Kievan Russia compared favorably with its neighboring states in Europe. Its economy was based on the small-scale agriculture of its mostly free peasants. Nonetheless, much of Kievan Russia's prosperity and character came from trade.

Trade.   The river network controlled by the Kievans was a major trade route linking Europe to the Middle East and beyond. The Kievan rulers encouraged and engaged in this trade. Their major trading partner, the richest and most culturally advanced of Russia's neighbors, was the Byzantine Empire to the south. This empire's capital, Constantinople,

RUSSIA AND THE WORLD

800–1918

800s	Kievan Rus established.
988	Prince Vladimir converts to Greek Orthodox Christianity.
1237	Mongols (Tatars) establish Golden Horde.
1453	*Ottoman Turks defeat the Byzantine Empire.*
1480	Ivan III frees Russia from Mongol rule.
1547	Ivan IV becomes the first Russian czar.
1598–1613	Time of Troubles
1613	Romanov dynasty begins.
1670–1671	Cossack Razin leads serf rebellion.
1721	Peter the Great is crowned emperor.
c.1760	*Industrial Revolution begins in Great Britain.*
1773	Cossack Pugachev leads peasant rebellion.
1776	*U.S. Declaration of Independence*
1789	*French Revolution begins.*
1812	Russia defeats France in the Napoleonic Wars.
1814–1815	*Congress of Vienna*
1825	Decembrist Revolt
1853–1856	Crimean War
1861	Alexander II abolishes serfdom.
1881	Alexander II assassinated.
1904–1905	Russo-Japanese War
1905	Revolution of 1905
	Nicholas II announces the October Manifesto.
1914–1918	*World War I*
1917	Riots break out in Petrograd (St. Petersburg).
	Czar Nicolas II abdicates.
	Duma elects Provisional Government.

was the most magnificent city in the Western world. Every year hundreds of boats sailed down the Dnieper to the Black Sea and then on to Constantinople. There they unloaded their furs, wax, honey, grain, slaves, and forest products, exchanging them for wines, perfumes, and other Byzantine luxuries.

In this way Byzantine culture, crafts, and religion were brought into Russia. The movement and borrowing of ideas, beliefs, objects, and customs between regions is called **cultural diffusion**. The interdependence between Kievan Russia and the Byzantine Empire led to a cultural diffusion that has helped to shape the modern nation-state of Russia.

The Byzantine religion was Greek Orthodox Christianity. When Kiev's Prince Vladimir converted to it in 988, it became the official religion of his realm. This event is one of the key events in Russian history. Greek Orthodoxy became the established religion in Russia, while the dominant religion in most of central and western Europe was Roman Catholicism. The head of the Greek Orthodox Church was the Patriarch

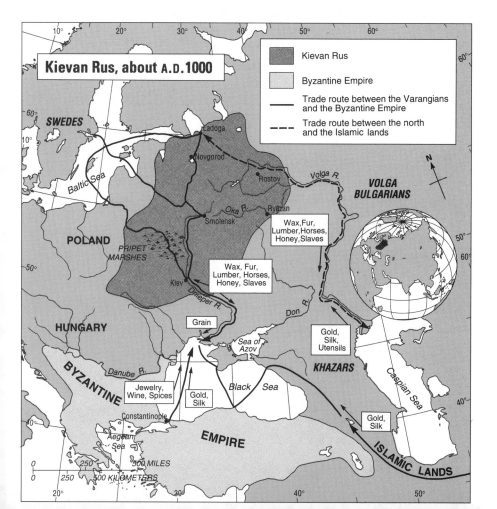

of Constantinople. He appointed the **metropolitan** (chief bishop) of Kiev, the religious leader of that city. The metropolitan was usually a Greek, not a Russian, although many of the lower clergy were Russian. In 1054, the Greek Orthodox Church broke away from the Roman Catholic Church because of a disagreement over the authority of the Pope in Rome. This helped to separate Russia from Western Europe.

This division was widened by another event. During the 800s, the missionary work of two monks, Cyril and Methodius, had led to the adoption of the newly devised Cyrillic (suh-RIL-ik) alphabet for writing Russian. The Cyrillic alphabet uses letters based on Greek ones. (See table below.) In contrast, Western Europe used (and still uses) the Latin alphabet. The major result of embracing the Greek Orthodox religion and the Cyrillic alphabet was that much of the learning and intellectual developments of Western Europe were inaccessible to educated Russians.

The Cyrillic Alphabet

CYRILLIC	TRANSLITERATION	PRONUNCIATION	CYRILLIC	TRANSLITERATION	PRONUNCIATION
А	a	as in father	С	s	as in sign
Б	b	as in bit	Т	t	as in ten
В	v	as in vote	У	u	as in pool
Г	g	as in goat	Ф	f	as in fit
Д	d	as in dog	Х	kh	as in Bach in German
Е	e	as in yes			
Ё	e	as in yoke	Ц	ts	as in cats
Ж	zh	as in azure	Ч	ch	as in cheer
З	z	as in zero	Ш	sh	as in shop
И	i	as in machine	Щ	shch	as in cash check
Й	i	as in boy			
К	k	as in kit	Ъ		hard sign, no pronunciation
Л	l	as in let	Ы	y	as in shrill
М	m	as in map	Ь		soft sign, no pronunciation
Н	n	as in not			
О	o	as in note	Э	e	as in bed
П	p	as in pat	Ю	iu	as in cute
Р	r	as in ravioli (rolled r)	Я	ya	as in yard

The Cathedral of St. Sophia in Novgorod, built between 1045 and 1052, is a fine example of early Russian architecture. Note the helmeted cupolas, sometimes called onion domes.

Still, in the 1000s Kiev was the largest city in Eastern Europe and as impressive in many ways as the major cities of Western Europe. With its many beautiful churches, Kiev compared well with the glorious city of Constantinople. Moreover, Kiev was merely one of several well-developed Russian cities. Novgorod (NAWV-guh-rud) was a major center of trade, and it contained one of the most magnificent of the many churches in Russia, the Cathedral of St. Sophia. Other vibrant cities were Rostov and Ryazan (ree-uh-ZAHN). These Russian cities all had citizen councils of self-government called **veches** (VYAY-chuhs), which shared power with the assemblies of nobles and the princes. Literature, architecture, and art flourished, much of it related to religious themes. A rich secular literature also developed. Even the Kievan law code was remarkably humane compared with the harsh laws elsewhere.

THE MONGOL CONQUEST

Kiev's achievements, however, were not enough to prevent its decline. Its strength was sapped by numerous wars and power struggles among its jealous princes. Its economic strength was undermined when the river trade route between Europe and the Middle East was replaced by a more direct route that was opened up by Italian merchants via the Mediterranean Sea. Finally, even at its height, Kiev was under constant pressure from nomadic peoples moving westward out of the Asian heartland. In the 1200s, with Kievan Russia already weakened, the Mongols—by far the most powerful of those nomads—burst out of Asia. In 1223, they gave Russia a brief but terrible taste of their power. They crushed a Russian army in a battle on the Kalka River near the Sea of Azov. Then, to Russia's relief, the Mongols returned home because their leader had died and a successor had to be chosen. Fourteen years later they returned. This time Russia received no relief. The Mongols— or Tatars, as the Russians called them—devastated the land. Kiev and most of Russia's other major cities were destroyed. In Ryazan, the first city to fall, it was said that "not an eye was left open to weep for those that were closed." Only Novgorod, protected from the Mongol cavalry by treacherous swamps, was spared. The suffering of the Russian people was immense, and it was only beginning. After enslaving perhaps 10 percent of Russia's population, deporting its best craftspeople, and carrying off whatever valuables they could, the Tatars established a state called the **Golden Horde** on the southern steppe. (See map on page 45.) They built their capital at Sarai (sah-REYE) on the lower Volga River. From there they controlled Russia with efficiency and brutality for almost 250 years.

The Impact of Mongol Rule.   The Mongol conquest had consequences for Russia that were far greater than the suffering it caused. It cut Russia's ties with Byzantium and with the West, contributing significantly to Russia's cultural decline. Russia's cities, cut off from outside trade, declined in size and importance. Tatar rule led to a three-part division of the Russian people. Those who later were called the Great Russians lived under Tatar control, while two smaller groups, the Ukrainians and the Belorussians, developed under Polish or Lithuanian influence. Mongol influence on the political system of Russia was also of prime importance. It was during the period of Mongol dominance that a powerful Russian autocracy began to develop.

The Mongol state was highly centralized, with power concentrated in its ruler, the **khan** (KAHN). Although the Mongols ruled Russia indirectly, their state provided the model for their local agents, the Russian princes. The Russians adopted Mongolian methods of administration, such as levying taxes, recruiting soldiers, and their extremely harsh administration of justice. Such methods destroyed the power of the *veches* and greatly reduced the independence and influence of Russia's nobility. The harsh realities of the Mongol conquest and political system created among the Russians a fear of foreign exploitation and domination that has lasted to the present.

The Mongols looked upon Russia primarily as a source of **tribute** (money payments). As long as the tribute was paid, they allowed the Russian princes to rule much as they had before. A noble class of *boyars* ran the local governments. The peasants lived in small villages and paid heavy taxes. The Tatars tolerated Christianity and allowed the Russian church to keep its lands as long as it paid tribute.

As it turned out, one minor princely state located in the forests of northeastern Russia did the best job of adapting to Mongolian rule. This principality also benefited and grew as a result of the many Russians who settled there when they fled from the Mongols. In addition, the principality's favorable location near the sources of the Volga and the Oka (ah-KAH) rivers strengthened its economy, as did the timber, tar, and other natural resources of its dense forests. Finally, it was blessed with a line of long-lived and able princes. Slowly, it annexed other Russian principalities. It eventually became strong enough to throw off the Mongol yoke as well. This state was Muscovy. Its major city, destined to become the capital city of Russia, was Moscow.

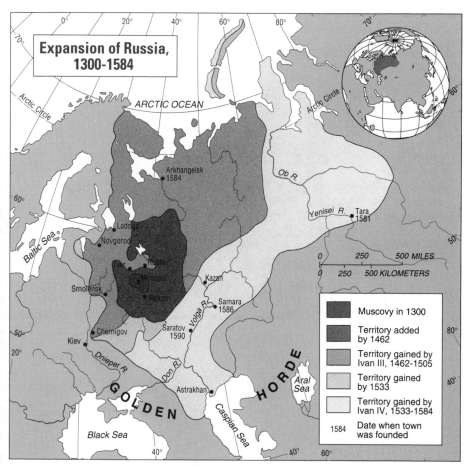

Expansion of Russia, 1300-1584

Legend:
- Muscovy in 1300
- Territory added by 1462
- Territory gained by Ivan III, 1462-1505
- Territory gained by 1533
- Territory gained by Ivan IV, 1533-1584
- 1584 Date when town was founded

THE RISE OF MOSCOW AND
RUSSIAN AUTOCRACY

Despite Muscovy's advantages, its success came only after a long, hard struggle. It faced many powerful enemies. In Russia itself there were rival principalities. To the west of Russia there were Poles, Lithuanians, Swedes, and Germans. To the south and east there were the Tatars of the Golden Horde. (See map on page 45.) The survival of Muscovy, let alone its success, required that all its resources be mobilized. Such a mobilization was achieved by the princes of Muscovy through a series of harsh measures. Over a period of several hundred years, Muscovy became an **autocratic state**—a state with virtually unlimited powers over its subjects. This state's ability to exploit its people exceeded anything that existed in Europe. As a Russian historian observed: "The state waxed [grew] fat, while the people grew lean."

Muscovy's fortunes improved noticeably during the reign of Ivan I (1328–1341). Ivan, nicknamed *Kalita* or Moneybags, convinced the Mongols to appoint him their tax collector for all of Russia. He also persuaded the Russian Orthodox Church to move its seat to Moscow. That gave Moscow prestige at a time when the Russians needed a beacon of hope.

Ivan III, the Great (1440–1505), established Moscow as the center of an expanding Russia, free of Mongol domination. He claimed to be the protector of Orthodox Christianity through his marriage to the niece of the last of the Byzantine emperors.

However, the decisive stages in the rise of Moscow and its autocracy came later, in the 1400s and 1500s. The two key men in that process were Ivan III, who ruled from 1462 to 1505, and his grandson Ivan IV, who ruled from 1533 to 1584, respectively named Ivan the Great and Ivan the Terrible. Under Ivan the Great, Moscow completed the job of uniting Russia, although considerable territory remained under foreign control. Ivan first conquered Moscow's remaining Russian rivals: the cities of Tver (teh-VER) and Novgorod. Then in 1480, he formally ended Russia's subordination to the Mongols by refusing to pay tribute to the Golden Horde.

Ivan was also successful in dealing with the internal obstacles to his autocratic power. The end of self-government in Russia came when he conquered Novgorod, which had been the home of Russia's most renowned *veche*. Next, Ivan turned on the old Russian nobility, who held their estates by virtue of heredity. He undermined their power by creating a new class of nobles to whom he awarded estates for their service to the state. The creation of Ivan's new state system demanded that all classes of society serve the state. Since there was little money but much land at Ivan's disposal, he paid for military or civil service with large grants of land. Ivan also dispossessed thousands of old noble families. This often bloody process included forcible evictions and mass deportations to remote regions.

Finally, Ivan married Sophia, a niece of the last Byzantine emperor. By then, the Ottoman Turks had stormed Constantinople and conquered the Byzantine Empire (1453). So Ivan claimed that Moscow was not only the capital of Russia but also the rightful center of Christendom. The reasons given for this claim were that Rome itself was in the hands of Roman Catholics (whom he regarded as heretics), and Constantinople, known as "the second Rome," was in the hands of the Muslim Turks. So the new slogan in Moscow was: "Two Romes have fallen, a third stands; and a fourth there shall not be."

Under Ivan the Great's rule, foreign architects rebuilt Moscow's Kremlin, a fortified area in the center of the city. Within its walls, Ivan ruled in splendor, surrounded by princes and *boyars* who became more and more dependent on him for favors and support.

The job of building the Russian autocracy was largely finished by Ivan's grandson, Ivan IV. This brilliant, unbalanced, and unbelievably brutal ruler is generally called Ivan the Terrible. It was Ivan the Terrible who gave Russia its first political police, the dreaded and merciless *oprichnina* (ah-PREECH-nee-nuh). To complete the job of crushing the hereditary-nobility's power, he used the *oprichnina* for a decade-long campaign of terror. Ivan's terror claimed thousands of lives, including—by Ivan's own hand—that of his son. Supported by the Russian Orthodox Church, which by now did the ruler's bidding, Ivan proclaimed himself the czar of all Russian lands. Ivan reformed the military and introduced a new legal code. He encouraged specialists in printing, mining, and medicine to come from Western Europe. Ivan IV expanded Russian power along the Volga River and eastward into Siberia. By the time of his death in 1584, there was no power in Russia that could challenge the absolute power of the monarch.

Serfdom.   Autocracy had become Russia's fundamental political institution. Serfdom became Russia's fundamental social institution. Serfdom developed gradually over a period of about 150 years, growing out of various measures taken by the autocracy. Serfdom assured a stable labor supply for the nobility. Serfdom also made it easier for the state to tax peasants and to draft them into the army. By 1649, Russian peasants, also called **serfs,** had been reduced to a condition that was like American slavery. Serfs could not move, marry, or learn to read without their owner's permission. They could be removed from the land, beaten, or sold by their owners. However, Russian serfs—unlike American slaves—had to pay taxes.

Russian serfdom was a cruel and brutal institution that injured Russian life for centuries. It kept the peasants under control, but also kept them totally ignorant. It also hurt Russian agriculture, which was no more productive up to the 1800s than Western Europe's had been in the Middle Ages. To understand the burden that serfdom placed on Russia, one should consider just how many problems slavery caused for

The city of Moscow dates from the 1100s, when most of the ordinary people lived in homes built of logs. Some log homes can still be seen in the present-day city.

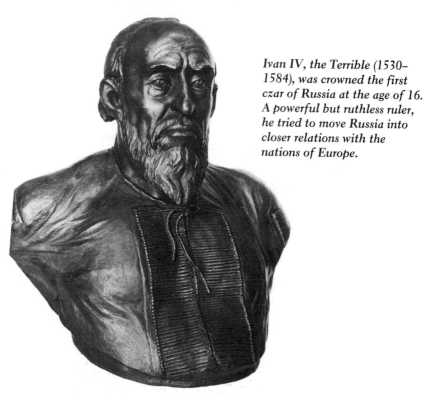

Ivan IV, the Terrible (1530–1584), was crowned the first czar of Russia at the age of 16. A powerful but ruthless ruler, he tried to move Russia into closer relations with the nations of Europe.

the United States. Consider, too, that in Russia serfs were a large majority, while slaves were a minority in the United States. Also, Russia's backwardness meant it had far fewer resources for solving its problems than the United States had before the Civil War. By the 1800s, serfdom had become a terrible burden that Russia could no longer carry but seemed unable to remove.

Expansion.   As the power of the Russian autocracy grew, it was able to bring people outside Russian borders under its control. Once Russia had become united and independent of the Golden Horde, it quickly expanded into territories occupied by non-Russian peoples. (See map on page 45.) There are no natural boundaries in the great plain that stretches from Europe into Asia, and there were rich prizes to be won.

Expansion has been a lasting theme in Russian history. The Russian people had been pushing outward into thinly settled regions of the forest and steppe since Kievan times. But under Ivan the Terrible, in the 1500s, the expansion became more organized. Ivan pushed in all directions. Besides the desire for land, there was the push to gain control of warm-water ports. However, in the south he was blocked by the powerful Ottoman Empire. In the west, despite a 25-year effort that cost Russia dearly, the Poles and Swedes blocked Ivan's efforts to reach the Baltic Sea and secure an ice-free port. Ivan's successes were in the southeast, where his armies destroyed two decaying *khanates*—lands ruled by a khan. These were Kazan and Astrakhan. Ivan's reign also saw the beginning of Russia's expansion into the vastness of Siberia. Within 60 years Russians had pushed across the breadth of Asia to the Pacific.

Russia continued to expand in the 1600s, 1700s, and 1800s by pushing south and west as well as east. In Europe, the territory that today is Ukraine was seized from Poland and the Ottoman Empire during the 1600s and 1700s. What today is Belarus was seized during the partitions of Poland in the 1700s. Southward expansion during the 1800s brought the Caucaus region, including Armenia and Azerbaijan, under Russian control. In Asia, Russia's expansion in the 1800s brought Kazakhstan, Uzbekistan, Turkmenistan, Kyrgyzstan, and Tajikistan into the empire.

Russia was gradually transformed into a **multicultural** empire. By the 1800s the ruling Great Russians amounted to less than half the country's population. Because Russia was composed of so many non-Russian nationalities, many of which were treated quite harshly, the Russian Empire came to be called the "prison house of nations."

Ironically, Russia's expansion did not make its people more tolerant of foreigners, or even more knowledgeable about them. Indeed, Russia's many wars helped make the Russian people deeply distrustful of foreigners. This feeling was reinforced by the state. Russia's rulers feared comparisons between local conditions and those in foreign countries. Every effort was therefore made to limit Russian contact with foreigners. Even highly placed Russians were subject to strict travel restrictions. Foreigners visiting or living in the country were isolated from the general population. Russia had emerged from the centuries-long Mongol shadow, but its people remained afraid of foreigners and ignorant of what other nations had accomplished.

Backwardness.   By the end of the 1600s, the Russian autocracy had made two notable achievements. It had established almost complete control over the Russian people and it had increased Russia's size and power through rapid expansion. It also survived a major crisis in the late 1500s and early 1600s when the ruling dynasty died out. Russia went through the "Time of Troubles"—15 years of disorder, civil war, and invasion.

By 1613 order had been restored, invaders from Poland had been repelled, and a new dynasty—the Romanovs (ROH-muh-nofs)—was on the throne. That dynasty soon faced and overcame major new challenges. It was able to use a rebellion against Poland in the Ukraine to take control of much of that rich farming region from Poland. (See map,

The coronation of Boris Godunov as czar in 1598, shown here, set off a period known as the Time of Troubles. Boris was the subject of a drama by the Russian poet Alexander Pushkin and an opera by Modest Mussorgsky.

on pages 70–71.) In 1656, when a split over doctrine occurred in the Russian Orthodox Church, Czar Alexis (1645–1676) sided with the reformers and won greater control over the church. Between 1670 and 1671 Alexis also managed to put down a great serf rebellion led by Stenka Razin, a **Cossack**, or southern Russian skilled as a horseman. Cossacks were free peasants who lived mainly in Ukraine. (See Chapter 8.)

But there was one problem that no force in Russia could solve. By the 1500s social, economic, and political changes in Western Europe were producing rapid strides in technology, organization, and military power. Russia's rulers were aware of this and worried about it, since both geography and Russian ambitions increasingly threw Russia into competition with the European powers to the west.

As early as the 1540s, technical specialists from the West had been imported by Ivan the Terrible for all sorts of civil and military enterprises. But the technological gap continued to grow. By the 1800s it had reached frightening proportions. Some czars tried to ignore it. Other czars tried to cope with it or became obsessed with it. But despite the enormous powers of the autocracy, no czar could overcome the gap. Russia's political and social institutions, especially the autocracy and serfdom, stifled the individual initiative that was promoting Europe's progress. Thus Russia's chronic backwardness began to destroy its strength from the inside, even as its immense mass and military machine made it appear powerful and menacing to its neighbors.

IMPERIAL RUSSIA

The Reign and Reforms of Peter the Great.   Peter I (1689–1725), known as Peter the Great, launched Russia as an empire when he had himself crowned emperor in 1721. Peter was the first czar who attempted to deal directly with the challenge of Western Europe's modernization and technical progress. He recognized that the technical gap with the West would have to be closed if Russia was to become a major European power and succeed in fighting Western neighbors. By all accounts, Peter was admirably suited to the task of driving his huge but reluctant country forward. Standing 6 feet 9 inches tall (2.07 meters), he was a powerful man with grandiose goals, extraordinary energy, and a wide range of abilities. Early in his reign Peter visited Western Europe, where he studied skills ranging from shipbuilding to dentistry with varied degrees of success. Thus he had first-hand knowledge of the technologies that he insisted his people must learn. Peter was capable of extreme ruthlessness and cruelty against those who opposed his plans. For instance, when he was forced to return from Europe in 1698 to suppress a rebellion, Peter served with enthusiasm as one of the executioners of the defeated rebels. Years later, Peter ordered the torture and execution of his own son, who had sympathized with Peter's conservative

Peter the Great cutting the beard of a protesting nobleman. Peter, who wanted to modernize Russia, believed that beards and the traditional style of dress were signs of Russian backwardness.

critics. The reign of Peter the Great, saw over 25 years of war, much social turmoil, and feverish building and experimentation. It was a time in which Russia made unprecedented progress, but according to some, the Russian people suffered more under Peter than they had under Ivan the Terrible.

Peter's plans to modernize Russia by copying the West were opposed by many conservative Russians. This opposition only seemed to make Peter more determined. As a symbol of his determination to end old Asian and Byzantine customs, Peter ordered all men to cut off their beards and to give up wearing their customary long coats. He himself wielded a razor and scissors on some of his courtiers in order to make them look more like Westerners. This was resented, as were similar reforms. Tradition-minded Russians complained that without their beards they looked not like Westerners but like dogs, cats, and monkeys. When Peter insisted that Russia adopt the Julian calendar in place of one that began with the presumed creation of the earth, he was accused of violating God's order.

Peter introduced many other far-reaching reforms. He invited foreign technical specialists to Russia and sent Russians to study in the West. Inside Russia he established schools, especially for the children of the nobility, and he founded an academy of science to promote higher learning. Peter did more to encourage industry in Russia than anyone before the 1800s. During his reign, over 200 industrial enterprises were established. Only 20 such industries had existed when he ascended the throne. He ordered the construction of canals and military roads between major cities. He created a civil service system in which able administrators advanced and acquired noble status, destroying the power of the *boyars*. Following Western models, Peter created a series of ministerial colleges, each geared to a specific responsibility of the government such as the army, the navy, foreign affairs, or state finances. Peter modernized Russia's army and founded its navy, and he brought the church under the direct control of the state.

Peter's reforms were expensive, and as usual, the burden of paying for them fell on the Russian peasants. It was the peasants who served in the ranks of Peter's expanded military forces. It was also the peasants who were conscripted to work under horrible conditions in Russia's new factories and mines. On top of that, Peter raised their taxes. In fact, he squeezed over five times more tax revenue from the hard-pressed Russian people than his predecessor had. Finally, to reinforce modernization and Westernization and give his country a "window to the West," Peter built a new capital. This was located on the Baltic coast, on terri-

Peter the Great spared neither money nor lives in building the new city of St. Petersburg as his "window to the West." The palace seen here and other public buildings designed by Western architects helped make St. Petersburg the most beautiful city in Russia.

tory recently conquered from Sweden. Thousands of pilings had to be sunk into this disease-ridden swampland to support the new city. Many thousands of peasants died while building this monument to Peter. He called his city St. Petersburg, after his patron saint. Others, remembering those who did not survive to see it, called it the "city built on bones."

Some of Peter's reforms brought immediate results, especially on the battlefield. As early as 1696, Peter's newly built naval force enabled him to reverse an earlier defeat by Turkey. Peter was also able to avenge some defeats that the Swedes had inflicted on Russia in the course of a 21-year struggle called the Great Northern War. In the end, Russia conquered all of Sweden's Baltic territory and established itself as a power on that sea.

But the long-term fruits of Peter's frantic and often disorganized campaign were less satisfying. By exposing Russia's upper class to Western influence, Peter's reforms opened a gap between them and the bulk of the population, which remained immersed in its traditional culture. Over the generations, this gap caused considerable misunderstanding and tension. Furthermore, there was much in Russia that did not change. Peter's endless wars meant that Russia's wealth and resources were constantly poured into the military—at the expense of dire civilian needs. Russia remained an autocratic state. In fact, it became more efficient at exploiting and oppressing the people than it had been before Peter modernized its bureaucratic apparatus. Russian agriculture remained backward and inefficient. Serfdom was more entrenched than ever. Thus Russia's social structure remained fundamentally the same. By itself, that structure could not generate the ongoing scientific and technical progress found in Europe. Therefore, once Peter's great driving force was removed by his death in 1725, Russia began to lag, and many of Peter's works began to erode. Nonetheless, his westward expansion had made Russia a major European power. It had also placed Russia into more direct competition with the West's major powers, and this made the problem of keeping up with the West even more urgent than it had been before.

The Era of Catherine the Great. The reign of Catherine II, or Catherine the Great (1762-1796), was similar in pattern to Peter's reign. During both periods Russia endured attempted reform, military successes, expansion, and continued mass poverty. Catherine, who was German by birth but Russian through her marriage to Czar Peter III, came to power in a **coup d'état**, or forcible overthrow of the government, that ended with the murder of her unpopular husband. Her rise to power solved one problem: it ended the political instability that followed Peter the Great's death. In those 40 years six ineffective rulers had succeeded one another. Like Peter the Great, Catherine gave Russia firm leadership. She also followed Peter's example by expanding Russia's borders. During her long reign, Russia expanded to the south at the expense of the Ottoman Empire, which had begun its long decline. Russia gained the northern coast of the Black Sea and the right to send ships through the straits leading to the Mediterranean Sea. (See map on pages 70-71.) Russia expanded to the west, too, at the expense of Poland—a country that disappeared as an independent state when Catherine cooperated with Austria and Prussia to dismember it.

Much of Catherine's reputation rests on her role of introducing Russia to the ideas of the Enlightenment, a European philosophical movement. She read the works of such Enlightenment thinkers as Voltaire and Diderot (DEE-duh-roh). Catherine established a commission to codify Russia's laws, supposedly on the basis of Enlightenment ideas. She expanded educational opportunities, built hospitals, initiated a reform of regional government, and tried to reform local government.

Catherine II, the Great (1729–1796), was a German princess who became ruler of Russia in 1762 after her husband's death. She favored many advanced Western ideas, but under her rule peasants lost rights and more peasants became serfs.

Catherine's contribution to Russian development should not be underestimated. During her long reign, Russia's power in its relationship with Europe improved dramatically. Russia's cultural and intellectual life grew among the upper class. Yet all the achievements of Catherine's reign were paid for by taxing the Russian peasantry. In addition, Catherine greatly expanded the area where serfdom existed. There were peasants in Russia who were state peasants rather than serfs. They were bound to the land, like the serfs, but lived on state-owned land and therefore did not serve private landlords. When Catherine gave vast tracts of state land to her nobles, state peasants who lived there became serfs. By 1773 conditions had become so bad for all the peasants that a massive rebellion erupted. Led by the Cossack Emelian Pugachev, the rebellion became the greatest one Russia had ever known. By 1775, the rebellion was finally suppressed. In a most unenlightened fashion, Pugachev was put in a cage and taken to Moscow, where he was executed in front of a large crowd.

Though Catherine wished to be known as a champion of progressive ideas, she was in reality terrified that ideas about personal rights and political liberty might spread to Russia. Two of Russia's outstanding intellectuals—the political thinker Alexander Radishchev (rah-DEESH-chev) and the publisher Nikolay Novikov (nuh-vee-KAWV)—were severely persecuted. One was exiled to Siberia, and the other was sent to prison. By the time Catherine died, Russia had a brilliant veneer of Western culture supported by a wretchedly poor peasant base. Catherine's favorite subjects and the nobility enjoyed the magnificent architecture she commissioned and the art treasures she collected in St. Petersburg. But most Russians continued to live in tiny, isolated villages, scratching the earth with wooden plows, and giving up most of their labor and income to their landlords and the state.

Russia's Crisis in the 1800s.   Catherine's unbalanced son Paul ruled for five years before he was murdered in 1801. After that, every czar was named either Alexander or Nicholas. These men had more in common than their names. They all enjoyed relatively long reigns. All of them were confirmed autocrats, determined to preserve the political system they had inherited. Their fear of change was shared by most of the bureaucrats who advised them and by most of the nobles on whom the czars depended for support. The reasons for this conservatism ranged from a dislike of all change to the fear that change, once begun, would be impossible to stop.

Russia in the 1800s was therefore in an awkward position. The need for change was even greater than before because Western Europe's strength had grown. However, change in Russia, whenever it came at all, was usually undertaken most reluctantly and by half measures. As a result, the changes Russia made during the 1800s were unevenly distributed across Russian society and did not catch up with the empire's growing problems. Russia was thus to pass through a number of major crises in the 1800s.

Alexander I and Nicholas I: Inaction and Reaction.   Alexander I (1801–1825) is noted for his victory over Napoleon. Certainly, the highlight of Alexander's reign was Russia's great victory over the French in 1812. Alexander began his reign by making a number of liberal reforms. He abolished torture in criminal cases, freed many political prisoners, permitted foreign books to be sold in Russia, and allowed serfs, under limited conditions, to buy their freedom. But his commitment to reform proved to be far more in words than in deeds. He left both serfdom and

CASE STUDY:

Serf and Master

The mood and temper of the Russian people in the 1800s is seen in Leo Tolstoy's great novel *War and Peace.*

> On all his estates Pierre saw with his own eyes stone buildings [built or being built,] all on one plan, hospitals, schools, and almshouses [poorhouses], which were in short time to be opened. Everywhere Pierre saw the steward's [manager of another person's property] reckoning [counting] of service due to him diminished in comparison with the past, and heard touching thanks for what was remitted [decreased] from deputations [visiting committees] of peasants in blue, full-skirted coats.
>
> But Pierre did not know that where they brought him bread and salt and were building a chapel of Peter and Paul there was a trading village, and a fair on St. Peter's day, that the chapel had been built long ago by wealthy peasants of the village, and that nine-tenths of the peasants of that village were in the utmost destitution [great poverty]. He did not know that since by his orders nursing mothers were not sent to work on their master's land, those same mothers did even harder work on their own bit of land. He did not know that the priest who met him with the cross oppressed [kept down] the peasants with his exactions [demanding and getting], and that the pupils gathered around him were yielded up to him with tears and redeemed for large sums by their parents. He did not know that the stone buildings were being raised by his laborers, and increased the forced labor of his peasants, which was only less upon paper. He did not know that where the steward pointed out to him in the account book the reduction of rent to one-third in accordance with his will, the labor exacted had been raised by one half. And so Pierre was enchanted by his journey over his estates, and came back completely to the philanthropic [charitable] frame of mind. . . .
>
> "How easy it is, how little effort is needed to do so much good," thought Pierre, "and how little we trouble ourselves to do it!"

Leo Tolstoy, *War and Peace*, translated by Constance Garnett. New York: The Modern Library, Random House.

1. According to this selection, was the master always aware of the plight of the serfs? Did his good will make their fate any easier?

2. How can ignorance of a real situation be almost as dangerous as ill will? What type of leader might oppressed serfs like these follow?

the autocracy untouched. Throughout his reign, Alexander was at times liberal but more often reactionary, especially during his later years.

Foreign affairs occupied much of Alexander's time. This was particularly true while Napoleon Bonaparte was emperor of France. Napoleon's attempts to dominate Europe included a successful campaign against the Austrians and Prussians that increased French territory and prestige. Although Russia joined them in the fight to stop Napoleon, the French defeated their armies in 1805, at the Austro-Hungarian city of Austerlitz, and again in 1807, in Friedland in East Prussia. But the great size of Russia, its large population and location, led Napoleon to strike a bargain and make an alliance with Alexander.

The two emperors met on a raft in the middle of the Niemen River, where they signed the Treaty of Tilsit (1807). The treaty left France and Russia supreme in much of eastern Europe. Alexander also agreed to join the continental system, a trade bloc against Britain. Through the continental system, Napoleon hoped to defeat Britain, which was the only country he had not been able to dominate.

Five years later Napoleon, angry with Russia for opening its ports to British ships, invaded Russia with an army of half a million soldiers. The Russians retreated before the invaders, destroyed everything behind them, and left Napoleon's troops little to find in the way of food or shelter. Napoleon entered Moscow in mid-September 1812. A few weeks later, the Russians burned the city down to deprive the French of food. Without supplies or shelter, Napoleon ordered a retreat. An unusually early and severe winter hindered the army's march back to western Europe. Cold, starvation, and attacks by Cossacks had reduced the army to 50,000 men when it finally staggered out of Russia. The disastrous Russian campaign hastened Napoleon's downfall.

The countries that had united to defeat Napolean met at the Congress of Vienna (1814–1815) to plan the peace. There, Alexander was able to secure Finland, Bessarabia, and additional Polish territory. (See map on pages 70–71.) Russia's defeat of Napoleon and success at the Congress of Vienna marked Alexander's "hour of glory." He persuaded the other European monarchs to agree to a "Holy Alliance." In it they pledged to perform their duties in a Christian manner, to treat their subjects as their children and their fellow rulers as their brothers. Through this alliance, Alexander hoped to stop the spread of liberal political movements that might threaten the conservative monarchies of Europe. Since there was no way to enforce it, this vague treaty had little meaning for those who signed it. However, in 1815, Russia became a member of the Quadruple Alliance with Austria, Prussia, and Britain.

Romanov Rulers of Russia, 1682–1917			
Peter I (the Great)	1682–1725	Catherine II (the Great)	1762–1796
Peter II	1727–1730	Paul	1796–1801
Frederick	1730–1740	Alexander I	1801–1825
Ivan VI	1740–1741	Nicholas I	1825–1855
		Alexander II	1855–1881
Elizabeth	1741–1762	Alexander III	1881–1894
Peter III	1762	Nicholas II	1894–1917

Neither alliance could prevent a split between Britain with its parliamentary traditions and Russia, Prussia, and Austria with their absolute monarchies. These three countries were determined to repress liberal ideas anywhere in Europe.

Decembrist Revolt, December 1825. When Alexander I died, the throne passed to his youngest brother, Nicholas, not to the logical heir, his brother Constantine (who did not want to be czar). A group of aristocratic Russian army officers, familiar with liberal Western ideas from their experiences in Western Europe during the Napoleonic campaigns, plotted against Nicholas. Most wanted reform and a constitutional monarchy, but a few wanted a revolution and a republic. Some of the plotters favored an elected legislature and a free press, neither of which existed in Russia.

When news of Alexander's death reached St. Petersburg, the rebels planned a revolt of the army. In December 1825, soldiers in the central square of St. Petersburg shouted "Constantine and Constitution," in their efforts to limit the power of the czar. However, the main body of troops, loyal to Nicholas, fired on and scattered the disloyal soldiers. The leaders were captured. Five of them were executed and 300 received lesser penalties. The revolt was over.

The Decembrist Revolt was a milestone in Russian history. A rebellion in Russia had had as its aim not simply to put one ruler in place of another but to change the very form of government. Even in defeat the revolt planted a seed of organized opposition to autocracy. Despite all attempts to get rid of that seed, it survived and took root and grew.

Nicholas I, 1825–1855. The Decembrist Revolt hardened Nicholas's resolution to prevent another such plot from endangering his position as absolute ruler. An officer at heart, Nicholas adopted militaristic methods to strengthen his autocratic power and to fight "dangerous ideas" in all forms. He stressed the triple doctrine of *orthodoxy* (the Orthodox Church preaching loyalty to the czar), *autocracy* (devotion to the person and to the police rule of the czar), and *nationalism* (patriotism and love for "Mother Russia").

A widespread secret police, called the **Third Section,** was set up to supervise all the people. Repressive measures over schools, newspapers, and the army silenced expressions of opposition or suggestions of reform. Foreign travel was frowned upon, and foreign books, papers, and people were carefully scrutinized, and even excluded from Russia.

A Polish revolt in 1830 was put down harshly by the Russians. The Polish constitution that had been granted by Alexander I was abolished, and the country was made part of the Russian Empire. A campaign of stern **Russification** followed. The use of the Polish language was restricted. The lands of the Polish Catholic Church were seized. Russian officials took control over many government functions in Poland. Nicholas, hating any form of liberalism, eventually carried this struggle beyond Russia's borders. He helped the Austrian emperor put down a democratic uprising in Vienna in 1848 and a nationalist uprising in Hungary in 1849. But not even Nicholas could stop the clock. Despite his efforts, Russia was changing. Russia's first railroad was built during his reign. An expanded educational system increased literacy significantly. This growing pool of literate people soon produced the first wave of great Russian writers, including Alexander Pushkin and Leo Tolstoy. (See Chapter 8.)

Crimean War (1853–1856). Czars since Peter the Great had tried to secure a warm-water port at Constantinople. Nicholas made another effort. The Ottoman Empire, weak and growing weaker, seemed particularly vulnerable. Nicholas demanded the right to protect all Ottoman subjects of the Orthodox faith. When this was refused by the sultan of Turkey, Russia declared war and destroyed a Turkish fleet in the Black Sea. This led Britain and France to go to war against Russia. Britain did not want Russian ships on the Mediterranean to threaten the important British route to India. Most of the fighting took place in the Crimean Peninsula which the Russians stubbornly defended. The war's most important battle was the siege of Russia's naval base at Sevastopol. In September 1855, it fell after a bitter year-long siege.

The great Russian writer Leo Tolstoy was a landowner who was deeply sympathetic to the plight of the Russian peasants. He started a school for his serfs and often worked with them in the fields. Shown here in his old age, Tolstoy believed the world would become a better place only when people learned to love one another.

Nicholas, meanwhile, had died in March of 1855. The war clearly was going against Russia. The next czar, Alexander II, ended the war. The Crimean War demonstrated the backwardness of Russia's military forces. Although Russia had been fighting on its own soil and against relatively small foreign forces, it was defeated. The Treaty of Paris (1856) cost Russia much prestige and influence in the Middle East. The Christian subjects in the Ottoman Empire were not placed under Russia's protection. The Black Sea was closed to Russian warships. Russia did not succeed in gaining the warm-water port it so much desired. The defeat and the social unrest caused by the war would lead directly to a series of new policies that became known as the Great Reforms.

Alexander II and the Great Reforms. Russia's unsuccessful war called attention to several long-festering domestic problems. The most severe of these was the poverty of the countryside. Although it was now the middle of the 1800s, Russia's peasants were no more productive than the peasants in Europe had been in the Middle Ages. Natural conditions were a part of the problem. But the bulk of the problem was caused by serfdom and by the farming methods that came along with it.

Most serfs belonged to what was called a *mir*, or commune. According to the traditional method of farming, farmers had collective use of the land, rather than owning it as private property. This system was in existence even before serfdom and state taxes. The peasant commune became the way the state made sure that the peasants met their tax and military obligations. The peasants were held responsible for meeting these obligations as a village commune rather than as individual families. The commune therefore had control over the land a serf farmed. To ensure that each family could bear its share of the commune's burden, the land was divided into many strips. Each family received some strips of good land, of average land, and so on. A family might therefore be farming 20 or 30 scattered strips of land, some of them no wider than 6 feet (2 meters). To ensure fairness, many communes redistributed these strips every few years. This helped guarantee equality and stability within the communes, but it did not allow for progress or change. The serfs distrusted innovation and therefore discouraged it. They feared that it would upset long-established habits they considered vital for their survival in a pitiless world. As a result, their farming methods remained the same from generation to generation.

Russia's state peasants were somewhat better off than the serfs. But the similarity of their lives far exceeded the differences. Like the serfs, they were bound to the land and were subject to heavy taxes and brutal military service. Most of them belonged to communes. In addition, they could be sent to work in state factories under inhuman conditions. They also could be given to private landlords and so become serfs.

Although there was no major uprising in the 1800s to compare with the Razin or Pugachev revolts, there was trouble enough. The years from 1800 to 1860 were marked by 1,500 disturbances of various sorts, creating the fear that another major upheaval was not far off. This fear, as well as worries about Russia's backwardness, especially in military matters, led to the Great Reforms.

On March 3, 1861, Alexander II, "Autocrat of All the Russias," abolished serfdom in Russia. Twenty million serfs were freed from the authority of their landlords in this emancipation, the largest in history. The Emancipation Edict was followed by several other major reforms. An edict in 1864 authorized the creation of new institutions of rural government called the *zemstvos* (ZEMST-vohz). That same year, the judicial system was overhauled. In addition, there were major educational and military reforms, and an attempt to overhaul city and town government. Together, these measures are known as the **Great Reforms.**

The Great Reforms enjoyed varying degrees of success. The *zemstvos* were composed of representatives of nobles, peasants, and inhabitants of small towns, with representation proportional to property ownership. Despite this obvious discrimination against the peasants, the *zemstvos* took their work seriously and made considerable progress in building and improving rural schools, hospitals, and other services. Representative councils did similar work in the cities. Military reform greatly improved conditions in the army. Judicial reform established an independent judiciary, a major step forward for Russia.

The peasants, who had been granted personal freedom and civil rights, were nonetheless subject to special courts. In effect, this gave their new freedom second-class status. Far more serious, though, were the economic problems now facing the emancipated peasants. When they were freed from the control of their landlords, they were not given enough land to farm—they had less land, in fact, than they had for their own use before 1861. The pieces allotted to them were not choice land. Moreover, these former serfs had to pay for their land, and the price the government set for it was higher than its value. The peasants were given 49 years to pay for their land, but they soon fell into debt. The government retained the *mirs* because they provided a ready mechanism of government control. Thus the peasants had no real control of the land for which they had paid so dearly. On top of all this came the ever-grow-

These peasant women are hauling a barge along a river, work that in most other countries was done by animals.

ing taxes, which were used to pay for the military, for the state's growing debt, and for industrialization.

Considerable industrial development took place between 1861 and 1900. But rural conditions hardly improved at all. In fact, they deteriorated in many regions. In 1891/1892, Russia experienced one of its worst droughts and famines. Moreover, most of the peasants' former oppressors, the nobles, could not adjust to a world without serfs. Many of the nobles fell into debt and sank into poverty.

The Great Reforms had raised some high hopes that had not been fulfilled. Disappointment with this state of affairs turned many young, educated people against the government. Some of them decided to use violence and terrorism to overthrow czarism. Among their targets was Alexander himself. Their first attempt to assassinate him, in 1866, was unsuccessful. But it helped to turn the czar away from liberalism, resulting in restrictions being put on some of his earlier reforms. After surviving several more attempts on his life, Alexander II was assassinated in 1881, when he was fatally wounded by a bomb.

Alexander III.   Alexander III (1881–1894) succeeded his father. The new czar was influenced by people who believed they could solve Russia's problems by returning to a stricter, more repressive government. Alexander's chief adviser, a former professor of law named Konstantine Pobedonostsev (puh-bee-dah-NAWS-tsev), was opposed to all progressive ideas and every liberal institution. Thus the reign of Alexander III was extremely reactionary. He reorganized the secret police and issued a series of regulations that undercut the legal and judicial system adopted during his father's reign. He repressed ethnic and religious minorities. His Russification policy imposed the Russian language and Russian schools on his Armenian, Polish, Finnish, Ukrainian and other non-Russian subjects. His harshest measures, however, were directed against the Jews. This religious minority had been a long-time victim of persecution in Russia. Alexander's new restrictions concerning Jews limited the areas in which they could live and excluded all but a small quota of Jews from higher education. Worse than that, however, were the anti-Jewish riots of murder and pillage known as **pogroms**. These the government either encouraged or did not try to stop.

Progress After the Emancipation.   Despite the economic difficulties and harshness of Alexander III's rule, the period from 1830 to 1900 was marked by great intellectual, artistic, and scientific achievements. (See Chapter 8.) The 40 years after emancipation also produced unprece-

Czar Alexander III tried to suppress all opposition to his reactionary policies. Here Russians accused of being revolutionaries are being shipped into exile in Siberia.

dented industrial growth. Some of this growth, particularly the rise of the cotton industry and the building of railroads, took place in the 1860s and 1870s. But the giant steps were taken in the 1890s. During that decade, the Russian government pursued a comprehensive industrialization policy. Between 1892 and 1903, Russia's railroad mileage increased by over 70 percent. Other major growth industries were iron and steel, textiles, metallurgy, coal, and oil. Overall, Russia's industrial growth rate was a spectacular 8 percent per year. This marked the real beginning of Russia's industrial revolution.

However, there were problems. The benefits of the industrial growth were very poorly distributed. The burden of paying for growth fell, as usual, on the peasants, who were taxed to the hilt. A heavy burden also fell on Russia's small but growing class of factory workers. In 1903, there was a wave of industrial strikes. Russia was making progress, but not nearly fast or fairly enough.

The Revolutionary Movement.   These difficult economic conditions helped stimulate growth in another new sector of Russian society: the revolutionary movement. Interestingly, this movement did not originate among the peasants or workers. Most peasants were illiterate and still in superstitious awe of the czar. There were too few workers and, until the end of the 1800s, they were virtually unorganized. The main force for radical change came from Russia's educated elite. Initially, in the 1820s and 1830s, these people were of noble origin. But as education spread in the 1840s, the revolutionary movement came to include more people of middle and lower-class origin. Whatever their background, these increasingly angry opponents of czarism shared the precious gift of education and the desire to change Russia quickly and drastically.

Aside from their hatred of the autocracy and the czar, the revolutionaries often found themselves in disagreement. Some of them wanted a constitutional, democratic regime. Others hoped to establish a dictatorship that would improve economic conditions dramatically and also guarantee equality. Both groups found themselves frustrated by the power of a state that seemed unable to improve Russian society but was strong enough to put down its opponents.

During the 1860s this frustration helped to produce a movement called **Nihilism**. Its adherents insisted that they were responsible only to their own moral code and that real change could come to Russia only when all of its existing institutions were destroyed. Nihilism was short-lived as a movement, but its ideas endured to influence later generations of revolutionaries.

During the 1870s and 1880s, a new generation of revolutionaries arose who were, for the most part, **populists**. The populists, influenced by Western thinking, were socialists with a Russian twist. **Socialism** is an economic system in which there is group or government ownership of the means of production and distribution of goods. Most Western socialists believed factory workers would control the takeover. However, the Russian populists believed that the Russian peasants and their communes provided the key for establishing socialism in Russia. The trouble was that the revolutionaries could not get that point across to the peasants. The peasants, it turned out, were highly suspicious of city intellectuals, frustratingly loyal to the czar, and preoccupied with everyday survival. Some populists responded by forming secret groups to stage a revolution on behalf of the peasants. They believed that only a tightly knit organization of revolutionaries, one that would control and direct the peasant masses, could carry out a revolution in Russia. These populists rejected democracy in favor of a dictatorship controlled by a few socialist leaders, a view that many later Russian socialists also would adopt. Other populists who rejected this view tried—in 1874 and 1875—to "go to the people" in the countryside, live with them, and educate them into starting a revolution. When those efforts failed completely, a small group calling itself the People's Will tried to use assassination to spark a revolution. In 1881, People's Will managed to assassinate Alexander II. However, instead of causing general upheaval, these efforts sent the revolutionaries to prison, to exile in Siberia, or to the gallows.

*Two contrasting settings of life in Russia in about 1900
are shown here. In the top picture, working class residents
of the rough, undeveloped Siberian city of Omsk are
gathered on a muddy street near their crude homes. In the
picture below, well-dressed middle-class city dwellers put
on a dramatization of a short story by Anton Chekhov.*

Eventually some of Russia's revolutionaries adapted the ideas of Karl Marx. (See Chapter 3.) **Marxism** held that the development of capitalism created a new revolutionary class—the factory workers, or **proletariat**. By the end of the 1800s Marx's ideas had spawned a small political movement. The Russian Marxists called themselves **Social Democrats**. They made their first attempt to set up a national organization in 1898. Interestingly, almost as soon as the Marxists had formed their party, it split in two. One side was called the **Mensheviks** (MEN-shuh-viks). Literally, this meant minority, referring to those who voted a certain way at the party's second congress in 1903. The Mensheviks looked to Western Europe for their model of how the party should be organized. Therefore they favored a party that had a democratic organization. The other faction was called the **Bolsheviks** (BOL-shuh-viks), meaning majority. The Bolsheviks were led by **Vladimir I. Ulyanov**, who called himself **Lenin**. In a 1902 pamphlet called "What Is to Be Done?" Lenin had outlined how he felt the party should be organized. He believed in a compact, strongly centralized party. Its membership would be limited to committed activists, or "professional" revolutionaries. The party would lead, direct, and control the working class, while a small group, the central committee, would control the party. As it turned out, this early split was to have profound implications, not only for the Social Democrats but for all of Russia.

The Russo-Japanese War.   Upon becoming czar, Alexander III's son Nicholas II (1894–1917) commented that he knew "absolutely nothing about matters of state." In addition, he was a man of reactionary views and little common sense.

The early years of Nicholas II's reign were not easy for Russia. Chronic economic problems as well as rapid social and economic changes caused a great deal of hardship and tension. Peasants and workers reacted with riots and strikes. Some revolutionary organizations, especially the Socialist Revolutionaries (a new political party that generally followed the old populist beliefs), conducted a campaign of assassinations of government officials. Nicholas, advised by reactionaries, responded with repression. Meanwhile, with Russia's expansionist goals blocked in Europe, Nicholas turned to the Far East, to Korea and to the Chinese province of Manchuria. There, thousands of miles from where most Russians lived, Nicholas and his advisers hoped for successes. Their plans for Korea and Manchuria were opposed by Japan. But Nicholas and his advisers assumed that a war with Japan would be short and victorious, that it would sweep Japan out of the way and unite

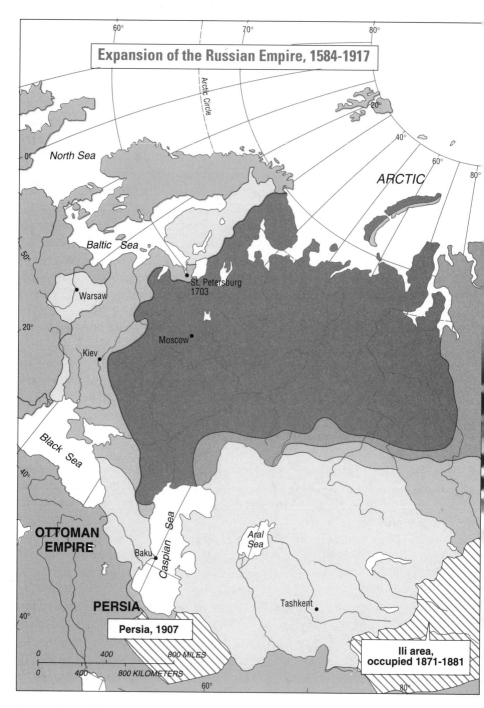

Expansion of the Russian Empire, 1584-1917

ARCTIC

North Sea

Arctic Circle

Baltic Sea

St. Petersburg
1703

Warsaw

Moscow

Kiev

Black Sea

OTTOMAN
EMPIRE

Baku

Caspian Sea

Aral
Sea

PERSIA

Tashkent

Persia, 1907

| 0 | 400 | 800 MILES |

| 0 | 400 | 800 KILOMETERS |

**Ili area,
occupied 1871-1881**

Russia behind Nicholas. Instead, the Russo-Japanese War, which began with a Japanese surprise attack in February of 1904, brought Russia a humiliating defeat. The suffering caused by the war produced riots and protests among the poor. It also united many middle-class and some

70

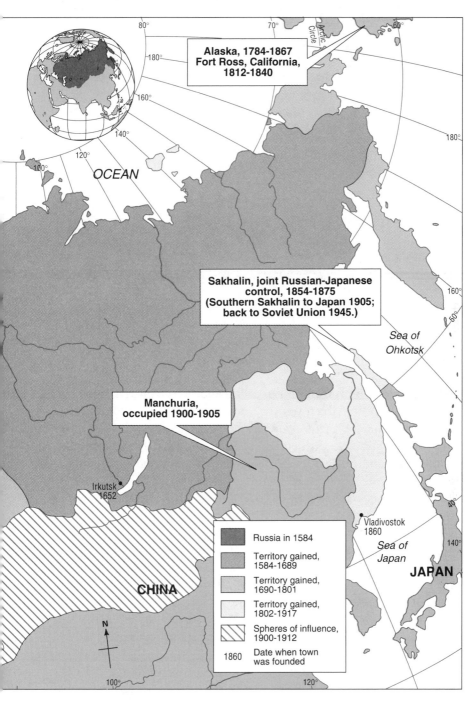

Alaska, 1784-1867
Fort Ross, California,
1812-1840

Sakhalin, joint Russian-Japanese
control, 1854-1875
(Southern Sakhalin to Japan 1905;
back to Soviet Union 1945.)

Manchuria,
occupied 1900-1905

OCEAN

Sea of
Ohkotsk

Irkutsk
1652

Vladivostok
1860

Sea of
Japan

CHINA

JAPAN

Russia in 1584

Territory gained,
1584-1689

Territory gained,
1690-1801

Territory gained,
1802-1917

Spheres of influence,
1900-1912

1860   Date when town
was founded

N

upper-class Russians in an effort that called for democratic reforms. But
Nicholas felt that calls for an elected assembly were "senseless dreams,"
and he refused to compromise. Public anger reached the boiling point
and exploded into the Revolution of 1905.

On Bloody Sunday in 1905, troops fired upon thousands of unarmed workers who had marched to the czar's Winter Palace in St. Petersburg to petition him for help.

Bloody Sunday, the Revolution of 1905, and the October Manifesto. The spark that ignited the revolution came on January 22, 1905. On that day a priest named Father Gapon led thousands of poor workers to the czar's Winter Palace in St. Petersburg to petition for help. They were met by troops and a hail of bullets that killed over 100 and wounded several thousand. As the news spread, Russia was swept by riots, strikes, angry meetings, assassinations of government officials, and even some mutinies in the armed forces. In October a general strike broke out in St. Petersburg. The workers of the city organized a **soviet** (meaning council) to press their demands. Pressured by organized protests that spanned the country both geographically and socially, Nicholas reached what he called his "terrible decision." On October 30, 1905, his **October Manifesto** promised the Russian people civil rights and a parliament, the *Duma*, with legislative power. Three generations after the Decembrists began the struggle, their dreams had begun to come true.

Results of the 1905 Revolution. The results of the Revolution of 1905 were decidedly mixed. In November, when he had finally ended the disastrous war with Japan and brought the army home, Nicholas arrested the St. Petersburg *soviet* and regained control of the capital. Then he embarked on the long, bloody process of restoring peace in the rest of the country. Since the army had remained loyal to him, he succeeded.

The revolution had been suppressed, but the clock could not be turned back completely. Russia's new parliament, the *Duma*, was a progressive force. Among its accomplishments were laws for the protection of workers and a program of universal primary education that would begin by 1922. Still, the *Duma* lacked many of the powers of Western parliaments. It was the czar, not the *Duma*, who appointed the ministers of the government; and these ministers were responsible only to the czar. The czar could also dismiss the *Duma* at will. Then, in the *Duma's* absence, he could issue emergency laws. In 1907, Nicholas and his prime minister, Peter Stolypin, used that power to rewrite the electoral laws in favor of the nobility and other conservative voters.

One important reform was undertaken after the Revolution of 1905 had been suppressed: Stolypin's agricultural program. Stolypin's program was designed to complete what the emancipation had left undone some 40 years earlier: to create an independent peasantry on the Western model. His program stipulated that the peasants themselves, not their communes, should be the owners of their land; that peasants could leave their communes; and that peasants could exchange their scattered strips of land for a single plot. Stolypin could do little about the peasants' need for more land, since he was unwilling to take the nobility's land away and give it to the peasants.

Although Stolypin was assassinated in 1911, his program continued to enjoy considerable success. Its implementation, like everything else in Russia, was interrupted by World War I. It took a long time to bring about these reforms, and that was a major shortcoming. By 1916, only 50 percent of the peasants had become the owners of their land, while 75 percent had not left their communes.

World War I: Imperial Russia's Last Crisis.   Overall, Russia made considerable progress between 1905 and 1914. The *Duma* had begun to perform its proper functions. Agriculture began to change for the better. Industry grew and modernized. Superb literature, art, music, and dance were produced in this "Silver Age" of Russian culture.

At the same time, Russia's agriculture and industry still lagged behind the West in productivity. The czar and his government were losing support even among the upper classes. In his choice of ministers, Nicholas was often influenced by his wife, Alexandra, and through her by a monk named Grigory Rasputin. As a result, most competent ministers did not last long in office. Though Alexandra believed that Rasputin was a "holy man," he was in reality a scoundrel whose actions undermined upper class confidence in the czar and his government.

Russia was thus unprepared for war when World War I broke out in August 1914. It lacked the industrial power and modern weapons to fight effectively. For two and a half years, Russia fought the modern army of Germany. Fifteen million men were drafted into the Russian army; over 8 million were killed, wounded, or captured. At home, shortages of basic goods crippled everything from railroad transportation to food distribution. By early 1917 the breaking point came. In the capital, which was now called Petrograd instead of the German-sounding St. Petersburg, riots began in early March. Troops sent to quell the riots joined the rioters instead. As disorder spread unchecked and generals began to doubt they could control their troops, the czar was told by his closest military and civilian advisers that only his abdication could prevent chaos. On March 12 the *Duma* ignored Nicholas's order to disperse and elected a "provisional committee" to cope with the crisis. That same day, the Petrograd Soviet of Workers' and Soldiers' Deputies came into being. On March 14 the Duma's provisional committee became the Provisional Government. The next day, powerless to do otherwise, Nicholas II abdicated. The monarchy's long rule over Russia had ended. A new age, full of hope and danger, was about to dawn.

Czar Nicholas II with his wife Alexandra and their five children in a photograph taken in 1914. Four years later the royal family was seized by the Bolsheviks and reportedly shot to death.

REVIEWING THE CHAPTER

I. Building Your Vocabulary

In your notebook, write the numbers from 1 to 6. After each number, write the word that matches the definition.

veche	autocracy	pogroms
khan	Nihilism	proletariat

1. self-governing council

2. anti-Jewish riots

3. state with unlimited power over its people

4. factory workers

5. movement advocating the destruction of all institutions

6. title of Mongol ruler

II. Understanding the Facts

In your notebook, write the numbers 1 to 5. Write the letter of the correct answer to each question next to its number.

1. By the 1400s, what city had become the capital of Russia?
   a. Novgorod   **b.** Moscow   **c.** St. Petersburg

2. Ivan the Terrible created Russia's first political police, called
   a. the KGB.   **b.** the *Kalita.*   **c.** the *oprichnina.*

3. The Cossack leader Pugachev led a revolt against what ruler?
   a. Catherine the Great   **b.** Ivan the Terrible   **c.** Fyodor I

4. The destruction of Sevastopol is associated with the
   a. Napoleonic Wars.   **b.** Russo-Japanese War.
   c. Crimean War.

5. Soon after the Social Democrats organized in 1898, they split into two groups called
   a. Mensheviks and Bolsheviks.   **b.** Nihilists and Marxists.
   c. czarists and Leninists.

III. Thinking It Through

In your notebook, write the numbers 1 to 5. Write the letter of the correct answer to each question next to its number.

1. The missionary monks Cyril and Methodius encouraged the use of
   a. the Cyrillic alphabet.
   b. secret police.
   c. the Roman Catholic Bible.
   d. the *Duma*.

2. The Mongol invaders of the 1200s swept into Russia from the central plains of
   a. Europe.
   b. Siberia.
   c. Asia.
   d. Sweden.

3. Which of the following was NOT an institution of rural government?
   a. the *mir*
   b. the *zemstvos*
   c. the Mensheviks
   d. the communes

4. What policy of the czars is best expressed in the phrase "One Czar, One Language, One Church?"
   a. socialism
   b. Russification
   c. cultural diffusion
   d. orthdoxy

5. The aim of the Decembrist Revolt was to
   a. assassinate Nicholas I.
   b. change the form of government in Russia.
   c. bring the Bolsheviks to power.
   d. protest the terms of the Congress of Vienna.

DEVELOPING CRITICAL THINKING SKILLS

1. Describe the impact of the Mongol invasion on Russia. How did it affect the political organization of the Russian states?

2. List the reasons that serfdom took hold in Russia. Then explain how the abolition of serfdom in 1861 created new problems for serfs.

3. Discuss the ways in which Peter the Great attempted to Westernize Russia. How did he open "a window to the West"? How was Catherine's reign an extension of Peter's?

4. Describe the steps taken to modernize Russia under Alexander II.

5. What were the outcomes of the Revolution of 1905? for the czar? for the Russian people?

INTERPRETING A MAP

Study the map on pages 70–71. In your notebook, write the letter of the choice that best completes each of the following sentences.

1. The major expansion of the Russian Empire from 1584 to 1689 was from
   a. north to south. **b.** east to west. **c.** west to east.

2. Which city was founded earliest?
   a. St. Petersburg **b.** Irkutsk **c.** Vladivostok

3. One area that was not part of the Russian Empire's sphere of influence during the period from 1900 to 1912 was
   a. Persia. **b.** China. **c.** Japan.

4. Which territory did Russia lose as a result of the Russo-Japanese War?
   a. the Ili area **b.** Fort Ross **c.** Sakhalin

ENRICHMENT AND EXPLORATION

1. The historic defeat of Napoleon's army in Russia resulted in the loss of a half million French soldiers. Research and prepare a report for the class on how the French army was stopped at Moscow.

2. Czar Alexander I played a significant role in the peace settlement at the Congress of Vienna in 1815. Using world history texts or encyclopedias, research and report on the Holy Alliance. Give its membership, its aims, and its results.

3 Fundamentals and Failures of Communism

Throughout history, philosophers and political thinkers have attempted to find a way to create a perfect society. In the ideal places they envisioned, there would be no poverty and everyone would have all his or her needs met. Two German thinkers of the 1800s named Karl Marx and Friedrich Engels, searching for a perfect society, developed a concept called communism. Although the ideas of Marx and Engels were new, their ideas reflected the thinking of philosophers as far back as the time of the ancient Greeks.

FORERUNNERS OF COMMUNISM

In the 400s B.C., the Greek philosopher Plato (c.427–c.347 B.C.) described his concept of an ideal society. In this society, a specially educated small group would rule and private property would be abolished. All wealth would be held in common. In 16th-century England, the statesman Sir Thomas More (1745–1833) described an ideal island he named Utopia. In Utopia everything was owned in common and there was no poverty. In 16th-century Germany, a religious leader named Thomas Müntzer (MOONT-ser), (c.1489–1525), preached the virtues of a collectivist society to his followers. In a collectivist society, the people as a group own and operate the means of production and distribution.

During the early 1800s, there were two well-known social philosophers in France: Claude Henri Saint-Simon (san-see-MOHN), 1760–1825, and Charles Fourier (foo-ree-YAY), 1772–1837. Saint-Simon (who fought on the side of the American colonists in their rebellion against England) advocated a planned society managed by a small group of technically trained people. Fourier proposed small communities in which about 1,600 people would live together in communal bliss.

Robert Owen (1771–1858), a Welsh contemporary of Saint-Simon and Fourier, was an industrialist who took matters one step further. In England, he established a factory village called New Lanark based on his ideas. At a time when factory workers—men, women, and children—worked and lived under horrendous conditions, Owen built adequate housing, for his workers. In New Lanark, children under the age of ten went to school instead of to work. The older children worked a 10 1/2-hour day, which was considerably shorter than the work load in other factories. The adults followed Owen's rules of morality and conduct, which required them to respect the rights of the community as a whole.

Some visions of the perfect society required not only the collective ownership of property, but also the abolition of the state. This ideology, called **anarchism**, had two outstanding advocates: the Frenchman Pierre Proudhon (proo-DOHN), 1809–1865; and the Russian nobleman Mikhail Bakunin (bah-KOO-nin), 1814–1876. The goal of abolishing the state could, in Bakunin's opinion, be reached only after terror and violence had been used to destroy the old order completely.

The various new societies that these thinkers envisaged had several common features. Most thinkers called for the abolition of private property. All of them supported the idea that the interests of the community carried more weight than did the interests of the individual. Another important and interesting feature is that most of these ideal societies were antidemocratic. Plato strongly rejected the democratic system of his native Athens. More, Saint-Simon, Fourier, Owen, Proudhon, and Bakunin all believed that decisions had to be made by an exclusive small group, not by the masses. There were, of course, exceptions like Müntzer, who believed that the masses had to take direct control.

THE BASIC PRINCIPLES OF MARXISM

By far the most influential theory of how to build the ideal society came from Karl Marx (1818–1883). Marx, born in Germany, came from a prosperous middle-class family and received an excellent education in law, history, and philosophy. During Marx's lifetime the Industrial Revolution was taking place in Europe. The miserable conditions under which workers lived—long hours and low wages, child labor, and the threat of unemployment—made a lasting impression on Marx.

The Communist Manifesto, written by Marx and his lifelong collaborator Friedrich Engels (1820–1895), appeared in 1848. It begins with the chilling, much-quoted warning, "A specter is haunting Europe—the

Karl Marx was the most influential of all the socialist thinkers. His ideas were adopted by revolutionaries in all parts of the world. They were the foundation of the Communist system of the Soviet Union.

specter of communism." It ends with the thunderous battle cry: "WORKERS OF ALL COUNTRIES, UNITE!" The manifesto is a bitter denunciation of capitalism and industrialization for maiming and destroying millions of lives and the entire social order of Europe.

Because of his political activities, Marx was forced to leave first Germany, then France, and finally Belgium. In 1849, he settled in England, where he spent the rest of his life. There he wrote *Capital*, a monumental three-volume study. (Actually, the last two volumes were completed by Engels after the death of Marx.) In it Marx and Engels attempted to prove that capitalism was doomed and that *communism*— a political and economic system that would guarantee equality, prosperity, and freedom for all—was inevitable. *Capital*, which became the bible of communism, was one of the most influential books of the 1800s and 1900s. Its influence on the social sciences and on the development and spread of communism is immeasurable. An understanding of Marx's theory requires some explanation of:

- the idea of dialectical materialism
- the class struggle
- the theory of surplus value and the crisis of capitalism
- the dictatorship of the proletariat
- the inevitability of communism

Dialectical Materialism. Marxism claimed that no human situation lasted forever. The world was always changing. According to Marx, change comes about through a process called **dialectical materialism**. **Materialism** is the idea that all human history—from everyday events to major historical developments—depends completely on what people do. It totally rejects all beliefs that gods or "spirits" of any kind affect what happens to human beings. In other words, the answers to why past events occurred or the solutions to present problems lie in the physical or "material" world of men and women.

Dialectical described the pattern of how changes occur. According to Marxism, any human situation—called the "thesis"—inevitably creates the seed of its own destruction, or "antithesis." The antithesis is the opposite of the thesis. As change occurs, there is a period of conflict. The conflict results in the destruction of the old order. This produces a new situation called the "synthesis" in which things are once more in balance. There is no rest, however, for the process begins again.

Marx applied this framework to the study of history. He believed that history could be understood by studying several areas. First was the **mode of production**. This was how people worked and used their technology at a given time to produce what they needed to live. Marx also believed it was important to learn about what he called the class struggle. According to him, this was the unending tension between those who controlled the wealth of a society and those who did not. Marx wrote that the way a society was organized economically (the mode of production or the **substructure**) determined everything else in a society. For example, a society might produce what it needed by hunting, farming, industry, or some combination of these activities. Whatever its economic system, a society developed laws, customs, political principles, and religious beliefs. Marx called these beliefs and rules the **superstructure**. These beliefs and rules supported and strengthened the position and privileges of the holders of wealth and power.

Marxism claimed that the mode of production or substructure—like any human institution—was constantly changing. This process of change was usually slow, but it was there nevertheless. For example, a new invention—a simple hoe perhaps—might gradually cause some members of a society to change from hunting to farming. As more people switched from hunting to farming, the ways of producing things (the substructure) were no longer in agreement with the old beliefs and rules (the superstructure). Thus customs and laws left over from times when hunting was most important might not have given enough credit and power to the growing group of farmers. This imbalance leads to a con-

CASE STUDY:

The Communist Manifesto

Karl Marx and Friedrich Engels were relatively unknown in 1848 when they issued their famous call to revolution, *The Communist Manifesto.* In these final paragraphs they repeat their major themes:

> ... the theory of the Communists may be summed up in the single sentence: Abolition of private property.... Communism deprives no man of the power to appropriate the products of society; all that it does is to deprive him of the power to subjugate the labor of others by means of such appropriation....
>
> We have seen ... that the first step in the revolution by the working class is to raise the proletariat to the position of ruling class....
>
> The proletariat will use its political supremacy to wrest by degrees all capital from the bourgeoisie; to centralize all instruments of production in the hands of the State, i.e., of the proletariat organized as the ruling class; and to increase the total of productive forces as rapidly as possible....
>
> The Communists disdain to conceal their view and aims. They openly declare that their ends can be attained only by the forcible overthrow of all existing social conditions. Let the ruling classes tremble at a Communist revolution. The proletarians have nothing to lose but their chains. They have a world to win.
>
> WORKERS OF ALL COUNTRIES, UNITE!

Karl Marx and Friedrich Engels, *The Communist Manifesto*, New York: Penguin Books, Inc., 1986.

1. According to the manifesto, what is the main goal of communism?

2. What is the first step in the revolutionary process?

3. What is the role of the proletariat?

4. Who are the exploiters, according to Marx and Engels?

5. Why do you think this document was so powerful?

Although the Revolution of 1905 caused much destruction, it did not change how the czar ruled Russia.

flict between the two groups. This Marx called the class conflict. When the conflict reaches the breaking point, Marx claimed there would be a revolution. The old ruling group (the hunters) is overthrown. The new group (the farmers) takes control. It then sets up a new superstructure—laws, customs, and beliefs—that strengthen the farmers' power.

The Class Struggle. In their *Communist Manifesto,* Marx and Engels wrote, "The history of all hitherto existing society is the history of class struggles." The class struggle they had found in every society was a struggle between those who controlled the wealth of a society and those who did not. Thus, the slaves struggled against their masters, feudal serfs struggled against their feudal lords, and factory workers struggled against their capitalist employers. But always it was the class that controlled the sources of wealth that had all the power. This class, the ruling class, sets up a political system to protect its own economic power. Governments are created to do the bidding of the ruling class, and laws are passed to protect its special position.

To justify a situation that is unfair and oppresses the majority of the people, the ruling class invents moral values and religious beliefs. According to Marx, religion plays a major role in fooling people into believing that life on earth is unimportant compared to heaven. "Religion," said Marx, "is the opiate (narcotic) of the masses."

Marx believed that change from one type of society to another was, by necessity, violent, because no ruling class would give up its position

83

without a fight. Yet every ruling class must lose. Gradually changes in the mode of production strengthen some other groups at the former's expense. Thus, the slaveholders had to yield to the feudal lords, and the feudal lords to the capitalists. From this Marx and Engels confidently predicted that the downfall of the capitalists was near.

The Theory of Surplus Value and the Crisis of Capitalism.   In Marx's time, it was common for a factory worker to work 80 hours a week. Wages were extremely low. Marx insisted that workers were paid far less than they were worth. For example, the goods that the worker produced in that week might be worth 50 dollars. Yet the weekly wage of the worker would be 10 dollars. The difference between these two values—in this case 40 dollars—was what Marx called **surplus value.** The capitalist who owned the factory regarded it as rightful profit. To Marx that amounted to stealing the surplus value from the workers. It left the workers miserably poor while the capitalists grew rich.

The theft, said Marx, was a two-edged sword. Because the workers were paid far less than the value they produced, they could not buy enough goods to keep all the capitalists in business. This led to increasing competition among the capitalists. To outsell his competitors, the capitalist will cut his prices, often by introducing machines to replace workers, or cut his workers' wages. But this allows the workers to buy even less. As the capitalists' profits fall, competition gets fiercer. Eventually, the merciless struggle reduces the number of capitalists, as the losers go bankrupt and economic crises become more severe.

The Dictatorship of the Proletariat.   The working class, which Marx called the **proletariat,** was exploited by the capitalists. But it was also gaining valuable experience. In the factories, many people had to cooperate in order to make a product. The workers were learning that their cooperation, not the activities of the capitalist, was the reason for society's wealth. Eventually, led by a group Marx called **communists,** the working class would unite and overthrow the tiny capitalist minority.

Immediately after their revolution, the victorious workers would control the **means of production**—the factories, railroads, mines, and farms. Then private property would be abolished. If the capitalists fought back, the workers would use their overwhelming numbers to crush them. The new society, the **dictatorship of the proletariat,** would own the means of production, and it would not exploit the workers.

Marx did not consider the dictatorship of the proletariat to be oppressive in the traditional sense. It would crush a small minority—the former oppressors—but not hurt the majority of the people. When the dictatorship of the proletariat had destroyed the capitalists once and for all, it would somehow dissolve. Then what Marx called the era of socialism would arrive. Marx said very little about how the dictatorship of the proletariat would function or how it would dissolve.

Socialism was the first stage of Marx's dream society, **communism**. Under socialism, there would still be some remnants of the old order, such as old habits of behavior and inefficient methods of organization. Therefore some kind of state would be needed to organize and to run things. In this state, people were to be paid according to the value of their labor. As the old ways of doing things disappeared, the socialist state would "wither away," said Marx. After that, wealth would be produced in great quantity. In this society, the amount of money or property one has would not depend on one's job. Rather, society would be run according to the principle: "From each according to his ability, to each according to his needs." Communism would have arrived. Social classes would cease to exist, for all people would be equal in a communist society. Crime, vice, and all other evils would disappear, since they are products of the old class society.

The Inevitability of Communism.   Marx claimed that his analysis with its promise of well-being was based on a scientific study of history. He and Engels had not simply complained that things were bad. They had carefully examined Western civilization, tracing its development and progress. Their predictions reflected that study. Marx and Engels criticized other socialists for basing their ideas on hopes rather than on reality. Socialism could not have been achieved before the 1800s, they pointed out. In earlier times, industry, essential for a universal high standard of living, had not existed. History had now reached a point where socialism (followed by communism) was inevitable. In 1848, they proclaimed

Lenin, shown here addressing a May Day rally in 1918, adapted the ideas of Karl Marx to suit conditions in Russia.

that capitalism was haunted by the "specter of communism." Both men spent the rest of their lives waiting for its arrival.

Leninism: The Application of Marxist Theory.   The first Marxist who had the opportunity to try out the master's ideas was Vladimir Ilich Ulyanov (ool-YAHN-uv), a Russian from an educated, middle-class family. Ulyanov was touched by revolutionary currents early in life. In 1887, when he was just 17, his brother was executed for participating in a plot to assassinate the czar. Ulyanov himself got into trouble as a university student for his role in student protests. By his mid-twenties, he was a committed revolutionary, known to his comrades in the movement—as he is now known to history—by his revolutionary alias "Lenin."

A number of differences exist between the Marxism of Karl Marx and the Marxism of Lenin, later known as **Leninism**. Leninism combined elements of Marxism with elements of Russia's revolutionary tradition. For example, Marx believed that the factory workers themselves would become revolutionaries and eventually take action to overthrow their oppressors. Lenin had much less faith in the workers' ability to act alone. He believed a group of professional revolutionaries functioning as a centralized political party would have to show the workers the way. Without such guidance, said Lenin, the workers would be satisfied with better wages and working conditions, and thereby ensure the continuation of capitalism. Lenin's plan for a revolutionary party stressed that the party would control the workers, and a small central committee would control the party. His plan met with some opposition. Many of Lenin's fellow Marxists feared that his party—if it ever came to power—would be as oppressive and dictatorial as the czarist regime.

Lenin also differed with Marx about the timing of the revolution. Lenin accepted Marx's idea that every society had to pass through a capitalist phase. But Lenin rejected Marx's belief that capitalism would have to run its course and completely decay before a society could pass on to the next stage. Lenin felt that the next stage could be reached sooner if the proletariat seized power in Russia and if the revolution quickly led to other socialist revolutions in Western Europe.

Stalinism: Marxism Forges a New Society.   Lenin combined Marxism with the Russian revolutionary tradition. Joseph Stalin (STAH-leen), who succeeded Lenin as head of the Communist party, added the governing methods of Ivan the Terrible. Stalin's real name was Dzhugashvili (joo-gahsh-VEE-lee). The name "Stalin" was derived from the Russian word for "steel." He was not an ethnic Russian. He was

*Joseph Stalin, shown here in police photographs, was
jailed several times for his revolutionary activities.*

from Georgia, a country in the Caucasus that was part of theRussian
Empire and then part of the Soviet Union until 1991. However, Stalin
tried to make himself seem as Russian as possible. He was born into
poverty and endured a brutal childhood. Defying his father, he drifted
into revolutionary activity. As a member of Lenin's Bolshevik party,
Stalin helped to raise funds by engaging in criminal activities, such as
bank robberies. Lenin approved but some of the revolutionaries did not.
They distrusted Stalin because they thought he was two-faced and
mean. Their fears proved to be justified. Once Stalin assumed power,
he employed unbelievably brutal methods. Millions who opposed Stalin
were executed, and his methods have been compared to those of Ivan
the Terrible and Peter the Great. The degree of violence that Stalin
brought to Marxist government would have shocked Marx, and probably even Lenin.

Stalin modified Marxism in other ways as well. Communist principles and practices were increasingly merged with the traditions and
methods of old Russia. He insisted that Russia could build socialism on
its own, without communist revolutions elsewhere, which other
Marxists considered essential. Furthermore, Stalin refused to accept
Marx's view that the state would wither away. While communism was
being built, he insisted, the state would have to grow stronger. Stalin
kept proclaiming that he was the faithful interpreter of Marx and Lenin.
Many historians think Stalin's state had more in common with Russia's
age-old tradition of autocracy than with Marxist theory. In Chapter 4 we
will see how this happened by turning to the history of Russia since
1917, the year Lenin led his small band of Bolsheviks to power.

CONTRADICTIONS AND PROBLEMS OF MARXISM

Marxism appealed to some who believed that its theories of human behavior and history provided the best available guide to the future. In reality, it did a poor job of predicting future circumstances and over the years, many became disillusioned by its failures.

The Successes of Capitalism. Marx's prediction that poverty would increase under capitalism did not occur. Instead, during the 1800s and 1900s, the standard of living in capitalist countries rose, not just for wealthy capitalists, but for ordinary workers as well. Even during Marx's lifetime, the industrialized, capitalist countries of Western Europe and the Americas were providing their people with the highest standard of living in the world. Because most of the working people in Western Europe and the Americas could see how their standard of living was better than that of the previous generation, they did not answer the revolutionary call of Marx and other communists. Of course, extreme poverty and other problems in capitalist societies persisted, but these problems did not create the amount of discontent that might have led to a socialist revolution.

Marxism did have its followers and by the late 1800s, there were several well established Marxist political parties in Western Europe. In Germany, the Social Democratic Workers' Party (SPD) did well in democratic elections, although it never was able to win a majority of the vote. It was ironic that the SPD got stronger as it abandoned the idea of revolution and turned increasingly to reform. It seemed to gain in popularity as it became less Marxist.

By the early 1900s, Marx's followers were struggling to explain why capitalism continued to survive and why Europe's workers seemed uninterested in overthrowing the system. Their explanations generally ignored certain developments that contradicted Marxist theory. Not only was capitalism a productive system that enabled workers to improve their standard of living, but capitalist countries were capable of making reforms that led to other improvements in workers' lives. A number of new laws improved working conditions in factories in Europe and the United States. Social welfare programs in some countries provided workers with benefits such as unemployment insurance and pensions. In addition, more people in the industrialized capitalist countries were winning the right to vote. This strengthened democracy and enabled workers to press for more reforms under capitalism. As a result, the workers' interest in overthrowing the capitalist and democratic systems in their countries decreased even more.

There were other problems with Marxist theory. No Marxist concept caused more problems than the dictatorship of the proletariat. Marx despised democracy as it existed in Western Europe and the United States because he considered it a tool of the ruling capitalist class. Under his theory of the dictatorship of the proletariat, the small minority of "capitalist oppressors" would have no rights. The new revolutionary government would have the power to do whatever it wanted to the defeated capitalists. But Marx and many of his later followers overlooked the possibility that a state without limits on its power, even a proletariat dictatorship, would become corrupt and oppressive. They assumed that revolutionaries were somehow incorruptible and that they would always use their power for good purposes.

The reality turned out to be very different, first in the Soviet Union, as you will learn in Chapter 4, and then in other countries where communists succeeded in setting up dictatorships. Instead of governments that were better than those in capitalist countries, these communist regimes were among the most corrupt and brutal in the world.

Russian Marxists were appalled by the conditions under which many Russian peasants worked. The peasants shown here are plowing a field—work that in most countries would have been done by animals or machines.

Another flaw in Marxist theory was its belief that it was possible to have a society where individuals worked "each according to his ability" and received "each according to his needs." Marx assumed that people under socialism would work without such incentives as higher wages. During the Soviet era, the government often relied on the goal of building the world's first socialist society to inspire people to work harder. Usually this approach failed and the Soviet government found it had to rely on incentives—higher wages that would enable people to buy more goods—to get its labor force to work hard. However, the Soviet economy had relatively few goods to offer its people. For decades the Soviet government devoted its resources to building modern factories and a powerful military; there was little left over to make the consumer goods people needed. Millions of Soviet workers refused to work hard, because there was little reward for their labor. Instead of working "each according to his ability" for a promised return of "each according to his needs," Soviet workers often repeated another slogan: "They pretend to pay; we pretend to work."

After World War II, the Soviet Union occupied Eastern Europe and set up communist regimes. (See map on page 129.) As a result, Europe was divided into a capitalist west and a communist east. The communist regimes did not receive the support of most people, and most of these governments depended on protection from the Soviet army to survive. The Soviet-imposed division of Europe caused great tension for over 40 years as an alliance of capitalist nations led by the United States faced a communist bloc dominated by the Soviet Union.

Ultimately, economic failure, corrupt and inefficient communist dictatorships, and the continued failure of communism to provide a better life than capitalism provided undermined most communist regimes. During 1989, most of the communist regimes of Eastern Europe collapsed, and the few remaining ones in the region fell shortly thereafter. Finally, communism in the Soviet Union collapsed in 1991. The struggle between capitalism and communism was over, but it ended differently from the way Marx and Engels had predicted in *The Communist Manifesto*. The next three chapters will discuss the rise of communism in the Soviet Union and its spread to other countries after World War II. You will learn about the effect Marxism had on Eurasia and on events all over the world since 1917. You will also learn how communism grew to be such a powerful force in world affairs and why it declined and eventually collapsed.

REVIEWING THE CHAPTER

I. Building Your Vocabulary

In your notebook, write the numbers 1 to 5. After each number write the word that best completes the sentence. (There are two extra words in the list.)

surplus value   socialism   Robert Owen   Utopia
anarchism   *Capital*   Ulyanov

1. The ideal community envisioned by the 16th-century English statesman Sir Thomas More was called _____.

2. _____, a British industrialist, founded a factory village in which children and adults followed his rules of work, morality, and conduct.

3. Some people believed the perfect society could only be achieved through _____, the abolition of the state.

4. Karl Marx explained his theories of communism in a monumental three-volume work entitled _____.

5. The difference between the worth of what a worker produces and his or her weekly wage is known as _____.

II. Understanding the Facts

In your notebook, write the numbers from 1 to 5. Write the letter of the correct answer to each question next to its number.

1. In *The Republic*, Plato described an ideal society for his native
   a. France.   **b.** Russia.   **c.** Greece.

2. The proletariat refers to
   a. the workers.   **b.** the nobles.   **c.** the peasants.

3. Karl Marx came from
   a. an English working-class background.
   b. a prosperous German family.
   c. a group of Russian revolutionaries.

4. Marx and Engels believed that when communism finally arrived
   a. there would be only two social classes.
   b. no one would work.
   c. crime, vice, and all other evils of society would disappear.

5. Marx believed that
   a. when the proletariat gained control, the workers would not be exploited.
   b. a small group of professional leaders should lead the masses.
   c. socialism would be established by peaceful means.

III. Thinking It Through

In your notebook, write the numbers from 1 to 5. Write the letter of the correct answer to each question next to its number.

1. According to Marx and Engels, the class struggle
   a. existed throughout history.
   b. was a product of the Industrial Revolution.
   c. was the fault of the czars.
   d. resulted from surplus value.

2. Religion, according to Marx,
   a. strengthened the government.
   b. was important to socialism.
   c. encouraged socialist ideals.
   d. fooled the people into accepting their lot.

3. The first stage of Marx's dream society was
   a. slaves and masters.
   b. the dictatorship of the proletariat.
   c. the crisis of capitalism.
   d. the era of socialism.

4. Lenin revised Marxist principles by
   a. introducing the idea of professionally trained leaders.
   b. denouncing the class struggle principle.
   c. adding the fundamentals of capitalism.
   d. renouncing the use of violence.

5. Stalin modified Marxism by
   a. building an autocratic government.
   b. advocating peaceful methods.
   c. insisting on worldwide revolution.
   d. declaring himself czar.

DEVELOPING CRITICAL THINKING SKILLS

1. Charles Fourier and Robert Owen each criticized economic injustices. Discuss how each proposed to find solutions to the plight of workers. Why do you think their programs did not last?

2. Compare and contrast the major ideas of socialism and communism.

3. What was the appeal of Marxism in the late 1800s? How did it reflect the changes brought about by the Industrial Revolution? Give two reasons that explain why Marxism did not take hold in the 1800s.

4. Evaluate Marxist theory. Give two reasons for the failure of Marxism in the former Soviet Union and the countries of Eastern Europe.

INTERPRETING VISUAL EVIDENCE

Study the photograph on page 89. Then answer the following questions.

1. Why do you think these Russian peasants from the 1800s are plowing without either horses or oxen?

2. What does this photograph tell you about Russia in the 1800s?

3. How might a Marxist have used this photograph for propaganda?

ENRICHMENT AND EXPLORATION

1. In the century since Karl Marx first proclaimed the goals of the proletarian revolution, many improvements have been made in working and living conditions, particularly in the Western world. List the changes advocated by socialists in the 1800s and determine which have been achieved.

2. Select two groups of volunteers to debate the statement, "The only hope for mankind is the creation of the socialist state." One group should represent the supporters of Karl Marx. The other group should represent the ideas of Mikhail Bakunin, the anarchist. The rest of the class should judge the effectiveness of the arguments of each side.

3. Prepare on a bulletin board or the chalkboard a diagram showing the stages of the class struggle, according to Karl Marx. Label each step and explain how Marx believed one would lead to the next.

THE GROWTH OF THE SOVIET UNION
1917–1953

1914–1918	*World War I*
1917	Bolshevik Red Guard overthrows Provisional Government.
1918	Bolsheviks close down the Constituent Assembly.
	Russia and Germany sign the Treaty of Brest-Litovsk.
	Bolsheviks execute Czar Nicholas and his family.
1918–1921	Civil war in Russia
1921	Rebellion breaks out at the Kronstadt naval base.
	Lenin announces New Economic Policy.
1922	The Union of Soviet Socialist Republics created.
1922	Stalin becomes the general secretary of the Communist party.
1929	Stalin becomes leader of the Soviet Union.
	Stalin announces the first Five Year Plan.
1932	Collectivization results in famine in the Ukraine.
1934–1938	Stalin conducts the Great Purge.
1938	*Hitler annexes the German-speaking region of Czechoslovakia.*
1939	Stalin and Hitler sign nonaggression pact.
1939–1945	*World War II*
1939–1940	USSR defeats Finland in Winter War.
1941	Hitler invades USSR.
1942–1943	Soviet troops stop German advance at the battle of Stalingrad.
1948	Yugoslavia breaks away from the Soviet bloc.
1949	USSR develops an atomic bomb.
	People's Republic of China is founded.
1953	Stalin era ends.

4 The Soviet Union Under Lenin and Stalin, 1917–1953

The Communist government officially took the name Union of Soviet Socialist Republics, or Soviet Union, in 1922. However, the Soviet regime actually began on November 7, 1917, when the Bolshevik party seized power in Russia. The history of the Soviet Union can be divided into four major periods: the Lenin era (1917–1924), the time of Stalin (1924–1953), the period of Stalin's successors (1953–1985), and the era of Mikhail Gorbachev and his reforms (1985–1991).

Between 1917 and 1924, the Communist party under Lenin's leadership established and solidified its political power. It eliminated all other political parties and established its dictatorship. After a power struggle within the party that lasted from 1924 to 1929, Joseph Stalin emerged as Lenin's successor. During the troubled period of Stalin's control the country underwent one of the most thorough economic and social transformations in history. This process, which involved immense human suffering, established the basic institutions that governed and managed the Soviet Union until its final days. From 1953 to 1985, Stalin's successors struggled to institute reforms to improve the life of the Soviet people and enable the Soviet Union to compete economically and militarily with the West. After 1985, Mikhail Gorbachev introduced radical reform in an attempt to modernize and democratize the Soviet system. However, his program came too late and rather than strengthening the system, undermined it.

THE SOVIET UNION UNDER LENIN: 1917–1924

When the czarist regime was overthrown in March 1917, it proved very difficult to establish an effective government in its place. The *Duma* formed a provisional committee, which then became the Provisional Government. (See Chapter 2, page 74.) It was dominated by liberals and moderate socialists. They were committed to establishing the rule of law and governing with the consent of the people. The Provisional Government granted civil rights and freed political prisoners. It also established an eight-hour workday. Meanwhile, the Provisional Government prepared for an election of a constituent assembly that was to provide the country with a constitution. Its commitment to democracy, however, prevented the government from acting rapidly and decisively on other matters. The Provisional Government did not pull Russia out of World War I, which was causing large numbers of casualties and much suffering. It also refused to authorize the immediate transfer of the nobility's land to the peasantry. This refusal came from the belief that land transfer would be illegal unless it had the approval of a nationally elected legislature. Furthermore, because it was reluctant to interfere with free political expression, the government was unwilling at first to crack down on groups, such as Lenin's Bolsheviks, that clearly wanted to overthrow the new order.

Despite its democratic intentions, the Provisional Government had little support among the workers and peasants. This fact is demonstrated by the existence and power of another body: the Petrograd Soviet. (St. Petersburg had been renamed Petrograd in 1914.) This body had no fixed membership. It was made up of representatives from the factories and military units and intellectuals from various socialist parties. Because of its close ties with the soldiers and workers, the Soviet—its formal name was the Soviet of Workers' and Soldiers' Deputies—had far

Russian soldiers marching in 1917 under the banner of "Communism" in Moscow during the Bolshevik Revolution.

more influence among them than did the Provisional Government. Therefore it was able to issue its famous "Order #1." That order told the military units to take commands only from the Soviet and to ignore the Provisional Government. Meanwhile, other soviets were springing up all over the country. None of them was listening to the Provisional Government.

The increasing confusion and hardship that developed during the summer and fall of 1917 weakened the Provisional Government. The government still refused to transfer noble-held lands to the peasantry. Its reputation suffered further after a disastrous military offensive in late June. The Bolsheviks saw their chance. All of the political parties associated with the new government lost influence. Only the Bolsheviks benefited since they were the only major political party that had refused to support the government. As the Provisional Government foundered, the Bolsheviks promised the people of Russia *Land, Peace, and Bread.* This slogan had great appeal for the land-hungry peasants, the suffering soldiers, and the hungry workers. At the very least, the Bolsheviks promised action, while the Provisional Government had become paralyzed. As the Bolsheviks' influence grew among the workers and soldiers, so did Lenin's confidence. Late in October, while soldiers were deserting their units, the Bolshevik party began to draw up its plan for seizing power. During the night of November 6–7, it acted. Armed Bolshevik units, known as the **Red Guards**, occupied the key parts of Petrograd and arrested the ministers of the Provisional Government. Russia's short experiment with democracy was over.

The Establishment of the Bolshevik Dictatorship. Lenin's new government was called the **Council of People's Commissars.** In addition to its chairman, Lenin, the new government included Leon Trotsky (1879–1940). Trotsky was a brilliant revolutionary agitator and a superb organizer, who served first as Commissar for Foreign Affairs and then as Commissar of War. (The Bolsheviks used the revolutionary term *commissar* instead of the more traditional *minister.*) Another of the Bolshevik commissars—though not yet a member of Lenin's inner circle—was Joseph Stalin, who served as Commissar of Nationalities.

The new government moved immediately. On November 8, it issued a land decree that transferred all of the nation's farmland to the peasants. It also issued a peace decree, which called for immediate negotiations between all involved nations to end the war. When its allies rejected the call, Russia negotiated with Germany alone. The negotiations were long and difficult. Finally, Lenin's government accepted the

Leon Trotsky, center, one of the leaders of the Bolshevik Revolution, at a parade of a Moscow army battalion.

harsh German peace terms. These terms called for Russia to give up a large amount of territory, but Lenin knew that only peace would ensure the survival of the new Soviet state. In March 1918, the Bolshevik government signed the Treaty of Brest-Litovsk (brest-lih-TOHFSK). In signing a separate peace with Germany, Russia was leaving its former allies—Great Britain, France, and the United States—to fight alone.

Consolidation of Political Power. On the political front, the Bolshevik government soon moved to eliminate its political rivals. To the surprise of almost everyone, Lenin excluded the other socialist parties from his government. Then most of the non-Bolshevik newspapers were closed down. In December 1917, the government created its own secret police, the **Cheka** (che-KAH). It was to suppress what the Bolsheviks called **counterrevolution**, meaning all popular dissent and criticism of the government.

In January 1918, the Bolsheviks moved against another potential rival: the Constituent Assembly. This body had been selected late in 1917 through the election organized by the Provisional Government. The Bolsheviks, who had already seized power, did not want the election to take place. However, they were afraid to cancel it and risk angry reactions from the public. It was the first and, as it turned out, the last free election in Russia for the next 70 years. Another socialist party, the Socialist Revolutionaries, won a majority of the seats. But the Constituent Assembly met for only one day. Then the Bolshevik troops closed it down by force.

Some of the Bolsheviks' policies, such as their land and peace programs, won them popular support. But their attempts to silence all criticism and their use of repression upset many people. The opposition included many who had been potential supporters. Other socialist parties turned against the government. So did many workers and soldiers.

The peace treaty with Germany brought much-needed peace. However, it offended many patriotic Russians, who resented the loss of land the treaty demanded. In addition, supporters of both the old czarist order and of the Provisional Government rallied to the anti-Bolshevik cause. So did the United States, Great Britain, and France. British, French, and American troops took control of Arkhangelsk in northwestern Russia. American and Japanese troops landed on the coast of eastern Siberia. At first they hoped to set up a new Russian government that would be willing to continue the fight against the Central Powers. After the Allies' victory over Germany in November 1918, they simply wanted to overthrow this dangerous new regime in Russia that was pledged to promote communist revolutions around the world.

The Civil War.   The result of all this upheaval was a terrible civil war that lasted almost three years. From the summer of 1918 until early 1921, it was a merciless fight to the death. The Bolsheviks were called the **Reds**; their opponents, the **Whites**. At first glance, the odds were against the Reds, just as the odds had been against the Provisional Government. This was the case with any government trying to function in strife-torn Russia. But the Bolsheviks did have several advantages. First, they controlled Petrograd and Moscow, and therefore the center of the country. The Whites, on the other hand, were scattered across the country and therefore found it difficult to coordinate their forces.

Second, the Bolsheviks had several superb and ruthless leaders. Foremost among them was Lenin, the man who held the party together. He was ably assisted by the brilliant Trotsky and other talented people. The Whites, in contrast, were a mix of diverse parties, factions, interests, and poorly disciplined military units, with nobody in charge.

Meanwhile, the Bolsheviks were organizing what resources they had. They used their new Red Army—hastily organized by Trotsky—to maximum advantage. To mobilize every economic resource, they took over all factories, seized food from the peasantry by force, and banned all private trade. Workers or peasants who resisted were crushed by force. These policies, which came to be known as **war communism**, destroyed the country's economy. Nevertheless, they enabled the Bolsheviks to keep the Red Army supplied and in operation.

Finally, the Whites handled their public relations poorly, while the Bolsheviks were expert propagandists. The Whites had no land program to present to the peasants. Nor did they have a program for the non-Russian peoples of the country. Some of these people wanted local self-government. Others wanted complete independence. During 1917 and

A woman's battalion prepares to defend the Bolshevik Revolution in the civil war that raged until 1921.

1918 Finland, the Ukraine, Georgia, Armenia, and Azerbaijan declared independence. The Whites had no unified response to these declarations. The Bolsheviks, on the other hand, had promised land to the peasants and independence to all the non-Russian peoples who wanted it. The result was that when the peasants or non-Russian minorities sided with anyone, they sided with the Bolsheviks.

Once they gained power, the Bolsheviks broke most of these promises and reconquered many of the people who had declared their independence. However, they were unable to conquer Poland during a short war in 1920.

In 1921, the Bolsheviks won the civil war. The Whites were not the only losers. Millions had been killed in the fighting or had died of starvation or disease. Millions more were homeless. Czar Nicholas and his family had been murdered by the Bolsheviks in 1918. When the fighting was finally over, the famine of 1921–1922 claimed additional millions.

Lenin's New Economic Policy. By 1921, the Bolsheviks had passed the test of seizing power and the far more difficult test of holding on to it during the civil war. But they were still not secure. The economy was in ruins. Millions of people lacked food and shelter. There were strikes in the cities and riots in the countryside. Food was especially scarce. During the civil war, the peasants had responded to food seizures by growing only what they themselves could eat. Then, in February and

March 1921, a major rebellion broke out at the Kronstadt naval base near Petrograd. This event was a serious setback because Kronstadt had long been a Bolshevik stronghold. Now the sailors were demanding an end to the Bolshevik dictatorship and its replacement by a government of several socialist parties. The Bolsheviks responded to these demands by putting down the rebellion with cruelty and great loss of life.

To deal with the economic crisis, Lenin drew up a bold new program, the **New Economic Policy (NEP)**. Because it included some measures that were clearly capitalistic, this program was unpopular with many Bolsheviks. But Lenin insisted that these measures were necessary to bolster food production and restore vital services. Unless these were restored, he warned, the regime would be in jeopardy.

The New Economic Policy put an end to the seizure of food from the peasants. Instead, the peasants turned over a certain percentage of their crops to the government and were free to sell the rest in the open market. This policy provided the peasants with an incentive to produce as much as they could. Major enterprises such as banks, railroads, mines, and large factories remained under government control. But small businesses were returned to private ownership. Thus the New Economic Policy restored a certain amount of private enterprise.

The results were impressive. Agricultural production increased quickly, and so the food crisis was overcome. Industrial production recovered more slowly, but progress was considerable. Nonetheless, the Bolsheviks were unhappy with this limited return to private enterprise. The more efficient peasants were outproducing their neighbors. Some were renting more land and hiring others to work for them. These so-called **kulaks** were becoming more prosperous than other peasants and were in fact small-scale capitalists. In the cities, too, private merchants and small manufacturers, called **NEPmen**, after the New Economic Policy, were spreading capitalist business methods. The Bolsheviks were also dissatisfied with the condition of major industries. Being Marxists, they believed that efficient modern industry was essential to a socialist society. They therefore believed the country's industry had to be modernized and greatly expanded. To do this, however, the government would need large sums of money, which it did not have. One reason for the lack of money was that the existing industries were too inefficient to produce large profits for the government. The traditional czarist method of raising funds—taxing the peasants more and more heavily—also had been eliminated by Lenin's New Economic Policy. Low tax rates had been set for the peasants so that they would have the incentive to produce as much food as they possibly could.

While Lenin's government was loosening some of its controls on the economy of the country, it tightened its political controls. Within the Communist party, as the Bolshevik party had been renamed in 1918, new rules adopted in 1921 severely restricted debate at party meetings. It became very difficult and dangerous to disagree with the party leadership, and those who did risked being thrown out of the party. These new rules, which Lenin totally supported, later became the tools that Joseph Stalin used to destroy his rivals and build his personal dictatorship.

The Union of Soviet Socialist Republics. In 1922, the party turned to reorganizing the government structure of the country it ruled. Until then, the party officially did not rule a unified country. Instead, in theory there were six "independent" republics under communist rule: Russia, Ukraine, Belorussia, Georgia, Azerbaijan, and Armenia. In reality, all of these countries were tightly controlled by Lenin's government in Moscow. In December 1922, the fictitious state of independence ended when all six republics signed a treaty creating the Union of Soviet Socialist Republics. The new union offically contained four republics: Russia, Ukraine, Belorussia, and the Transcaucasia, which combined the territories of Georgia, Azerbaijan, and Armenia.

The constitution of the new state asserted that the Soviet Union was a "voluntary union of equal peoples." One clause even stated that any republic could "secede freely" from the new union. Within a few years more republics were added to the union. The Transcaucasian Republic was again broken up into Georgian, Azerbaijian and Armenian republics, and four new republics in Central Asia were carved out of the Russian Republic. In 1940, four new republics were created out of territory the Soviet Union had seized along its western border as a result of its 1939 treaty with Nazi Germany. That brought the total number of Soviet republics to 15. As before, the Union of Soviet Socialist Republics remained a centralized communist dictatorship under which millions of non-Russians were tightly controlled from Moscow.

Lenin's Last Struggle. There was little or no check on government officials after public criticism of Bolshevik rule was suppressed. Without fear of reproach, many government officials were high-handed and inconsiderate in their dealings with the public. Many also used their official positions for personal gain. Lenin found these developments both disturbing and surprising. He seems to have assumed that revolutionaries would be above corruption.

102

One revolutionary who was not above corruption was Joseph Stalin, who early in 1922 became general secretary of the Communist party. As such, he selected party members for positions within the party. By the fall of 1922, it was becoming clear to Lenin that Stalin was using this function to promote his own political future instead of the party's interests. Lenin's disapproval of Stalin is clear from the political testament Lenin wrote after suffering two strokes that year. In the postscript to the testament, written in January of 1923, he wrote: "I propose to the comrades . . . to remove Stalin from that post [general secretary] and to appoint to it another man who in all respects differs from Stalin . . . more patient, more loyal, more polite, and more attentive to comrades." In March 1923, Lenin suffered another stroke, which left him virtually disabled. In January 1924, he died. The fate of the party Lenin had founded and led now passed into other hands.

STALIN: THE SECOND BOLSHEVIK REVOLUTION

At Lenin's death, the party faced two great problems. First, it had to choose a leader to replace Lenin. Initially, Leon Trotsky, who had been Lenin's right-hand man since 1917, seemed the logical choice. But other party leaders, among them several who feared and hated Trotsky, united against him. Thus began a struggle for power that lasted several years. It was complicated by the other great problem that faced the party—what should be done about the New Economic Policy and the issue of industrialization?

Trotsky was the most vocal critic of the New Economic Policy. He believed the policy would not permit the government to industrialize the country. According to Trotsky, the existing industrial and agricultural systems were inefficient and outdated. They would never earn the profits necessary to build new, modern enterprises. The predominantly small peasant farms were too inefficient for that, said Trotsky. Moreover, the peasants were being taxed too lightly. This left the peasants with too much to spend on themselves, and the government with too little to spend on building new industries.

There were leaders who defended the New Economic Policy. Among them were Stalin and Nikolai Bukharin (boo-KAHR-een), the party's leading economic theorist. Bukharin argued that NEP could provide for industrialization, but at a slower pace than many party members considered necessary. What distinguished Stalin in these debates was the way he used them to his own advantage. Others took sides on

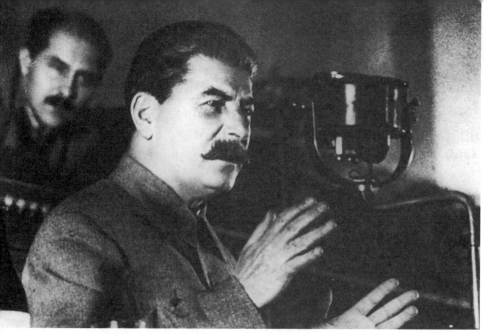

Joseph Stalin made few public speeches. Here in 1936 he discusses the new Soviet constitution, the first of several such documents.

the basis of their convictions. Stalin, by contrast, formed his alliances with the intent of undermining his rivals, one by one. By 1929, the struggle for power was over. Trotsky was exiled outside the Soviet Union. Other would-be leaders were discredited and made powerless. Stalin stood alone at the top as Lenin's successor.

Stalin's Industrialization Drive.   Stalin's victory settled the question of the New Economic Policy. He supported it until 1928. Then he suddenly changed course. With the party now dominated by his supporters, Stalin began a full-speed drive to establish modern industry in the Soviet Union. The goal was to catch up with the West within ten years. This would firmly establish socialism in the Soviet Union and also enable it to resist any attacks by the capitalist nations.

This apparently impossible task could be accomplished, said Stalin, because the industrialization process would be thoroughly planned. In fact, the Soviet Union, he announced, would have the world's first fully planned economy. Economic development would proceed according to a series of Five Year Plans. The first **Five Year Plan**, which contained over a thousand pages, was issued in 1929. It called for phenomenal increases in production of most goods. Heavy industry, such as coal, steel, and machine tool production, was to jump by 330 percent.

The plan also called for the **collectivization** of agriculture. This meant that the small farms the peasants owned would be taken over by the state and combined to form much larger collective farms. Peasants on these farms would pool their tools and their labor as they jointly cultivated the land. Working on larger fields than before, they would be able to use modern machines and techniques. This would raise the productivity of the land so that there would be enough to feed the millions who worked in the cities. There would also be grain for export, which would provide funds to allow the country to import industrial machinery. The first Five Year Plan intended to turn 20 percent of the peasant-owned land into collective farms. The remainder was to be collectivized under later plans.

Collectivization. Collectivization was a vital part of the first Five Year Plan. Stalin believed it would not only increase production on the farms but also allow the government to exercise greater control over them. Clearly, it would be easier to control and tax 200,000 large collective farms than 20 million small peasant farms. There was one major problem, however. The peasants were deeply attached to their land and resisted collectivization. The conflict caused terrible slaughter. Soviet troops and police tore peasants from their farms by force. Those who tried to resist were shot.

No attempt was made to collectivize the more prosperous peasants, the *kulaks*, who were the country's most efficient farmers. The *kulaks* were killed or deported by the millions to remote areas of the Soviet Union or to the ever-growing network of slave labor camps. This pitiless massacre was blandly called **dekulakization**. Resisting collectivization, many peasants slaughtered their animals rather than give them up. More than half the Soviet Union's horses, nearly half its cows, and about two thirds of its sheep were killed in this way or died from poor care on the new collective farms. It took Soviet agriculture more than a generation to recover from these losses.

By brute force, the government managed to collectivize Soviet agriculture. Under the circumstances, it is not surprising that agricultural production actually declined rather than grew during the first Five Year Plan. Nonetheless, the government, now in control of the collectives, took what it needed for the cities and for exporting. In 1932, this policy produced a horrible famine in the Ukraine, the country's most vital agricultural area. Instead of trying to ease the famine, Stalin used what he called "war by starvation" to break the peasants' continued resistance. In the end, 5 million people died in the Ukraine and northern Caucasus in what some have called the "terror famine." Across the entire nation, collectivization had caused an even greater loss of lives.

To increase agricultural production, collective farms needed tractors and other mechanized equipment. Here farmers drive tractors made in the United States.

By the mid-1930s, private farms had been replaced by two kinds of farms: collective farms and state farms. A collective farm, or **kolkhoz** (kahl-KHOZ), technically was owned and operated by its members. But they were forced to deliver a large part of their crops to the state at prices fixed by the state. These prices were low, even at times below cost. So the peasants earned little from their work on the collective. Their only incentive to work was the small plot each family was allowed to cultivate for its own use. Here the family could raise what it needed and sell the surplus on the open market. Added together, these tiny plots came to one twenty fifth of the total farmland. But they produced over one third of the nation's fruit, milk, meat, eggs, and vegetables.

A state farm, or **sovkhoz** (sahv-KHOZ), was even larger than a collective farm. Here the peasants were simply employees and were paid a straight salary. Neither the state nor collective farms were an efficient alternative to private farming. Soviet agriculture remained unable to feed the nation properly. Still, the state was able to control and regulate these farms. Therefore it could take what it needed for its industrialization programs. Whatever the cost, from Stalin's point of view, his collectivization policy achieved its main goals.

Industrialization. The resources squeezed from the peasants and the state's other resources were thrown into a crash program to build up heavy industry. The first two Five Year Plans were to make the Soviet Union the industrial and military equal of the capitalist West. But the incredible tempo resulted in numerous breakdowns and bottlenecks that threw both plans into chaos. At best, the country operated according to its short-term goals. Even these were often not met. In fact, no single major target of the first two plans was achieved.

While Stalin fell short of meeting his impossible goals, a great deal was nevertheless achieved. Everyone—women as well as men—was enlisted and pressured to work hard. For many, this was a period of upward mobility. Party members threw themselves into their work with extraordinary enthusiasm. Thousands of foreign technical experts were brought in to do key jobs and to train Soviet citizens.

Focusing on a few key projects and directing all resources to them helped get the most important jobs done. The Soviet people were forced to do without basic consumer goods while the "industries of the future" were built. Housing, clothing, furniture, and other consumer goods were hardly produced. During the 1930s, the Soviet Union experienced the greatest peacetime decline in standard of living in history.

Finally, coercion and force were used by the government on a huge scale. Workers were denied the right to strike. They were forced to work long hours. They were fined—or even sent to prison—for being late or absent from work. Many of the new railroads, canals, and factories were constructed by forced labor. Millions of people were sent to the largest network of forced-labor camps in history. There they lived and worked under such severe conditions that many died. The camps were run by Stalin's secret police. Reaching into all corners of Soviet society, the secret police crushed all opposition to Stalin's regime and policies.

Results of the Industrialization Drive.   The results of the industrialization drive were dramatic. Between 1928 and 1937, oil production tripled; coal production increased 350 percent; steel production quadrupled; and the production of electricity increased 700 percent. Overall, heavy industry quadrupled. In less than 10 years, the Soviet Union had built a modern industrial base. By the late 1930s, its industry was producing military hardware that was competing with that produced in the West. This military equipment helped the Soviet Union in World War II. The industries built during the 1930s provided the basis for further economic growth during the postwar years.

Along with industry, Soviet education was being overhauled and expanded to meet the needs of a modern industrial society. A population that had been largely illiterate became largely literate. A country that had been predominantly rural was quickly becoming urban. In short, the industrialization drive of the 1930s modernized key areas of

CASE STUDY:

Soviet Industrialization

Stalin believed that the Soviet Union had to industrialize at the greatest possible speed. These are the reasons he gave in 1931.

> To slacken [slow up] the tempo [speed] would mean falling behind. And those who fall behind get beaten. We do not want to be beaten. No, we refuse to be beaten! One feature of the history of old Russia was the continual beatings she suffered because of her backwardness. She was beaten by the Mongol khans. She was beaten by the Turkish beys. She was beaten by the Swedish feudal lords. She was beaten by the Polish and Lithuanian gentry. She was beaten by the British and French capitalists. She was beaten by the Japanese barons. All beat her—because of her backwardness, military backwardness, cultural backwardness, political backwardness, industrial backwardness, agricultural backwardness. They beat her because it was profitable and could be done with impunity [without fear of punishment].... Such is the law of exploiters—to beat the backward and the weak. It is the jungle law of capitalism. You are backward, you are weak— therefore you are wrong; hence, you can be beaten and enslaved. You are might—therefore you are right; hence, we must be wary of you. . . .
>
> That is why we must not lag behind. . . .
>
> We are fifty or a hundred years behind the advanced countries. We must make good this distance in ten years. Either we do it, or we shall be crushed. . . .

Stalin, A Documentary History of Communism, edited with introduction, notes, and original translations by Robert V. Daniels; Vol. 1. Hanover, N.H.: University Press of New England, rev. ed., 1984, p. 230. Reprinted by permission. Copyright c 1984 by the Trustees of the University of Vermont.

1. Who has beaten Russia in the past? Why was Russia beaten?

2. Does Stalin believe there can be any reason for slowing the pace of his industrialization program? What did his determination to move so quickly mean for the Soviet people?

3. Do you agree with Stalin about the "jungle law of capitalism"?

Soviet society. It enabled the Soviet Union to become the world's second largest industrial nation, surpassed only by the United States. It was an achievement of major historical importance, but one achieved at a terrible cost in ruined lives.

The Great Purge.   One other major event took place during the 1930s: the **Great Purge.** A **political purge** usually refers to the expulsion from a political party or government of members whose conduct has become unacceptable. In the Soviet Union during the 1930s, it meant much more than that. Stalin's purge, which began in 1934 and went on until 1938, swept through the Communist party like a tornado. Among its victims were nearly all the leaders who had been close to Lenin. Hundreds of thousands of loyal members of the party were accused of crimes they could not possibly have committed. Then they were sent to the labor camps or executed. This was only the beginning. Millions of innocent citizens who did not belong to the party were arrested and shipped to labor camps, where they were worked to death or executed outright. Of the people who had been elected to the Communist party's Central Committee in 1934, nearly three-quarters became the victims of Stalin's purge. So did half of the officers in the Red Army. Estimates of the total number of people arrested begin at about 8 million. About 1 million people were shot. Uncounted millions died in the camps.

How can the purge be explained? There had been party purges before. They had involved power struggles, disagreements, or corruption, but none had ended in a bloodletting. Of course, violence was nothing new to the party. Violence had been used to seize power and to maintain it during the civil war. Violence had also been used on a much larger scale during the collectivization and industrialization drives. But what purpose did the enormous and seemingly pointless violence of the Great Purge serve? To find an answer, if any can be found, we must turn to Stalin himself. Stalin intended to have total and absolute power over the Soviet people and the Communist party as well—and he got it as the result of the Great Purge. He unleashed a reign of terror in which everyone was terrorized, nobody was secure, and the entire Soviet Union was subject to his whim.

How Could This All Have Happened?   Regardless of how important or powerful Stalin was, not even his motives or personal cruelty can explain how the Great Purge could have taken place. The reason is simple: he could not have done these things himself; whether the event in question is collectivization, the famine of 1931–1932, or the Great

Purge. Sometimes there is a tendency to blame horrible acts or events only on the individual tyrant who stood at the top. Thus, the murder of 6 million Jews during the Nazi era in Germany is blamed solely on Hitler, while the Great Purge is blamed exclusively on Stalin. Yet it is absolutely vital to understand that these men, who were surely guilty of dreadful crimes, did not act and could not have acted alone. Their policies required the active support and participation of large numbers of people. A key question therefore arises. How could ordinary people have done these terrible things to one another?

Part of the answer in the case of the Soviet Union is that the country had passed through terrible times, both before and after 1917. World War I, the revolutions of 1917, and the civil war destroyed millions of lives, and with them many traditional values and beliefs. Many people therefore became capable of doing things they would not even have considered during normal times. On top of this, the Soviet people were subject to the steady drumbeat of a new morality. It insisted that anything was justified if it served the revolution. Also, during events such as collectivization and the purges, there were careers to be made by people ruthless enough to seize the opportunity. Nikita Khrushchev (KROOS-chev), Leonid Brezhnev (BREZH-nev), Yuri Andropov (ahn-DROH-pawf), and Konstantin Chernenko (chuhr-NEN-koh), all future leaders of the USSR, first made their marks during the 1930s, at the expense of other party members and ordinary citizens. Although specific conditions were different, the general pattern was similar in Nazi Germany. In other words, the underlying reasons for the events that occurred in the USSR during the 1930s were not uniquely Russian. They were circumstances that could have—and have—occurred in other countries, with similar tragic results.

A New Phenomenon: The Totalitarian State. What emerged from all this building and brutality was not simply a modernized country or socialist society. It was something new to the 20th century: a **totalitarian state**. In a totalitarian state, almost every aspect of human life is tightly controlled. The state controls every institution: the army, police, trade unions, factories, farms, youth organizations, even sports clubs. The state itself is controlled by a single party, in this case the Communist party. All information is controlled. There is only one version of news and developments: the official version.

The Soviet Union under Stalin was not the only totalitarian state of the 1930s. Nazi Germany, under Hitler, was another. After World War II, others, such as the People's Republic of China and the Soviet-controlled states of Eastern Europe, emerged. The development of Soviet-style totalitarianism proved to be as important as the economic developments of the industrialization drive.

World War II. In 1938, the international situation became increasingly tense as Hitler insisted on adding the German-speaking part of Czechoslovakia to Germany. That September, the prime minister of Great Britain and the premier of France went to meet Hitler, who assured them that he had "no other territorial ambitions." To avoid a war for which their countries were ill-prepared, the prime ministers granted Hitler the highly industrialized portion of Czechoslovakia he was claiming.

Having thus allowed the totalitarian dictator of Germany to carve up a small democratic country, the British prime minister said, "I have brought back peace with honor. . . . There will be peace in our time. Hitler has given me his word, and Hitler is a Christian gentleman." After this, Stalin feared that Great Britain and France would stand by and do nothing if Germany attacked the Soviet Union. Since the Soviet Union was unprepared for such a war, Stalin played for time.

In August 1939, Stalin, hoping to buy time and turn Germany against the West, signed a nonaggression pact with his archenemy, Adolf Hitler. Hitler's troops marched into Poland on September 1, and thus began World War II. Seventeen days after the Germans invaded Poland from the west, Soviet troops invaded Poland from the east. When the two armies met at Brest-Litovsk, Hitler and Stalin divided

Soviet troops fighting amid ruined factories during the siege of Stalingrad (now Volgograd) in the winter 1942–43.

Poland and then each added his agreed-upon share to his own country. The Soviet Union defeated Finland in the short Winter War of November 1939 to March 1940, gaining land from that country. The Soviet Union maintained friendly relations with Germany while Hitler overran France and most of western Europe and attacked Britain. Through 1940 and 1941, raw materials Germany bought from the Soviet Union helped keep the Nazi war machine running.

However, in June 1941, Hitler stunned Stalin by invading the Soviet Union. The Soviet Union now joined the Allies, which included France and Britain, in their fight against Nazi Germany. The turning point of the invasion of the Soviet Union came at the battle of Stalingrad, in the winter of 1942–1943. Here the advance of the Nazi armies was finally stopped, and the Germans were forced into a slow retreat. In all, the Soviet Union fought Germany for four dreadful years before the Nazis were finally beaten in 1945. (See Chapter 5.)

World War II added greatly to the Soviet Union's power. The borders the victorious Soviets drew in 1945 added to their territory in Europe. (See map on page 129.) The war left two of the Soviet Union's rivals, Germany and Japan, defeated. In addition, the advance of the Red Army during the war put the Soviet Union in a position to control most of the countries of Eastern Europe. After the war, Poland,

A memorial service for the victims of the Germans at Babi Yar, near Kiev. Here more than 100,000 civilians, mostly Jews, were killed and buried in a mass grave between 1941 and 1943.

Romania, Bulgaria, Hungary, Czechoslovakia, East Germany, Albania, and Yugoslavia became part of a Soviet-dominated bloc of communist states. Although Yugoslavia broke away from the Soviet bloc in mid-1948, the spread of communism into Eastern Europe was the great prize of the Soviet Union's victory over Germany in World War II.

Yet, the price of victory was enormous. Most of the war against Germany had been fought on Soviet soil. Entire cities and hundreds of thousands of villages and collective farms had been destroyed. For the Soviet Union, the cost of the war in human lives was staggering: at least 20 million men, women, and children died. By contrast, the army of the United States lost about 400,000 men in World War II.

Stalin's Last Years: 1945–1953. Not even this victory in the war brought relief to the long-suffering Soviet people. Although the Soviet Union had fought on the same side as the Western powers, this wartime alliance did not last. Trouble began almost immediately, when the Western powers objected strongly to Soviet domination of Eastern Europe. Led by the United States, the West argued that the Soviet domination violated the principle of **self-determination**, allowing a country to decide its own political future. Moreover, the West saw Soviet control over Eastern Europe as a dangerous increase of Soviet power. This was further seen as a threat to the security of Western Europe.

The Soviets in turn distrusted the capitalist West. Most of all, they feared the United States, the only nation in the world that had produced an atomic bomb. As soon as the war was over, Stalin resumed his industrialization drive. All efforts went into repairing the country's heavy industry and expanding it. A crash program was set up to develop an atomic bomb. The program succeded in 1949. Very little effort was devoted to raising the Soviet people's low standard of living.

At the same time, Stalin launched further campaigns and purges to preserve his absolute power. Millions of citizens and soldiers whom the war had brought into contact with the West were sent to slave-labor camps. Artists and intellectuals of all kinds, accused by Stalin and the party of expressing Western values, were persecuted, imprisoned, or executed. Stalin's suspicions fell especially heavily on the Jewish community. Jewish intellectuals and community leaders were arrested and executed in large numbers. So again were members of the Communist party leadership. Then, in 1953, while Stalin was planning another large purge, he suffered a massive stroke. He died on March 5, 1953. The Stalin era, with its unique combination of growth and brutality, had finally come to an end.

Chapter 4:
CHECKUP

REVIEWING THE CHAPTER

I. Building Your Vocabulary

In your notebook, for each term in Column A, write the letter of the best description in Column B.

Column A	*Column B*
1. soviet	a. the right of a country to decide its future
2. *Cheka*	b. state-owned farm
3. *kulaks*	c. Bolshevik secret police
4. NEPmen	d. collective farm
5. collectivization	e. private merchants who used capitalist business methods under Lenin's economic policy
6. *sovkhoz*	
7. Great Purge	f. state control over every aspect and institution of life
8. totalitarian state	g. well-to-do peasants
9. self-determination	h. elimination of all who might oppose Stalin's leadership
10. *kolkhoz*	i. revolutionary committee of workers and soldiers
	j. uniting small, independent farms into one large farm

II. Understanding the Facts

In your notebook, write the numbers from 1 to 5. Write the letter of the correct answer to each question next to its number.

1. The Provisional Government, which took over in March 1917,
   a. granted voting rights to all.
   b. established the eight-hour workday.
   c. elected the country's president.

2. The Provisional Government's policies included all the following measures *except*
   a. establishing an eight-hour workday.
   b. the freeing of political prisoners.
   c. the transfer of land to the peasants.

3. The Treaty of Brest-Litovsk
   a. brought peace to Russia and its allies.
   b. gave Germany large territorial concessions.
   c. was well received by patriotic Russians.

4. "Land, Peace, and Bread" was the slogan of the
   a. Duma.   b. Bolsheviks.   c. kulaks

5. The long struggle for power after Lenin's death was won by
   a. Leon Trotsky.   b. Joseph Stalin.   c. Nikolai Bukharin.

III. Thinking It Through

In your notebook, write the numbers from 1 to 5. Write the letter of the correct answer to each question next to its number.

1. Under Lenin's New Economic Policy
   a. peasants were heavily taxed.
   b. all crop production was seized by the government.
   c. titles and power of nobility were restored.
   d. a certain amount of private industry was restored.

2. The goals of the first Five Year Plan included all of the following *except*
   a. increased industrial productivity.
   b. collectivization of all farms.
   c. the return of land to kulaks.
   d. a 330 percent increase in the production of heavy industry.

3. One indirect result of Stalin's agricultural policy was
   a. a famine in the Ukraine.
   b. peaceful collectivization of farming activities.
   c. increased production of consumer goods.
   d. surplus wheat to export.

4. Shortly after Stalin and Hitler signed a nonaggression pact in August 1939
   a. Britain and France sought a military alliance with the Soviet Union.
   b. the Soviets stayed out of World War II.

c. the United States broke off diplomatic relations with the Soviet Union.

d. the two leaders divided Poland.

5. Which of the following was not a result of World War II?
   a. The Soviet added to its territory in Europe.
   b. Two of the USSR's rivals, Germany and Yugoslavia, were defeated.
   c. Much of Eastern Europe became a part of the communist bloc.
   d. The Soviet Union lost at least 20 million people.

DEVELOPING CRITICAL THINKING SKILLS

1. Discuss the Russian experiment with democracy in 1917 and some reasons for its failure.

2. Although the odds were against them, the Reds were the victors in the civil war. Analyze some of the reasons they succeeded.

3. Describe the different views held by Trotsky and Stalin toward the New Economic Policy.

4. What results did the first Five Year Plan have on Soviet agriculture? How effective was collectivization?

INTERPRETING GRAPHS

The first Five Year Plan was issued in 1929, as part of Stalin's efforts to modernize the Soviet Union. On the next page, the graphs for steel and tractors represent industrial growth, while the graph for cattle reflects agricultural production. Study the graphs and answer the questions below.

1. During which 20-year period was there greatest industrial growth?

2. During which period did agriculture suffer? Give some reasons for the decline in the number of cattle.

3. What effect could the increase in steel production have on military developments in the Soviet Union?

4. In what ways was the slow agricultural growth the result of the industrial program?

116

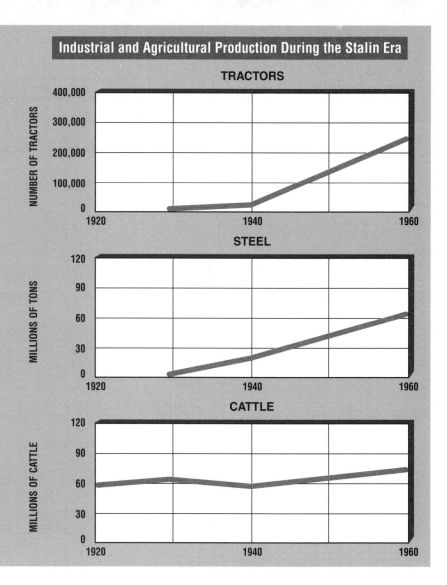

Industrial and Agricultural Production During the Stalin Era

TRACTORS

NUMBER OF TRACTORS

400,000
300,000
200,000
100,000
0

1920 — 1940 — 1960

STEEL

MILLIONS OF TONS

120
90
60
30
0

1920 — 1940 — 1960

CATTLE

MILLIONS OF CATTLE

120
90
60
30
0

1920 — 1940 — 1960

ENRICHMENT AND EXPLORATION

1. Prepare a short written or oral report on the life of one of the leaders of the Russian Revolution: Trotsky, Lenin, or Stalin. Include biographical information, how your subject developed his revolutionary ideals, and his part in the creation of the new Soviet government.

2. In *One Day in the Life of Ivan Denisovich* Alexander Solzhenitsyn draws a vivid picture of life in a Stalinist work camp. Read this fictional account of an experience in a forced labor camp and prepare a brief oral report or dramatic reading to share with the class.

THE SOVIET UNION AND THE WORLD
1914–1953

1914–1918	*World War I*
1917	Bolshevik Revolution
1918	Treaty of Brest-Litovsk
1918–1921	Civil War in Russia
1919	Comintern organized.
1921	Soviets sign trade agreement with Great Britain.
1922	Treaty of Rapallo
1934	Soviet Union becomes member of League of Nations.
1935	Soviet Union forms alliances with France and Czechoslovakia.
1936	*Germany and Japan sign Anti-Comintern Pact.*
1938	*Germany annexes Austria.*
1939	Hitler-Stalin pact formed.
	Germany invades Poland.
1939–1945	*World War II*
1941	German army invades Soviet Union.
1942–1943	Battle of Stalingrad
1945–1949	Communist governments installed in Eastern Europe.
1949	*Mao Zedong founds People's Republic of China.*
1945	Yalta and Potsdam Conferences
1947	Cominform founded.
	Truman Doctrine and Marshall Plan
1948	Berlin Blockade begins.
1949	*NATO formed.*
	Soviet Union organizes COMECON.
	Soviet Union explodes atom bomb.
1950–1953	*War in Korea*

5 Soviet Foreign Policy, 1917–1953

When the Bolsheviks seized power in Russia in 1917, they inherited the old Russian Empire's relationships with other countries. The leaders of the new government deeply opposed some of these relationships. Although Russia was still involved in World War I fighting against capitalist Germany, it was fighting on the same side as other capitalist countries. The new regime had to develop a **foreign policy**, or a way to relate to other nations, that met the need to preserve and protect the Bolshevik state and was in harmony with its Marxist ideals.

THE NEW REGIME AND OLD FOREIGN POLICIES

Foreign policy was a problem for both the czarist government and the Bolshevik regime. Some of the complexity was a result of problems of the times, such as World War I. But much of the complexity was because of the sheer size and diversity of the country and the Communist ideals of the government.

The Bolsheviks, like the czars, had to consider relationships with Russia's many neighbors in Europe and Asia. Although many of the USSR's aims were very different from those of the Russian Empire, in many ways the Bolsheviks followed czarist foreign policy after 1917. The Bolsheviks continued to try to weaken their rivals and to expand their influence in the world. One goal was to increase Soviet territory from northern Europe and the Balkans to Central Asia and East Asia. The Bolsheviks continued to press the long-standing aim of the czars to possess warm-water ports.

Communism, a New Complication. The Bolshevik Revolution, however, did add one complication to the country's foreign policy. Lenin

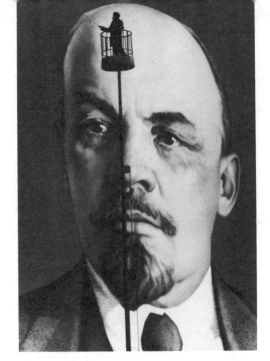

A worker retouching a giant mural of Lenin. Paintings, posters, and statues of Lenin and Stalin were on view in public places throughout the Soviet Union. What impact do you think these images had?

and his comrades were determined to turn their own revolution into a world revolution against capitalism. This goal created enemies among governments all over the world. Russia's capitalist allies in World War I did not welcome attempts to overthrow their systems. In the years following the revolution, several of them tried to help overthrow the Bolshevik government in an attempt to stop a world revolution.

Historians do not agree about the Soviet Union's commitment to communist world revolution after Joseph Stalin took control of the country. It is clear that the Soviet Union promoted revolutionary change in Europe and Asia between 1924 and 1953. It is not clear whether this was done to promote world communism or simply to establish governments that supported Soviet interests.

BETWEEN TWO WORLD WARS

Immediately after the Bolshevik Revolution, foreign policy goals were very modest. The new regime was simply trying to survive. Continued participation in World War I, with its many Russian losses, made the new government's survival more difficult. To help establish the Soviet government, the Bolsheviks signed the Treaty of Brest-Litovsk with Germany in March 1918. (See page 98.) In that treaty, the Soviet government gave up a great deal of territory to get the country out of the war and gain a chance to establish its power firmly. In November 1918, after the Germans had been defeated by the Allies, the Soviet government declared that the Treaty of Brest-Litovsk was no longer valid. The Soviet army then reclaimed much of the territory the Bolsheviks had given away in the treaty.

The end of World War I was not a cure for all of the USSR's troubles. The new Soviet government faced other problems as well. Between 1918 and 1921, Russia was torn by a bitter civil war. Russia's former allies—Great Britain, France, the United States, and Japan—sent troops to Russian territory to support the anti-Bolshevik cause. (See page 99.) They hoped that the revolution could be overturned and that a government more to their liking would replace the Bolsheviks.

While struggling to survive, Lenin's government stressed its commitment to world revolution. To this end, it organized the **Communist International** (or **Comintern**) in 1919. Although the Comintern was supposedly an organization of independent communist parties, the government in Moscow really controlled it. It worked to promote communist revolutions in Europe, especially in Germany. But every attempt ended in failure.

Making Peace with Other Countries. Even while it was trying to promote worldwide revolution, Lenin's government had to deal with the nonsocialist nations of the world. As early as 1920 and 1921, it signed peace treaties with many of its neighbors. Treaties were signed with countries that had been independent, such as Persia (present-day Iran), Turkey, and Afghanistan. Lenin's government also recognized the independence of several countries that had been part of the Russian Empire but had broken away between 1917 and 1921. These countries included Estonia, Latvia, Lithuania, Poland, and Finland.

More nations of the world began to accept the existence of the USSR. On May 16, 1921, the Soviets signed a trade agreement with Great Britain. This agreement ended the trade **boycott** that many Western nations had been conducting against the Soviet state. The next major diplomatic move was the Treaty of Rapallo in April 1922, a trade and political agreement with Germany. By 1924, most Western nations had granted the Soviet Union recognition. The only major exception was the United States. The official U.S. reason was that the Soviets refused to honor czarist debts owed to U.S. citizens or to pay for U.S. property that had been nationalized, or brought under Soviet control, since 1917. It was not until 1933 that the United States recognized the Soviet Union.

THE 1930S: ON THE BRINK OF WORLD WAR II

During the 1920s, the Soviet Union had enemies, but it did not face any direct threats of war with powerful countries. This situation changed during the 1930s, when Adolf Hitler and the Nazis came to power in Germany. The Nazis believed that Germans were members of a "master race" and that other people were inferior. Along with their bitter hatred for Jews and contempt for other "inferior" people such as Poles and Russians, the Nazis were hostile to communism and the Soviet Union. Hitler made it clear that someday he would attack the Soviet Union to provide "living space" for his "master race."

Threats from East and West. Meanwhile, in East Asia, Japan was growing increasingly powerful and aggressive. Between 1931 and 1937, Japanese aggression was directed against China. However, it was no secret that Japan wanted a large part of Soviet Siberia. The international situation became even more threatening in 1936, when the Germans and the Japanese signed an Anti-Comintern Pact. Italy joined this alliance, in 1937.

During this time, the Soviet Union was in the middle of its industrialization drive. (See pages 104–109.) It had many problems at home and could not afford a war, especially after Stalin began his Great Purge. To protect his regime and the Soviet Union, Stalin chose to follow a foreign policy of **collective security**. This meant that despite their differences, nations that were threatened by German or Japanese aggression would cooperate against those two dangerous powers. Beginning in 1935, the Soviets supported **united front** movements in France and other countries. United fronts meant that local communist parties would cooperate with socialist and other left-wing parties. The goal was to establish antifascist governments that were prepared to challenge German, Italian, and Japanese aggression.

Stalin also signed alliances with France and with Czechoslovakia, a small democratic country wedged along Germany's southeastern border. These treaties called for the Soviet Union to help Czechoslovakia against German aggression, but only if France also did so. In 1936, when civil war broke out in Spain between the democratically-elected left-wing and the fascist right-wing forces, Stalin sent military aid to the leftists, while Germany and Italy supported the rightists.

Germany's Move for Power. During the 1930s, the nations of the world were coping with the effects of a worldwide economic depression.

With the devastating effects of World War I still fresh in their memories, European nations and the United States refused to take action against German, Italian, and Japanese aggression. In 1936, in violation of the Treaty of Versailles, German troops occupied a part of western Germany called the Rhineland. In March 1938, Germany annexed the small German-speaking country of Austria. In September of the same year, Hitler forced Czechoslovakia to give up a heavily industrialized part of its territory to Germany.

While Germany was growing stronger and more aggressive, the United States chose to follow a policy of isolation. It had decided to stay out of Europe's problems. The leaders of Great Britain and France, hoping to avoid war, did little or nothing against Germany. They sent some help to the antifascist forces in Spain, but not enough to defeat the fascists, who won in 1939.

The key event, however, was the Czechoslovak crisis of 1938. The Soviet Union was ready to help the Czechoslovaks resist the German territorial demands. The French and the British were not. Instead, the leaders of France and Britain met with Hitler in the German city of Munich but Stalin was not invited. In an attempt to appease Hitler, the French and the British submitted to Hitler's demands. In March 1939, Hitler's troops invaded Czechoslovakia.

The Hitler-Stalin Pact. As soon as Hitler had taken Czechoslovakia in 1939, he made demands for more territory. This time his target was Poland. At last, the French and British realized that Hitler could be stopped only by force. They began negotiations with the Soviets for an anti-German alliance. However, the talks produced no results because each side distrusted the other.

The Soviets suspected that Great Britain and France hoped that Hitler would attack the Soviet Union. Stalin's main interest was in keeping his country out of war, at least for the time being. With those interests in mind, he began secret negotiations with Germany. On August 23, 1939, Stalin and Hitler stunned the world by announcing that the Soviet Union and Nazi Germany had signed a nonaggression pact. Each country publicly pledged not to attack the other. A secret clause in the pact divided Poland between Germany and the Soviet Union and assigned Estonia, Latvia, Lithuania, and part of Romania to the USSR.

Relieved of the threat of war with the Soviet Union, Germany attacked Poland on September 1, 1939. Britain and France then declared war against Germany. World War II had begun, but as yet the USSR was not a participant.

Soviet Occupation of Eastern Europe.   The war began well enough for the Soviet Union. After only two weeks, the Soviets occupied eastern Poland, more than 75,000 square miles (194,250 square kilometers) and inhabited mainly by Lithuanians, Belorussians, and Ukrainians. When Finland refused Soviet territorial demands, the Soviet Union invaded that country. After a short, bloody war during the winter of 1939-1940, Soviet forces overcame heroic Finnish resistance, and Stalin gained the territory he wanted. In 1940, the Soviets annexed a part of Romania that had once been part of the Russian Empire. They also seized all of Lithuania, Latvia, and Estonia. In addition, the Soviets deported more than 1 million people to Soviet labor camps.

Meanwhile, Hitler conquered Western Europe as far as the English Channel. The Soviet Union provided Germany with many of the raw materials it needed for its war machine. The Soviets also gave the Nazis diplomatic support and allowed the German navy use of important naval ports. In return, Stalin gained two more years to prepare for a war he knew was coming.

WORLD WAR II: THE STRUGGLE TO SURVIVE

In those two years, the Soviet Union built up its military forces, introduced new weapons, and constructed new factories far from its exposed western borders. However, much was still needed, and some of Stalin's policies impaired the country's ability to prepare for the coming war. The purges had eliminated thousands of army officers as well as many

In August 1939, as Soviet leader Joseph Stalin looks on, his foreign secretary, Vyacheslav Molotov, signs a nonaggression pact with Nazi Germany.

scientists and engineers who might have helped develop better weapons. Though Nazi Germany actively opposed the Soviet Union's expansion into Finland and other areas, Stalin refused to believe that Hitler would turn on him so soon. Even though warned by Western sources, he refused to prepare for the attack. When the German army invaded the Soviet Union on June 22, 1941, the Red Army was caught completely unprepared. It suffered huge losses in the initial stages of the war.

The German Invasion. The German invasion of 1941 did what the crises and negotiations of the 1930s could not do. It brought the Soviet Union and the British together to fight the Germans. (France had already been defeated and occupied by Germany.) After the Japanese attack on Pearl Harbor in December 1941, the United States joined what came to be called the **Grand Alliance**.

At first, help from its allies did the Soviet Union little good. Much of the fighting between Germany and the USSR took place on Soviet soil. The German army attacked in three ways. It destroyed Soviet forces. It killed Soviet civilians who resisted. It terrorized the rest of the population. The Nazis also began systematically murdering hundreds of thousands of Soviet Jews. By the end of 1941, Leningrad was under a siege that would last for two and a half years.

In the winter of 1941, the Germans also stood at the outskirts of Moscow ready to take the city. A combination of freezing weather and Soviet resistance stopped them at the last moment. The Germans renewed their advance in 1942 despite the Soviet's **scorched-earth policy**. Under this policy, Soviet forces destroyed everything in the Nazi invaders' path to prevent the enemy from using it. The battle of Stalingrad in the winter of 1942-1943 finally halted the Germans. However, before the Red Army could counterattack in 1943, the Germans had occupied valuable Soviet territory—territory that produced 38 percent of the nation's grain and 58 percent of its steel and contained 41 percent of its railroads.

Assistance from the United States to the USSR had begun in November 1941 in the form of **lend-lease**. Lend-lease was a U.S. wartime program that provided the Allies with food, machines, and other material they needed for the war effort. Some of the assistance was considered a loan, while other assistance was to be repaid in goods, services, or money. In fact, the United States never asked for or received payment for most of the $50 billion worth of goods it provided its allies during World War II.

The War's High Costs.   The struggle to drive the Germans out of the USSR was long and bitter. The Germans were not forced out of Soviet territory until 1944, and they were not defeated until April 1945. By then, the Soviet people had paid a terrible price in lost lives and property damage. The fighting had destroyed 1,100 cities, 70,000 villages, 32,000 factories, and 40,000 miles (64,370 kilometers) of railroad track. The human cost was unimaginably high and remains uncounted to this day. The best estimates are that at least 20 million Soviet citizens, including 13.6 million soldiers, and 1 million Jews lost their lives.

World War II, which the Soviet Union called the **Great Patriotic War**, was a national nightmare. Although the Soviets were on the winning side, their country was in ruins. The fierce fighting, the German brutality and destructiveness, and the suffering caused by the lack of food, clothing, and shelter left deep scars. The war reinforced the people's distrust of foreigners and made many of them more willing to accept the government's policies for the sake of stability.

For years after the war, the Soviet government did everything it could to remind its people of the losses they suffered in World War II. Yet the government told the Soviet people only part of the story. Officials omitted any mention of the millions of Russian men who could not fight the Germans because Stalin had imprisoned them in Soviet labor camps. Unmentioned were the thousands in "penal battalions" who died when troops of special secret police drove them virtually unarmed against German fortified positions.

Postwar Settlements.   The Grand Alliance was never very solid. The Soviets and the Western democracies distrusted one another. Only the German menace had held them together. During the war, Stalin complained bitterly that the British and the Americans had delayed a direct attack on German-held Western Europe until the Germans had exhausted themselves fighting the Soviet Union. The Western leaders denied the accusation. They pointed out that this so-called second front had been delayed because of the extraordinary technical difficulties involved in transporting a large army from Great Britain across the English Channel to France. On their part, many Western policymakers were worried that the advance of the Red Army would leave the Soviet Union in control of large parts of eastern and central Europe. Such control would lead to what Western leaders considered a dangerous increase in Soviet power once the war was over. Several conferences during the war failed to reduce these mutual suspicions.

126

Yalta and Potsdam.   The key Allied conference of the war was held in February 1945 at the Soviet Black Sea resort of Yalta. The Soviets agreed to join the war against Japan once Germany was defeated. Germany itself was to be occupied by the Allies. It would be divided into four occupation zones, one each for the United States, Great Britain, the Soviet Union, and France.

At Yalta, the sticking point was what to do with Poland, the country whose fate had sparked the war in 1939. The Soviets wanted a "friendly" government in Poland. They pointed out that their country had been invaded through Poland in 1812, 1914, and 1941. They intended to avoid allowing such an invasion to happen again by installing a communist government controlled by Moscow. The West wanted a noncommunist government in Poland, a government that would help limit Soviet influence in Eastern Europe. Since, at the time, the Red Army controlled Poland, the "compromise" reached at Yalta favored the Soviet Union. Stalin promised "free and unfettered" elections in Poland. He had no intention of keeping that promise, but Western leaders—at least in public—pretended to believe him.

Another conference was held in Potsdam from July 17 through August 2, 1945. The Potsdam conference only deepened the problems left by the Yalta meeting.

In February 1945, Winston Churchill of Great Britain, Franklin D. Roosevelt of the U. S., and Joseph Stalin of the USSR met at Yalta to decide the future of postwar Germany and Eastern Europe.

The Postwar Spread of Communism. Poland was not the only territory under Soviet control after the war. The Red Army had driven the Germans from Hungary, Czechoslovakia, Romania, and Bulgaria, and it had occupied those countries. Between 1945 and 1948, Soviet-backed groups established communist dictatorships in all of them.

Meanwhile, in 1945, communists loyal to the Soviet Union were able to seize power and establish dictatorships in Yugoslavia and Albania. The methods of gaining control varied slightly from country to country. They ranged from rigged elections to outright terror and murder. But everywhere the results were the same. By 1948, an area of more than 560,000 square miles (1.45 million square kilometers), which was home to about 100 million people, was under Soviet control in eastern and central Europe. This area included the Soviet occupation zone in Germany, where the Soviets set up a communist regime in 1949 called the German Democratic Republic, or East Germany.

What came to be called the Soviet **satellite system** was established. (See map on page 129.) Satellites are countries whose political and economic systems are controlled by a more powerful country. With the satellite system, communism had spread from the Soviet Union to other countries. The only bright spot was that Yugoslavia, while remaining communist, broke away from Soviet control in 1948.

The Soviet Union believed that it had earned these postwar gains through its sacrifices during the war. It had fought the German army on the eastern front almost alone from June 22, 1941, to June 6, 1944, the day the Western democracies landed their armies in France. It therefore seemed reasonable for the Soviet Union to enjoy the security of "friendly" governments along its western border.

The communist domination of Eastern Europe and the Western reaction to it set the stage for a Soviet-American confrontation. This confrontation dominated international politics for 45 years. Only the United States was in a position to challenge the Soviet Union. Germany and Japan were defeated. Great Britain and France were exhausted after the war. At first, the United States hoped that some form of cooperation with the Soviet Union could be maintained after the war. But by 1946, the United States was threatening to use force if the Soviets did not drop their demands on Turkey and withdraw their troops from northern Iran, as previously agreed. In 1946, former British Prime Minister Winston Churchill made a dramatic speech in Fulton, Missouri. He warned that an **Iron Curtain** had descended on Europe. Behind this iron curtain were the imprisoned countries of Soviet-dominated Eastern Europe. The term Iron Curtain countries stuck.

The Soviet Union's Territorial Gains in Europe after World War II

From Finland

From Finland

SWEDEN

FINLAND

NORWAY

ESTONIA

SOVIET UNION

North Sea

LATVIA

DENMARK

Baltic Sea

LITHUANIA

GREAT BRITAIN

From Germany

NETH.

EAST GERMANY

POLAND

From Poland

BELG.

LUX.

WEST GERMANY

CZECHOSLOVAKIA

From Czechoslovakia

FRANCE

SWITZ.

AUSTRIA

HUNGARY

From Romania

ROMANIA

N

ITALY

YUGOSLAVIA

Black Sea

BULGARIA

ALBANIA

GREECE

TURKEY

Territory of the Soviet Union before World War II

Territory added to the Soviet Union by 1945

Communist countries of Eastern Europe, 1945-1991

200   400 MILES

0   200   400 KILOMETERS

Mediterranean Sea

Arctic Circle

Arctic Circle

The Truman Doctrine and the Marshall Plan. The U.S. reaction to Soviet control of Eastern Europe grew stronger in 1947 and 1948. Early in 1947, the British told the United States that they no longer had the resources to support the anticommunist Greek government in its civil war against communist rebels. The United States responded quickly. In March, President Harry Truman announced his **Truman Doctrine**. It stated that the United States would provide $400 million in military aid to Greece and its neighbor Turkey to prevent communist takeovers in those countries. Truman committed the United States to defend "free peoples who are resisting attempted subjugation by armed minorities or by outside pressure." In saying this, Truman clearly extended U.S. protection beyond Greece and Turkey. A few months later, a State Department official, George Kennan, gave Truman's policy a name. He wrote that the United States would adopt a policy of "long-term, patient but firm and vigilant containment." **Containment** meant that the United States would actively oppose any attempt by the Soviet Union to extend its influence. The United States would see that Soviet influence would be contained within the area in which it then operated.

The policy of containment went beyond the use of military methods. At first, the emphasis was on rebuilding the economies of war-torn countries. During 1947 and 1948, the West feared that the Soviet Union might not have to do very much to expand its influence. Economic conditions were so bad in Western Europe that local communist parties found it fairly easy to increase their strength, especially in France and Italy. The United States responded with the **European Recovery Act**, better known as the **Marshall Plan**. This plan, which was proposed in 1947 and funded by Congress in 1948, provided more than $12 billion in economic aid over a four-year period. The money would help rebuild the economies of Europe from Great Britain to the Western-controlled part of Germany. Although the United States invited the Soviet Union to join the Marshall Plan it refused. The Marshall Plan was a remarkable success, certainly one of the most successful U.S. foreign policy programs since World War II.

The Berlin Blockade. Soviet reaction to the Truman Doctrine and the Marshall Plan came quickly. In 1947, Stalin set up a new international organization to replace the Comintern (see page 121), which had been disbanded in 1943. The new organization was called the **Communist Information Bureau**, or **Cominform**. Cominform was designed to promote communist ideas and foster the growth of communist parties outside the Soviet Union.

CASE STUDY:

A Soviet View of the Truman Doctrine

On March 12, 1947, President Truman addressed Congress about crises that had developed in Greece and Turkey. The Greek government, which was fighting a civil war against a communist minority, had appealed to the United States for help. Turkey, which felt threatened by its neighbor the Soviet Union, asked for financial help in order to strengthen itself. In his speech, Truman asked Congress not only for financial aid but also for military personnel to come to the aid of Greece and Turkey. Three days later, the Soviet newspaper *Izvestia* responded with the following criticism.

> The U.S. government has no intention of acting in the Greek question as one might have expected a member of UNO [the United Nations], concerned about the fate of another member, to act. . . .
>
> Truman, indeed, failed to reckon either with the international organization or with the sovereignty of Greece. What will be left of Greek sovereignty when the "American military and civilian personnel" get to work in Greece? The sovereignty and independence of Greece will be the first victims of such singular "defense." The American arguments for assisting Turkey base themselves on the existence of a threat to the integrity of Turkish territory—though no one and nothing actually threatens Turkey's integrity. This "assistance" is evidently aimed at putting this country also under U.S. control. . . .
>
> We are now witnessing a fresh intrusion of the U.S.A. into the affairs of other states. American claims to leadership in international affairs grow parallel with the growing appetite of the American quarters concerned. But the American leaders, in the new historical circumstances, fail to reckon with the fact that the old methods of colonizers and die-hard politicians have outlived their time and are doomed to failure. In this lies the chief weakness of Truman's message.

Adapted from *Great Problems in European Civilization*, edited by Kenneth M. Setton and Henry R. Winkler, Englewood Cliffs, NJ, Prentice Hall, 1966

1. Why do the Soviets think that the U.S. policy will fail?

2. What reasons besides the communist-democratic conflict do both nations have for wanting the two Mediterranean nations as allies?

Berliners greet the arrival of a supply plane during the
Berlin Blockade. In 11 months the Berlin Airlift flew over
2 million tons of goods into West Berlin.

Then the Soviet Union made a far bolder and more threatening move in the city of Berlin. Berlin, the former German capital, was 110 miles (177 kilometers) inside the Soviet occupation zone. Like the rest of Germany, it had been divided into four occupation zones. In June 1948, the Soviets blockaded all the land routes leading to Berlin. Stalin's strategy was to starve the Western powers, especially the United States, out of Berlin. If the Soviets succeeded the blockade would prove to the Germans and the rest of Europe that the United States could not protect them in a crisis. The lack of U.S. assistance, the Soviets reasoned, would make Europeans reconsider cooperation with the United States, and the policy of containment would collapse.

The **Berlin Blockade** brought the world's two greatest powers dangerously close to war. The United States managed to defeat the blockade by flying over it. Many people had doubted that this "Berlin Airlift" could supply a city of 2 million people with all the supplies it needed, but the Berlin Airlift did the job. Meanwhile, the shock of the blockade helped lead to the formation of the **North Atlantic Treaty Organization,** or **NATO.** NATO was founded in April 1949 as a defensive military alliance meant to defend Western Europe against any Soviet military threat. Its formation was led by the United States, and it included many of the countries that had fought against Germany in World War II. NATO gave containment an organized military arm and a multinational structure. Realizing that his blockade had backfired, Stalin lifted it in May 1949.

COMECON. In 1949, the Soviet Union organized **COMECON** (the Council for Mutual Economic Assistance). Member nations were supposed to help one another with economic development. Members included the Soviet Union, Bulgaria, Czechoslovakia, Hungary, Poland, and Romania. Albania was active in COMECON from 1949 to 1961. East Germany joined in 1950, and Mongolia in 1962. Cuba became the ninth full member in 1972.

The Cold War.   The events of 1945 through 1949 left Europe divided into two opposing camps: one led by the United States, and the other dominated by the Soviet Union. They also led to the **Cold War**. The term Cold War, first used in 1947, refers to the continued state of tension and hostility—but no outright war—between the Soviet Union and the United States. The two countries were careful not to engage in open warfare largely because they had become the world's first nuclear powers (the United States in 1945 and the Soviet Union in 1949). As they expanded their nuclear arsenals, both countries began to recognize the dangers of a nuclear war. Both understood that, win or lose, each would find it impossible to avoid terrible destruction.

The Cold War therefore had to be fought in other ways. The two sides used diplomacy against each other. Each supplied economic aid to other countries that might support its interests. Each side armed its allies against the other's allies. Each helped its allies fight the other side's allies. Sometimes one side even fought the other side's ally. However, Soviet soldiers never fought U.S. soldiers.

The U.S.-Soviet Cold War lasted from the late 1940s until 1990. By then, the Soviet satellite system had collapsed and dramatic reforms had taken place inside the Soviet Union itself. (See Chapter 6.)

Stalin's Last Years—Rising Tensions.   The last years of Stalin's life saw Cold War tensions rise. The Soviet Union's explosion of its first atomic bomb in 1949 came well before U.S. experts expected it. That nuclear shock was soon followed by some great political shocks. In China, communist rebels led by Mao Zedong (mow dzoo-doong) won a civil war. The People's Republic of China was established in 1949. Another large nation had become communist. Then, in 1950, war broke out in Korea. Korea had been divided into a communist northern half and a non-communist southern half after World War II. The war began when Soviet-backed North Korea attacked U.S.-backed South Korea. Forces sent by the United States and the United Nations intervened directly to drive back the invasion. Later that year, China intervened to help North Korea. The Korean War dragged on for more than three years. An armistice ended the fighting in 1953. Korea remained divided, with approximately the same boundaries it had in 1950.

REVIEWING THE CHAPTER

I. Building Your Vocabulary

In your notebook, write the numbers from 1 to 5. After each number, write the word that matches the definition.

Comintern   Iron Curtain   lend-lease
containment   NATO   Cold War

1. Western Europe's defensive military alliance

2. an organization of independent communist parties controlled by Moscow

3. U.S. policy to keep the USSR from expanding its influence

4. term for Soviet-controlled countries of Eastern Europe

5. state of tension and hostility without military confrontation

II. Understanding the Facts

In your notebook, write the numbers from 1 to 5. Write the letter of the correct answer to each question next to its number.

1. The way one nation relates to other nations is called its
   a. foreign policy.   b. united front.   c. collective security.

2. Just after World War II began, the Soviet Union invaded
   a. China.   b. Austria.   c. Poland.

3. The Soviet policy to destroy everything in the path of the invading Nazi army to prevent the enemy from using it is known as
   a. the scorched-earth policy.   b. containment.
   c. appeasement.

4. Countries whose political and economic systems are controlled by a more powerful country are known as
   a. united fronts.   b. Third World countries.   c. satellites.

5. The United States managed to overcome the Soviet blockade of Berlin by
   a. military threat.   b. peaceful negotiations.   c. an airlift.

III. Thinking It Through

In your notebook, write the numbers from 1 to 5. Write the letter of the correct answer to each question next to its number.

1. After World War I, Russia's former allies tried to
   a. help establish the Bolshevik regime.
   b. overthrow the Bolshevik government.
   c. encourage Soviet gains abroad.
   d. make Russia sign the Treaty of Versailles.

2. During the 1930s, the Soviet Union faced threats from
   a. Great Britain and France.
   b. Great Britain and the United States.
   c. Germany and Japan.
   d. Italy and Turkey.

3. In its effort to resist fascist aggression, the Soviet Union
   a. supported united front movements.
   b. signed the Anti-Comintern Pact.
   c. started a huge military build up.
   d. asked to become a part of the Marshall Plan.

4. The aim of the Truman Doctrine, was to
   a. end World War II.   b. initiate worldwide communism.
   c. contain Soviet influence.   d. start the Cold War.

5. The Soviet Union and eight other communist countries joined in an alliance to help one another with economic development known as the
   a. Comintern.   b. Non-Agression Treaty.
   c. League of Nations.   d. COMECON.

DEVELOPING CRITICAL THINKING SKILLS

1. In what ways did the Soviet Union continue the foreign-policy patterns of the Russian Empire? How did communism alter these goals?

2. After World War II, what grounds did the USSR's former allies have for fearing that communism would spread to Western Europe? Explain the steps they took to combat this spread. What policies did the United States adopt to limit Soviet influence?

3. What threat of world disaster made the Cold War different from other conflicts? How was the Cold War fought until 1953?

Step on it, Doc!

Roy Justus, *The Minneapolis Star*, 1947.

ANALYZING A CARTOON

Study the cartoon and review pages 128–133 about the Cold War. Then answer the following questions.

1. What international political situation is the cartoonist illustrating?

2. What nation is represented by the vulture?

3. What does the baby represent? Why does the baby hold a wrench?

4. From what nation's point of view has this cartoon been drawn? How do you know?

5. What is the cartoonist saying about the political situation?

ENRICHMENT AND EXPLORATION

1. List five facts about how Soviet civilians suffered during World War II. Use encyclopedias or history books from the library. Write an essay, poem, short story, drama that uses the five facts. Conclude with a statement about how the suffering affected the Russian people.

2. Using the *Readers' Guide to Periodical Literature* for references, prepare a report on one of the following topics: appeasement, "penal battalions," the Yalta conference, the Berlin Airlift.

136

6 The Soviet Union from Khrushchev to Gorbachev

Stalin's death raised a host of new problems and disagreements for Soviet leaders. Who would become the new party leader? Should the emphasis on heavy industry and the military be reduced in order to raise the standard of living? How should the dangerous tensions with the West be reduced?

Nikita Khrushchev, who emerged as the Soviet leader in 1955, wanted to reverse many of Stalin's policies and institute reforms. He succeeded in making the Soviet government at least a little more responsive to the needs of its citizens. Leonid Brezhnev, Khrushchev's successor, concentrated on maintaining stability in domestic and foreign policy. Mikhail Gorbachev (GOHR-buh-chawf) became general secretary in 1985. His term of office brought enormous changes in the economic, political, and social systems of the Soviet Union—changes that contributed to the breakup of the USSR in 1991.

DOMESTIC POLICIES IN THE SOVIET UNION UNDER STALIN'S SUCCESSORS

Whatever their disagreements, Stalin's successors agreed that Stalin's system of rule by terror had to end. Shortly after Stalin's death, his secret police chief, Lavrenty Beria (BER-ih-yah), was arrested and executed. The power of the secret police was reduced. For the first time since the 1920s, it was brought under the control of the party leadership. This leadership could and did use the secret police to crush anyone who criticized or defied the system. But after 1953, those who were loyal to the system and accepted the party's control were safe from arrest. This might seem to be small comfort to U.S. citizens, whose government is based on freedom of expression and the ability to turn

FROM THE SOVIET UNION TO THE COMMONWEALTH

1953	Joseph Stalin dies.
1955	Nikita Khrushchev becomes leader of the USSR.
	Warsaw Pact formed.
1956	Riots in Poland
	Hungarian uprising
1957	*Sputnik I* launched.
	European Economic Community forms.
1959	*Castro gains control in Cuba.*
1961	Berlin Wall constructed.
1962	Cuban Missile Crisis
1964	Leonid Brezhnev becomes secretary general.
1968	Soviet army invades Czechoslovakia.
1972	United States and Soviet Union sign SALT I.
1979	Soviets invade Afghanistan.
	Ayatollah Khomeini gains power in Iran.
1980	Striking workers in Poland organize Solidarity.
	United States invades Grenada.
1985	Mikhail Gorbachev becomes head of the USSR.
1989–1991	Communist governments collapse in Eastern Europe.
1990	Gorbachev wins Nobel Peace Prize.
1991	*Persian Gulf War*
	Conservative communists stage a coup against Gorbachev.
	Commonwealth of Independent States formed.
	Gorbachev resigns.

unpopular officials out of office. However, to Soviet citizens, it was a giant step forward—a major reform and a great relief.

Reforms and Reversals of Nikita Khrushchev. The struggle for power after Stalin's death led to the formation of a collective leadership headed by Georgii Malenkov (mahl-yen-KOHF), who held the posts of prime minister and general secretary. The collective leadership masked a continued struggle for power. Nikita Khrushchev, a member of the collective leadership, became first secretary of the Communist party in 1953. In 1955, Malenkov resigned, and Khrushchev emerged as the new Soviet leader.

Once in power, Khrushchev established new political ground rules in the Soviet Union. Unlike Stalin, Khrushchev did not kill his rivals or his opponents—he only demoted them. The era of rule by an absolute dictator was over. Khrushchev was, to be sure, the most powerful politician in the Soviet Union, but there were others, too, who held considerable power. Khrushchev needed them as allies if he was to stay in power and implement his policies.

Khrushchev's job was made more difficult by disagreement between him and some other important officials over political and economic reform policies that he wanted to adopt. Khrushchev's high-placed opponents objected, fearing that too many reforms would undermine their own power. They felt that Khrushchev's policies might threaten the entire Soviet system. They had supported Khrushchev in putting an end to Stalin's terror because that ensured their own security. Apart from that, they wanted most policies left as they were.

Retracting Stalinist Policy: De-Stalinization. Khrushchev responded with a policy that came to be called **de-Stalinization**. De-Stalinization was an attempt to reverse most of Stalin's repressive policies. Khrushchev's first major attack on Stalin came in 1956, at the 20th congress of the Communist party. He made a four-hour speech denouncing Stalin as a tyrant who had murdered thousands of innocent members of the Communist party. Significantly, Khrushchev said nothing about the millions killed by Stalin who had not belonged to the party. Nor did he mention the peasants killed during collectivization. To do so would have incriminated the whole Communist party, including himself and his associates.

Khrushchev's speech was supposedly given in secret to the delegates at the 20th party congress. However, news of the so-called "Secret Speech" and what Khrushchev had said soon spread and became widely known throughout the communist world and the West. De-Stalinization increased the pressure for speeding up reform and Khrushchev moved to eliminate one of the most notorious symbols of the Stalin era: the Soviet Union's gigantic system of forced labor camps. During 1956 and 1957, Khrushchev closed many of the camps and released most of their prisoners, about 8 million people.

Khrushchev's de-Stalinization speech had explosive consequences in Eastern Europe. Riots shook the communist regime in Poland, and an anticommunist uprising swept Hungary. (See page 149.) The troubles in Poland and Hungary provided ammunition for Khrushchev's opponents in the party leadership and nearly cost him his job. In June 1957, his enemies attempted to remove him from office, but failed when Khrushchev succeeded in rallying his supporters at a decisive meeting of the party leadership. At this crucial point, Khrushchev confirmed his control of the government. His opponents, while disgraced politically, suffered no worse than being sent into retirement.

Khrushchev's Domestic Programs.   Khrushchev was committed to raising the standard of living of the Soviet people. He recognized the sacrifices the people had made to build the Soviet Union's industrial and military might. He believed the time had come for the people to enjoy the fruits of their labor. Khrushchev also believed that the struggle between communism and capitalism would come down to which system could provide a higher standard of living for its people.

Nikita Khrushchev visiting a collective farm. Khrushchev made a determined effort to increase the country's farm output. What other domestic programs did Khrushchev implement?

Writer Boris Pasternak won the Nobel Prize in Literature in 1958, but was forced to reject it by the Soviet authorities.

Khrushchev's first reform program, designed to raise agricultural output and the standard of living, was called the Virgin Lands Program. Introduced in 1954, it involved farming millions of acres of previously uncultivated land in Central Asia. The program did raise food production in the Soviet Union, but its success was limited. As you have read in Chapter 1, rainfall in Central Asia is unreliable and often inadequate for farming. In the early 1960s, the region was hit by disastrous dust storms that destroyed crops.

Khrushchev tried to build new housing for the Soviet people. The destruction suffered by the Soviet Union during World War II had left many without adequate housing. Stalin had done virtually nothing to relieve the resulting housing crisis. Khrushchev's crash program yielded impressive results. Although the new Soviet housing was poorly constructed and unattractive, by the time Khrushchev left office in 1964, the Soviet Union had twice as much housing as it had had in 1950.

Other reforms lifted some of the suffocating censorship of the Stalin years. This was considered potentially dangerous by many in the party who feared that too much truth and freedom would threaten the Soviet system. Khrushchev's policies therefore were often inconsistent. What seemed permissible one day might suddenly be prohibited the next. In 1957, a distinguished poet named Boris Pasternak allowed his book, *Doctor Zhivago*, to be published in the West after it was denied publication in the Soviet Union. The book was about the Russian Revolution and the resulting civil war and was critical of many groups, including the Bolsheviks. Pasternak was bitterly criticized, especially after he won the Nobel Prize for Literature in 1958. Yet in 1962, a writer named Alexander Solzhenitsyn (sohl-zheh-NEET-sin) was allowed to

141

*Soviet science scored a triumph when Cosmonaut
Yuri Gagarin became the first human to orbit the earth
in 1961. Here he is greeted by Nikita Khrushchev.*

publish a book called *A Day in the Life of Ivan Denisovich,* which told
about Stalin's labor camps. Solzhenitsyn's later books, none of which
was published in the Soviet Union until the Gorbachev era in the late
1980s, established him as one of Russia's greatest writers.

One of Khrushchev's most successful policies was his support of
research in science and technology. He encouraged the development of
rocket technology for military purposes and for space exploration. In
1957, the USSR became the first country to launch a satellite—*Sputnik
I*—into outer space. In 1961, the Soviet Union was the first to put a person in orbit around the earth. Khrushchev further promoted scientific
research by building special communities where scientists and scholars
could live and work.

Khrushchev's Fall.   Eventually Khrushchev went too far. He tried to
overcome opposition in the party by introducing organizational changes
that cost his opponents their positions. This antagonized the party elite.
People at all levels of the power structure were fearful of losing their
power and privileges. Some of Khrushchev's domestic programs ran into
trouble or failed completely. His foreign policy also suffered a number
of reverses. One was the rift between the USSR and communist China.
Another was Khrushchev's embarrassing defeat in 1962 by the United
States in the Cuban Missile Crisis. As a result of the missile crisis, the

Soviet Union had to withdraw offensive missiles and missile bases from Cuba. (See pages 151–152.) Some party leaders began to see Khrushchev as a bumbling dictator.

In October 1964, the **Politburo**, the party's top decision-making body, voted Khrushchev out of office. All public mention of him ceased immediately. Nothing was said of his efforts to make life in the Soviet Union more comfortable and stable. No important official attended Khrushchev's funeral in 1971. Yet, some of the people whom Khrushchev had freed from Stalin's camps went to his funeral, though they risked punishment by doing so.

Brezhnev: Stability at the Helm. Khrushchev was succeeded by a team led by Leonid Brezhnev, who had been one of Khrushchev's top aides. Brezhnev's mandate was reasonably clear. The party elite wanted to ensure stability in the system. Thus, Brezhnev was to try to raise the people's standard of living, for this would win broader support for the party. He was also to try to improve relations with the United States, for this would increase Soviet security. Brezhnev did both of these things.

Brezhnev's mandate also required that his policies not threaten the power and privileges of the party elite. Any new policies or reforms had to have the approval of the important interest groups—the managers of heavy industry, the managers of the agricultural sector, or the military. He was expected to conserve and improve the existing system. Brezhnev did just that as he held back some key reforms that might have disturbed the system in the short run, while making it more efficient in the long run. In industry as well as agriculture, Brezhnev did not interfere with the established methods of operation. These became therefore more and more outdated in comparison with the methods of the West.

Brezhnev directed increased resources to the production of consumer goods. Under him, the government spent money on farm machinery, fertilizer, and irrigation. This doubled production of grain, milk, vegetables, meat, and eggs between the 1950s and the 1970s. He also raised the people's real wages (meaning the purchasing power of the wages) by 50 percent between 1965 and 1977. This rise in the standard of living was not enough, though, to close the gap with the West.

In attempting to catch up, Brezhnev was more successful with his military programs. By the mid–1970s, the Soviet Union was, for the first time, the equal of the United States in nuclear weapons. Relations between the Soviet Union and the United States improved during the 1970s. As a result, approximately 225,000 Soviet Jews who had long been prevented from leaving the Soviet Union were finally permitted to

Scientist Andrei Sakharov helped the Soviet Union develop a hydrogen bomb, but he later became one of the country's most outspoken dissidents. What types of reform did Sakharov call for?

leave. But after 1979, relations between the United States and the Soviet Union again deteriorated. This occurred largely because of the Soviet Union's tremendous buildup of nuclear weapons and an aggressive foreign policy, which included the invasion of Afghanistan in 1979.

The Dissident Movement. The Brezhnev government reversed de-Stalinization. There was a crackdown on artists and writers, and even some steps to restore Stalin's reputation. These steps met with an unexpected reaction. Some Soviet people became extremely upset. They had hoped that Khrushchev's more tolerant policies would be expanded, not reversed. With Stalin's terror gone, some of these people took the risk of openly criticizing their government. Although not united in any way except by their anger and courage, these people came to be known as the Soviet **dissident movement**. Among the leading dissidents were Andrei Sakharov, Alexander Solzhenitsyn, and two brothers named Roy and Jaurès (zhah-RES) Medvedev (med-veh-DEV).

Sakharov was the Soviet Union's leading nuclear physicist and he enjoyed all the privileges the Soviet system could provide. He gave them all up when he spoke out in favor of democratic reforms. In 1968, he warned the Soviet leadership that without democracy as it existed in the West the Soviet Union would decline and become a second-rate power. Solzhenitsyn also wanted changes, but not the ones Sakharov advocated. Instead, Solzhenitsyn called for the end of communism and for Russia to return to its prerevolutionary religious, cultural, and political traditions. The Medvedev brothers supported yet another path of change. They believed the Soviet system could be reformed along the lines that Khrushchev had tried before he was overthrown.

During the 1970s, mainly because the Soviet Union wanted to improve relations with the United States, the dissident movement enjoyed a few small successes. It was able to get some publicity and to secure emmigration rights for a number of Jews and Germans. Beginning in the late 1970s, however, Brezhnev cracked down. By the early 1980s, most dissidents had been imprisoned, exiled abroad, or frightened into silence.

Economic Problems and Inequalities in the Soviet Union. Although the Brezhnev regime was able to control the dissident movement, it could not come to terms with many of the Soviet Union's other problems. Because the government refused to consider economic reforms, the economy worsened. The Soviet economy was extremely inefficient and, by the 1960s, it had become far too complex to manage under the central planning system. Collective farming had also proved to be a failure. Soviet farmers did not care about the collectives, over which they had no control. Most of their effort went into their tiny private plots, while the crops in the collective farm fields often went untended. Therefore, despite its vast expanse of farmland, the Soviet Union could not produce enough grain to feed itself. As a result of these and other economic problems, by the late 1970s and early 1980s the Soviet standard of living had stagnated.

Unsolved problems in other areas added to the Soviet Union's difficulties. Ordinary people resented the privileges and higher standard of living enjoyed by the party elite. They knew that party officials shopped in well-stocked special stores, while they stood in line for hours in front of half-empty shops. They were aware that the party elite lived in luxury apartments while they lived in tiny apartments in poorly-constructed buildings. These inequalities undermined morale even more so because the Soviet Union was a society that promised equality according to communist ideals. This demoralization was reflected in serious social ills, such as alcoholism on a massive and destructive scale. Yet Brezhnev did little to solve any of these problems, since that would have required challenging the system he was pledged to defend.

After leading the Soviet Union for 18 years, Leonid Brezhnev died in 1982. He was succeeded by Yuri Andropov. Andropov, who was not much younger than Brezhnev, was in office for only 15 months when he too died. His successor, Konstantin Chernenko, was another elderly member of the Brezhnev generation. He lived only until 1985. Chernenko was replaced by a man in his early fifties, Mikhail Gorbachev. Gorbachev was the first of a new generation of leaders

Important Rulers of the Soviet Union, 1917–1991			
Vladimir I. Lenin	1917–1924	**Leonid Brezhnev**	1964–1982
Joseph Stalin	1929–1953	**Yuri Andropov**	1982–1983
Collective leadership headed by **Georgii Malenkov**	1953–1955	**Konstantin Chernenko**	1983–1985
Nikita Khrushchev	1955–1964	**Mikhail Gorbachev**	1985–1991

faced with the job of solving the Soviet Union's problems. (See page 154.)

FOREIGN POLICY UNDER NEW LEADERS

Changes in Soviet foreign policy occurred almost immediately after Stalin's death in 1953. With an uncertain political situation at home, the new Soviet leaders wanted to ease tensions with the West. This desire helped lead to an armistice, or truce, in the Korean War in July 1953. In 1955, the Soviet Union agreed to withdraw the Red Army from the eastern part of Austria, where it had remained since the end of World War II. The troop removal allowed Austria to be unified in exchange for Austrian neutrality. A summit meeting with Khrushchev and several Western leaders followed. So did Khrushchev's call for **peaceful coexistence**—living peaceably with one another. This policy recognized that the existence of nuclear weapons made open warfare between the United States and the Soviet Union too dangerous. Therefore, Khrushchev reasoned that competition between the communist and capitalist worlds would occur primarily in the economic sphere.

Winning Soviet Friends in Africa and Asia. Beginning in 1955, Soviet foreign policy took another new direction. Khrushchev and Nikolai Bulganin, the Soviet prime minister, made a friendship tour of several countries in Africa and Asia. These were areas that Stalin had ignored. Over the next few years, the Soviets increased their influence in many of these countries, most of which were just gaining their independence from colonial powers such as Great Britain, France, and

Belgium. During the 1960s, these countries in Africa and Asia came to be known as the **Third World**, largely because they had not sided with either the United States and Western Europe (the "First World") or the Soviet Union and its allies (the "Second World").

The Soviets encouraged the hostility that the newly freed former colonies felt for the Western colonial powers. Like the United States, the Soviet Union gave economic and military aid to various countries. During the 1970s, the Soviets helped install Marxist regimes in Angola, Mozambique, and Ethiopia.

Relations in Asia. The Soviet Union had far less success with the People's Republic of China, another communist country. In the 1950s and 1960s, China's leader, Mao Zedong, and Khrushchev disagreed over several issues. Relations between the two communist nations continued to worsen through the 1960s. In 1969, bloody battles broke out along the Soviet-Chinese border. Eventually most of the fighting stopped, but the Soviet Union faced a new threat to its relations with China. Early in the 1970s, relations between the People's Republic of China and the United States began to improve dramatically. The United States, which had refused to recognize the communist government of China after Mao Zedong came to power in 1949, established full diplomatic relations with the People's Republic of China in 1979. Although these developments did not place China in the U.S. camp, China gradually began to have better diplomatic relations with the United States than with its communist neighbor, the USSR.

Afghanistan, a small nation located in central Asia, developed into the Soviet Union's most painful foreign-policy problem. The trouble began when the USSR tried to turn Afghanistan into a Soviet satellite. In 1978, the Soviets engineered a communist coup in Afghanistan. But the new government had little public support. Armed resistance seemed likely to bring down the communist government. In response, the Soviets invaded Afghanistan in 1979 to preserve communist rule. But a resistance movement forced the Soviets to send over 100,000 troops to Afghanistan. Yet the Soviets were unable to defeat the anticommunist Afghan guerrillas. The United States supplied arms to these guerrillas. Over the years, the brutal fighting took hundreds of thousands of Afghan lives and about 15,000 Soviet lives. Many Afghans fled the country. By the mid-1980s, several million Afghans were refugees. Most of these Afghan refugees lived in camps in neighboring Pakistan. Yet the bloody war went on until the communist government was overthrown in 1992.

Growing Soviet Influence in Latin America. Khrushchev's most spectacular foreign policy success occurred in the Americas. In 1959, a revolution in Cuba brought Fidel Castro to power. Shortly after Castro overthrew the dictatorship that had been in power since 1933, he announced that he was a communist. He moved quickly to align Cuba with the Soviet Union. The Soviets greeted him warmly and offered abundant economic and military help.

Soviet influence in Latin America continued to grow during the 1970s and the early 1980s. In 1979, Nicaraguan revolutionaries overthrew the government of a pro-U.S. dictator and installed a Marxist government. It removed other parties that had been its allies during the revolution. It limited political rights, limited freedom of the press, and strengthened its ties with the USSR.

There were two major Soviet defeats in Latin America during the Brezhnev era. In 1973, a coup, supported by the United States, overthrew the democratically elected socialist government in Chile, headed by Salvador Allende. In 1983, the United States invaded the island nation of Grenada. The invasion eliminated a would-be pro-Soviet communist dictatorship in Grenada.

Changes in Influence in the Middle East. The reliance of the West on the vast oil reserves in the Middle East sparked the Soviet Union's interest in the region. The Soviets met with mixed results in the Middle East. They continued to support the Arab states. They also encouraged the Palestine Liberation Organization, or PLO, a group established in 1964 for the purpose of destroying Israel and establishing a Palestinian state. Although the Soviet Union recognized Israel's right to exist, the Soviets sided with the Arabs in wars with Israel.

Egypt had been receiving Soviet economic and military assistance for some time. During the late 1950s, for example, the USSR had helped Egypt build its huge Aswan Dam. Then, in 1972, Egypt turned against the Soviet Union and forced most Soviet advisers to leave. Egypt began to improve its relations with the United States. This left the USSR without its most important area of influence in the North African part of the Middle East.

Nevertheless, Soviet influence remained strong in Syria, Libya, Iraq, and South Yemen (now part of Yemen), as well as with the PLO. The Soviets also benefited indirectly when a 1979 revolution in Iran overthrew the shah, a pro–U.S. ruler. U.S. influence, once strong in Iran, was eliminated. But Iran did not place itself in the Soviet camp. The Soviet advantage in having U.S. influence out of Iran was offset in that same year (1979) when Israel and Egypt signed a peace treaty, arrived at with U.S. help. The treaty increased stability in the region, which in turn reduced Soviet influence to some degree.

Warsaw Pact.   In 1955, West Germany joined NATO, significantly strengthening that alliance. Later that same year, the Soviet Union reacted by forming its own military alliance called the Warsaw Pact. Besides the Soviet Union, its members included its satellite nations, Albania (which withdrew in 1968), Bulgaria, Czechoslovakia, East Germany, Hungary, Poland, and Romania. The unified military command was under the control of the Soviet Union.

Soviet Problems with Its Satellites.   During the 1950s, the Soviet Union had to deal with problems within its Eastern European satellite nations. In East Germany, nationalist feelings combined with hatred for the Soviet puppet government to produce massive riots in East Berlin in 1953. Riots also took place in other parts of East Germany. Soviet tanks were used to put down the uprisings. The Soviet government also had to use force to suppress several uprisings in labor camps at home.

In 1956, even greater trouble erupted in the satellite nations. In October, riots broke out against the unpopular communist regime in Poland. Khrushchev was forced to agree to some concessions, such as cancellation of a large debt Poland owed to the Soviet Union. However, the Polish government pledged their loyalty to the Soviet Union and promised to support Soviet foreign policy.

No such compromise was possible in Hungary, where a reform movement led to an outright rejection of communism. In October 1956, pressure for change led to Imre Nagy, a reform-minded communist, being appointed prime minister. When Nagy's new government announced that it was going to establish a democracy and become a neutral country, Khrushchev responded with Soviet tanks. Nagy had hoped for help from the UN, but help never came. Thousands of Hungarians were killed in their unsuccessful attempt to resist the Soviets. More than 200,000 Hungarian refugees fled to the West.

More Problems Within the Communist Bloc.   In Czechoslovakia in 1968, a reform movement won control of Czechoslovakia's Communist party. The reform group insisted that they were loyal communists and friends of the USSR. But they planned to do away with censorship, permit freedom of the press, establish civil liberties, and allow other political parties to exist. After several failed attempts to convince the

Lech Walesa led Poland's Solidarity movement in its struggle against the Soviet-dominated Polish government.

Czechoslovaks to give up their plans, the Soviet leadership decided to use force before these dangerous ideas spread to other communist countries. In August, more than 400,000 Soviet, Polish, Bulgarian, Hungarian and East German troops invaded Czechoslovakia and crushed the reform movement.

Despite Soviet suppression, the reform movement in Poland continued to grow and gain momentum. In 1980, workers rioted and went on strike in Gdansk (gih-DANSK), an industrial city. The strike was illegal, as were all strikes in Soviet-dominated countries. Because Poland's Communist regime was corrupt and had little popular support, it was unable to act. The workers then organized a labor union called **Solidarity**. It was the first trade union in the Soviet bloc that was not controlled by the Communist party. For a while the Communist government of Poland and Solidarity stood deadlocked. Even the Soviet Union hesitated and took no direct action. Its leaders were worried that the Poles would fight back if their country were invaded. Then, in December 1981 under growing pressure from the USSR, the Polish government acted. It proclaimed martial law, arrested Solidarity's leaders, and suppressed the union.

Agreements and Tension with Western Europe. Western Europe was one of the areas most important to the Soviet Union. Under Brezhnev, the Soviets made some advances there. Relations improved with both France and West Germany. There was increasing economic cooperation between those countries and the USSR. In 1975, 35 nations on both sides of the Iron Curtain signed the Helsinki Accords. This series of agreements recognized the post-World War II boundary changes that had been so favorable to the Soviet Union. In return, the Soviet Union made guarantees about such basic human rights as freedom of thought, conscience, and religion. In the following decade, the Soviet Union was repeatedly accused of violating these human rights agreements.

Other developments strictly limited Soviet influence in Western Europe. In addition to NATO, a military alliance organized in 1949, six European countries had formed an economic alliance in 1957 called the **European Economic Community**, or the **Common Market**. Other European countries joined the original group and by 1991, there were 12 member nations. The Soviets failed in their attempts to weaken the Common Market and NATO. The USSR was especially upset when NATO allies decided to allow the United States to deploy new, advanced missiles in their nations. These missiles balanced the new Soviet missiles aimed at Western Europe.

Clashes with the United States. There was constant friction between the United States and the Soviet Union over Berlin, much of it caused by the Soviets. The Soviets were embarrassed because West Berlin, which was not separated from East Berlin by any physical barriers, had become an escape route for thousands of East Germans. To put an end to their flight, the Soviets and East Germans, in August 1961, closed off West Berlin and soon started building a wall around it. The Berlin Wall cut the city in two and further isolated West Berlin within East Germany. This stopped the escaping East Germans, but also increased tensions with the United States. The Berlin Wall stood as a symbol of the Cold War until it was opened in 1989.

The most serious U.S.–Soviet incident arose in the Caribbean, in Cuba, just 90 miles (145 kilometers) from Florida. By 1962, Cuba was firmly in the Soviet camp. Khrushchev decided to use his ally to overcome a military disadvantage the USSR faced. The Soviet Union did not have many long–range nuclear missiles that could hit the United States from Soviet soil. But the United States could hit the Soviet Union by using missiles and bombers launched from its bases in allied countries in Europe and elsewhere. The United States could also use its

In October 1962, photos taken by U.S. reconnaisance planes showed that the Soviet Union was installing missile bases in Cuba. The U.S.-Soviet confrontation that followed brought the two nations to the brink of war.

long-range bombers to attack the Soviet Union. Khrushchev reasoned that he could close the missile gap with the United States by putting intermediate-range missiles in Cuba. That way the Soviet Union would have missiles within striking distance of the United States. Soviet missiles also would help protect Cuba against the United States, which in 1961, had assisted Cuban exiles opposed to Castro in an unsuccessful invasion of the island.

In fall 1962, the United States discovered that the USSR had been building missile bases in Cuba and was about to install the missiles. President John F. Kennedy dealt with what became known as the Cuban Missile Crisis by demanding that the missile bases be dismantled. He ordered a naval blockade to quarantine the area and prevent the shipment of the missiles. Faced with superior military strength, Khrushchev backed down. The Soviets stopped building the missile bases in Cuba.

Khrushchev's embarrassment over the outcome of the Cuban Missile Crisis undermined his position at home and contributed to his fall from leadership in 1964. It also led to his successors' decision to launch a massive military buildup to catch up with the United States. That buildup continued into the early 1980s, long after the Soviet Union's goal was achieved.

Out of the missile crisis, two positive results emerged for both nations. Shocked by how close they had come to a nuclear war in 1962, the United States and the Soviet Union set up a direct telephone hotline between the White House and the Kremlin in that same year. In 1963, the two nations signed a treaty that banned nuclear tests in the atmosphere. That treaty is still in force.

Further Challenges to the United States. During the Brezhnev era, the Soviet military buildup continued through the mid-1960s until Brezhnev's death in 1982. This buildup was the most important means of challenging U.S. power. Because of its advanced technology, the United States often developed and deployed new, advanced weapons before the Soviets did. But the Soviets remained in the **arms race.** The arms race refers to the continued build up of huge nuclear arsenals in the United States and the Soviet Union. During the 1970s, the Soviet Union outspent the United States. In many categories they built more, though not better, weapons than the United States did.

Brezhnev's policy toward the United States was to try to reduce the danger of nuclear war while building up the Soviet Union's arms. Brezhnev's attempt to achieve stable relations between the USSR and the United States coincided with similar U.S. efforts. These produced the policy of **détente** (day-TAHNT), meaning a relaxing of tensions between countries.

Détente involved a variety of agreements. These included cultural exchanges and expanded trade. But the heart of détente was an attempt by both sides to control the arms race. An early step toward détente occurred in 1968. Both nations signed a treaty to prevent the spread of nuclear weapons to other countries. Then, in 1969, the two superpowers began to discuss their own weapons in the **Strategic Arms Limitations Talks,** or **SALT.**

In 1972, these talks produced an agreement known as SALT I. SALT I limited antiballistic missile systems. It also placed a temporary limit on strategic weapons, in other words, weapons that have an intercontinental range. The theory was to limit defensive systems because without a defense neither side would dare attack the other. Each knew that it would be destroyed in a counterattack. This theory is known as **mutually assured destruction,** or **MAD.**

In 1974, under the second phase of SALT I, both sides agreed to limit their strategic weapons to 2,400 bombers and missiles. In 1975, a U.S. spacecraft and a Soviet spacecraft met and docked in space; on earth, both nations signed the Helsinki Accords.

Soviet troops in the war in Afghanistan met stiff resistance from Afghan guerrillas. How did Soviet invasion of Afghanistan affect détente?

Détente began to crumble after 1975. One reason was the concern many U.S. experts and political leaders expressed over the Soviet military buildup. The fall of South Vietnam to communist North Vietnam and the aggressive Soviet support of the Marxists in the Angolan civil war contributed to the decline of détente. The final blow came when the Soviet army invaded Afghanistan in 1979. After the invasion of Afghanistan, President Jimmy Carter withdrew the newly signed, but not yet ratified, SALT II treaty from consideration in the Senate, where it faced certain defeat. Additional signs of deteriorating U.S. Soviet relations came from a series of events that included a U.S. embargo on shipments of grain to the Soviet Union, a U.S. boycott of the 1980 Olympics held in Moscow, and the indirect Soviet suppression of the Polish Solidarity union in 1981.

GORBACHEV'S REFORMS AND THE COLLAPSE OF COMMUNISM

The process of change in the Soviet Union began immediately after Brezhnev's death in 1982, although in a narrow and limited way. Yuri Andropov, Brezhnev's successor, began a series of reforms that attempted to fight corruption and replace old party leaders. When Andropov died in 1984 after only 15 months in office, he was succeeded by Chernenko and reforms ground to a halt. Less than a year later, Chernenko died and Mikhail Gorbachev was named general secretary. Gorbachev was to unleash changes that would sweep the old system away.

Gorbachev's Reform Program.   Gorbachev came into office believing the Soviet system needed change. At first, however, he had no intention of undertaking the radical reforms he later sponsored. His program for change developed over time, as he began to realize that small changes could not solve the Soviet Union's immense problems. During 1985 and most of 1986, Gorbachev did not go much beyond Andropov's program of reform.

Gorbachev tinkered with the economic system, mainly by attacking corruption. The new general secretary launched a campaign to curb alcoholism, but was disappointed with its limited results. Gorbachev also continued to force the old guard into retirement. One of his most important moves was to appoint Eduard Shevardnadze (sheh-vahrd-NAHD-zuh), a strong supporter of reform, as the new Soviet foreign minister. However, not until the disastrous explosion at the Chernobyl nuclear power plant in April 1986 did Gorbachev go beyond minor reforms to radical change. The Chernobyl disaster, which contaminated thousands of square miles of land and damaged the health of hundreds of thousands of people, was the worst nuclear power plant disaster in history. This disaster seems to have convinced Gorbachev that bolder steps were necessary to restore the Soviet system to health.

The program of reform that gradually emerged included *perestroika* (restructuring), *glasnost* (openness), and *demokratizatsia* (democratization).

Perestroika. The word *perestroika* (peh-ruh-STROIY-kuh) often was used to describe Gorbachev's entire program of reforming the Soviet system, including problems in the economy, politics, and society. However, *perestroika* referred most directly to the economy. The centrally planned Soviet economy was extremely inefficient and unable to provide an adequate standard of living. Equally important, due to its sluggish economy, the Soviet Union could not compete with the United States in the arms race. As the ideas of *perestroika* evolved, Gorbachev called for limits on central planning. Market forces such as supply and demand would determine, at least in part, what goods would be produced, how many, and at what price. Eventually advocates of *perestroika* called for major changes in the collective farm system, and even its abolition.

Glasnost. *Glasnost* meant opening up the flow of information in the censored Soviet world. At first, it did not mean the end of all censorship. Under *glasnost,* the Soviet people were allowed to know more about

Mikhail Gorbachev visiting a steel mill in Dnepropetrovsk, an industrial city in Ukraine, in 1985. The iron and steel mills of the city by this time had become technologically outdated.

problems in their own society and about events in the outside world. They were told a more truthful version of their nation's history. Some previously banned books and films became available for reading and viewing. But *glasnost* soon caused as many problems as it solved. Once the people were told part of the truth, they wanted to know the rest.

Demokratizatsia. *Demokratizatsia* (day-moh-KRAH-tee-zah-tsee-ah) led to the same problems as *glasnost*. When Gorbachev came into office, he did not believe in democracy as it exists in the West. He only wanted to introduce some choice into the Communist system, such as allowing more than one candidate to run for certain lower-level party offices. The goal was to get the Soviet people involved in the reform program by allowing them a limited voice in deciding new policies. However, like *glasnost,* small doses of democracy quickly led to demands for more, and *demokratizatsia* ran far beyond what Gorbachev had originally intended.

Reactions to Reform. Aside from having to solve the enormous problems of a failing system, Gorbachev and the reformers faced powerful forces that opposed reform. Much of the Communist party was against far-reaching change because real change threatened the power and privileges the party members and leaders enjoyed. Opponents of reform were especially strong in organizations like the military and the KGB. The power of these organizations was directly threatened by policies that decreased military spending or introduced democratic reforms. Making matters worse, as Gorbachev began proposing more radical changes, the ranks of his opponents within the party leadership grew. The most powerful party leader opposing reform was Yegor Ligachev. He had supported limited reforms similar to Andropov's, but by 1987 increasingly turned against Gorbachev. This opposition forced Gorbachev to slow down and even reverse some of his reform policies.

During 1987, Gorbachev intensified his struggle to remove conservatives opposed to reform from powerful positions. He succeeded in breaking their grip on the Communist party's two most powerful bodies: the Politburo and the Central Committee, mainly by forcing older officials into retirement. The Central Committee then finally endorsed Gorbachev's economic reform package. It called for limiting central planning and allowing factory managers to set prices based on their costs. However, passing a law was far from making the actual changes it called for. Party members in key positions throughout the economy continued to resist change. In October 1987, a reformer named Boris Yeltsin publicly denounced the slow pace of change. He attacked conservatives like Ligachev, and even criticized Gorbachev himself. Gorbachev was furious, and Yeltsin was fired from his post as head of the party organization in Moscow.

Despite Yeltsin's complaints, by 1987 a great deal of change already was occurring in several areas. *Glasnost* had gained momentum and was radically changing what Soviet citizens knew and what they could say. News broadcasts began to carry news about disasters and scandals. Many political prisoners were released, including Andrei Sakharov, who had been under house arrest since 1980. Books, plays, and films that had been banned for years finally became available, including the Nobel Prize-winning novel *Doctor Zhivago*. By the end of 1988, over 6,000 previously-banned works of all kinds had been published. Religious music and rock 'n' roll finally were allowed to emerge from their underground existence. The most popular rock group in the Soviet Union was finally allowed to record an album in a government studio. Its 200,000 copies sold out within hours without the benefit of a single advertisement.

Glasnost was closely and inevitably tied to the advance of democracy. Gorbachev's strategy was to use small and controlled doses of democracy to appeal directly to Soviet citizens. After a difficult struggle, he got the party leadership to agree to set up a new parliament, called the Congress of People's Deputies. The new congress would have some real power, unlike the old Soviet parliament, which obediently followed party orders. Just as important, for the first time in Soviet history, more than one candidate could run for each seat in the elections to the congress. The 2,250 members of the congress also would elect a smaller body of 542 members called the Supreme Soviet to govern the country on a day-to-day basis. Gorbachev's political program also called for the abolition of the current post of Soviet president, a ceremonial post with no real power. In its place would be a new post, also called president. However, this president would have power.

The Election of 1989. In 1989, the Soviet Union had its first relatively free election since 1917. The election and its results shocked almost everyone. Candidates campaigned, disagreed, and argued with each other. Party reformers won many congressional seats while conservatives were defeated across the country. Among those elected to congress were Andrei Sakharov and Boris Yeltsin, who crushed a party conservative by winning an amazing 89 percent of the vote in his Moscow district. Even more unexpected, nonparty candidates won 20 percent of the seats in the new congress.

When the congress met, it became clear that the process of *demokratizatsia* was continuing at full speed and that Gorbachev was not always in control of it. While the congress elected Gorbachev president, its members openly disagreed with him on many issues. Delegates angrily criticized the Soviet regime for past abuses. After the congress elected the Supreme Soviet, over 200 delegates got together to form an independent organization they called the Interregional Group. For the first time in over 60 years, the Communist party faced a political organization openly opposed to its dictatorial rule.

In 1989, the Soviet Union's first free election drew spirited electioneering for candidates. The poster at the lower right calls for the election of Boris Yeltsin.

In March 1990, the Congress of People's Deputies struck another blow at the Communist dictatorship. It repealed the article of the Soviet constitution that guaranteed the Communist party absolute political power. The growing opposition to the Communist party was further illustrated in March 1990, when noncommunists swept to power in local elections held throughout the country.

Foreign Policy and the Collapse of Communism in Eastern Europe. Foreign policy reform was central to Gorbachev's plans. He wanted to reduce tensions with the West and control the arms race so that the Soviet Union could devote its resources to making repairs at home. A summit meeting with President Ronald Reagan held in December 1987 produced some results. For the first time since the start of the Cold War, the United States and the Soviet Union agreed to eliminate their intermediate-range nuclear missiles based in Europe. Early in 1988, Gorbachev announced that the Soviet Union was withdrawing its troops from Afghanistan, where they had been defending an unpopular communist government against a widespread rebellion since 1979. That withdrawal was completed in February 1989 and further improved Soviet relations with the United States and Western Europe. (See page 147.)

The international event of 1989 that did the most to change U.S.-Soviet relations took place in Eastern Europe. Despite over 40 years of repression, propaganda, and limited reform, the Soviet-dominated communist governments of Eastern Europe were despised by the people they ruled. Gorbachev had warned the leaders of these governments that they had to undertake major reforms, but his warning had come far too late. In April, the communist regime in Poland started to collapse. That began a chain reaction that by December ended not only communism in Poland, but in Hungary, East Germany, Czechoslovakia, Bulgaria, and Romania as well. Gorbachev had not wanted these regimes to collapse; he had wanted only reform. However, when the collapse of communism began, he made it clear the Soviets would do nothing to stop it. Given the choice between Soviet control of Eastern Europe and a chance to end the Cold War and establish better relations with the West, Gorbachev chose better relations and peace. In November 1990, all the nations of Europe (except Albania), along with the United States and Canada, signed the Paris Charter, that proclaimed the end of the Cold War. Gorbachev received deserved recognition for his extraordinary contributions when he was awarded the Nobel Peace Prize for 1990.

In 1990, the Soviet Union joined an international effort to solve a crisis in the Middle East, where Iraq had invaded and occupied oil-rich Kuwait. Iraq for years had been friendly to the Soviet Union and was heavily armed with the most modern Soviet weapons. The invasion caused great concern in the West. Iraq was known to be developing nuclear weapons and its modern million-person army was a direct threat to Saudi Arabia, which borders on Kuwait and has the world's largest oil reserves. When it became clear in 1991 that only force could budge the Iraqis, the Soviets made no effort to stop a coalition led by the United States from expelling the Iraqis from Kuwait in the Persian Gulf War.

Nationality and Economic Problems.   Conservative forces within the Communist party were not the only threats to Gorbachev's reform efforts. Disorder and hardship caused by ethnic conflict and economic crisis both distracted and weakened Gorbachev as he struggled to control the quickening pace of change in the Soviet Union.

There were two types of ethnic problems: minority nationalities trying to break free of Soviet control and conflict between various minority ethnic groups. The struggle for independence from Soviet control was strongest in the Baltic republics of Latvia, Lithuania, and Estonia. By 1988, what were called "popular fronts" had formed in all three republics. Although these organizations did not yet dare to use the word independence, they spoke openly of loosening their ties with the authorities in Moscow. In 1990, Lithuania declared its independence, although it had no way of enforcing that declaration given the presence of thousands of Soviet troops on its soil. What Lithuania did manage to do was to undermine further Gorbachev's authority. Meanwhile, the movement to break free from Russian dominance expanded to the other Soviet republics, from Moldavia in the west to the Caucasus in the south and Central Asia in the east.

As Soviet power weakened, the old hatreds it had kept smothered flared. Ethnic violence exploded into a crisis in the Caucasus, where Armenia and Azerbaijan fought over a territory called Nagorno-Karabahk, a region inhabited mainly by Armenians but located inside Azerbaijan. Other parts of the Soviet Union were also plagued by violent ethnic conflict. Gorbachev was unable to stop this ethnic conflict. Nor could he stop the Soviet economy from sinking into crisis. Most of Gorbachev's economic policies were half-measures that compromised between those people who opposed change and those who wanted real reforms. As a result, the old centrally planned system fell apart before a market economy could develop to replace it.

By autumn 1990, there were shortages of many goods, including food. Prices for food available in private markets shot up beyond what many ordinary people could afford. During the first half of 1991, production of oil, coal, and basic household goods all fell. Reports circulated that the harvest would be poor, in part because of shortages of tractors and fuel. These reports drove food prices even higher.

The August Coup. In the late afternoon on August 18, 1991, Communist party conservatives staged a coup against Gorbachev. They placed him under house arrest in his vacation home in the Crimea and removed him from office. The next day heavily armed troops entered Moscow. Soviet news broadcasts announced that Gorbachev had been replaced by an eight-man "State Committee for the State of Emergency." However, the coup was poorly planned and had few supporters. Opponents to the coup rallied behind Boris Yeltsin, who a few months earlier had been elected president of Russia. While most of the nations of the world waited anxiously, hundreds of thousands of Soviet citizens poured into the streets in protest. In Moscow on the first morning after the coup, Yeltsin climbed atop an armored truck and called on the Soviet people to stand firm against the coup. Faced with unexpected resistance, the coup plotters hesitated. At the same time, some of their troops began to join the resistance. Yeltsin received support from foreign leaders, including U.S. President George Bush. Three days after it had begun the coup collapsed. In the predawn hours of August 22, a shaken but smiling Mikhail Gorbachev returned to Moscow, once again the president of the Soviet Union.

Although the leaders of the August 1991 coup against Gorbachev ordered tanks into Moscow, civilians persuaded soldiers not to open fire. Some troops even joined the defense of the city.

CASE STUDY

Founding the Commonwealth of Independent States

On December 21, 1991, 11 newly independent republics of the former Soviet Union formed the Commonwealth of Independent States. Below is the declaration that founded the Commonwealth. The declaration proclaims an end to the Soviet Union and confirms some of the rights and obligations of the member states.

> THE INDEPENDENT STATES—the Azerbaijani Republic, the Republic of Armenia, the Republic of Byelorussia, the Republic of Kazakhstan, the Republic of Kirghizia, the Republic of Moldavia, the Russian Federation, the Republic of Tadzhikistan, Turkmenia, the Republic of Uzbekistan and Ukraine,

SEEKING to build democratic law-governed states, the relations between which will develop on the basis of mutual recognition and respect for state sovereignty [independence] and sovereign equality, the inalienable right to self-determination, principles of equality and non-interference in internal affairs, the rejection of the use of force, the threat of force and economic and any other methods of pressure, a peaceful settlement of disputes, respect for human rights and freedoms, including the rights of national minorities, a conscientious fulfillment of commitment and other generally recognized principles and standards of international law;

RECOGNIZING and respecting each other's territorial integrity and the inviolability [sacredness] of the existing borders;

BELIEVING that the strengthening of the relations of friendship, good neighborliness and mutually advantageous cooperation, which has deep historic roots, meets the basic interests of nations and promotes the cause of peace and security;

BEING aware of their responsibility for the preservation of civilian peace and inter-ethnic accord [peace];

BEING loyal to the objectives and principles of the agreement on the creation of the Commonwealth of Independent States;

ARE MAKING the following statement:

Cooperation between members of the commonwealth will be carried
out in accordance with the principle of equality through coordinating
institutions formed on a parity basis and operating in the way
established by the agreements between members of the
commonwealth, which is neither a state nor a superstate structure.
In order to insure international strategic stability and security, allied
command of the military-strategic forces and a single control over
nuclear weapons will be preserved, the sides will respect each other's
desire to attain the status of a non-nuclear or neutral state
The commonwealth of independent states is open, with the agreement
of all its participants, for other states to join - members of the former
Soviet Union as well as other states sharing the goals and principles
of the commonwealth.
The allegiance to cooperation in the formation and development of the
common economic space, and all European and Eurasian markets is
being confirmed.
With the formation of the Commonwealth of Independent States, the
Union of Soviet Socialist Republics ceases to exist.
Member states of the commonwealth guarantee, in accordance with
their constitutional procedures, the fulfillment of international
obligations stemming from the treaties and agreements of the former
USSR.
Member states of the commonwealth pledge to observe strictly the
principles of this declaration.

The New York Times, December 22, 1991, p. 12.

1. What form of government do the independent states of the
   Commonwealth want to establish?

2. Who may join the Commonwealth of Independent States?

3. According to this document, who is responsible for the control of
   nuclear weapons?

4. Who is responsible for maintaining civilian peace and inter-ethnic
   accord?

5. How is the agreement among the members of the Commonwealth
   different from the agreement among the states of the United States
   as stated in the U.S. Constitution?

After the August 1991 communist coup failed, Boris Yeltsin quickly assumed a leadership role, while Mikhail Gorbachev's power ebbed away.

The End of the Soviet Union. The August coup proved to be the final blow that shattered both Soviet communism and the Soviet Union itself. Immediately after the coup's collapse the Communist party was suspended in most parts of the country. Much of its property was seized and many of its activities were banned. Gorbachev resigned as its general secretary, leaving the party without a leader. Both the KGB and the military, two key underpinnings of the party's power, were purged of coup supporters. Symbolic changes underscored the end of over 74 years of communist rule, as cities and towns all over the Soviet Union dropped communist-era names in favor of their pre-1917 names. In the most significant of these changes, Leningrad reverted to its prerevolutionary name of St. Petersburg.

Gorbachev meanwhile began a desperate attempt to hold the Soviet Union together. But the forces of disintegration were too strong. In September, the tottering Soviet government recognized the independence of Lithuania, Latvia, and Estonia. Then, one-by-one the remaining republics of the Soviet Union declared their independence. On December 8, 1991, Boris Yeltsin, representing Russia, along with representatives from Ukraine and Belarus, announced the formation of a new organization: the Commonwealth of Independent States. The Commonwealth was a loose confederation of independent nations. On December 21, eight other newly independent republics of the former Soviet Union had joined the Commonwealth. The nation of Georgia, torn by internal strife, did not join. Lithuania, Latvia, and Estonia declined membership in the Commonwealth as well.

On December 25, 1991, Mikhail Gorbachev bowed to reality. He announced his resignation as president of the Soviet Union. Immediately after his speech, the Soviet flag was lowered from atop the Kremlin. In its place flew the flag of Russia. The Union of Soviet Socialist Republics suddenly belonged to the past.

REVIEWING THE CHAPTER

I. Building Your Vocabulary

In your notebook, write the numbers from 1 to 6. After each number, write the word the matches the definition.

Politburo	hotline	*perestroika*
glasnost	*demokratizatsia*	peaceful coexistence

1. restructuring

2. the Communist party's top decision-making body

3. openness

4. the direct telephone between the White House and the Kremlin

5. Khrushchev's foreign policy

6. democratization

II. Understanding the Facts

In your notebook, write the numbers 1 to 5. Write the letter of the correct answer to each question next to its number.

1. Krushchev's first action in his policy of de-Stalinization was
   a. a speech that denounced Stalin as a murderer.
   b. ending a riot in Poland.
   c. sending missiles to Cuba.

2. People who openly criticized the Soviet government were known as
   a. Soviet guerillas.   b. dissidents.   c. Marxists.

3. The first trade union in the Soviet bloc that was not controlled by the Communist party was called
   a. Solidarity.   b. Gdansk.   c. *Demokratizatsia.*

4. Gorbachev's policy of *glasnost* led to all of the following except
   a. free elections in the Soviet Union in 1989.
   b. the Soviet invasion of Afghanistan.
   c. the distribution of *Doctor Zhivago.*

5. Which republic did not join the Commonwealth when it formed?

a. Ukraine   b. Georgia   c. Russia

III. Thinking It Through

In your notebook, write the numbers 1 to 5. Write the letter of the correct answer to each question next to its number.

1. An important reform instituted by Nikita Khrushchev was

a. putting an end to purges and forced-labor camps for political enemies.

b. opening Party membership to all who wanted it.

c. permitting dissent in satellite states.

d. introducing the policy of *glasnost.*

2. The Soviet response to NATO was the formation of what organization?

a. Solidarity   b. Warsaw Pact

c. MAD   d. *glasnost.*

3. Which of the following statements is NOT true about the arms race?

a. It is defined as the continued buildup of huge nuclear arsenals.

b. The policy of dètente was developed in an effort to stop the arms race.

c. The Soviets were the clear winner in the arms race.

d. Strategic weapons were limited by both sides by SALT I.

4. Which of the following is NOT true about Third World countries in the mid 1900s?

a. The Soviet Union tried to win the support of many Third World countries.

b. The Third World countries were ones that had just gain their independence from nations such as Great Britain and France.

c. Most of the Third World countries were in South America.

d. Many Third World countries did not side with either the United States or the USSR.

5. One reason for the failure of the coup of August 1991 was that

a. Gorbachev lacked popular support.

b. Yeltsin supported the coup.

c. the United States sent troops to crush the coup.

d. it lacked popular support.

DEVELOPING CRITICAL THINKING SKILLS

1. Nikita Khrushchev instituted a number of changes in the Soviet Union. Give examples of the changes and discuss how they were received by others who sought power in the Soviet Union.

2. Soviet dissidents had different ideas about how Soviet society should be changed. Explain the ideas of each of the following dissidents: Andrei Sakharov, Alexander Solzhenitsyn, and the Medvedev brothers.

3. Identify three components of Gorbachev's reform program. Which parts of his program achieved success? Which did not?

CREATING A TIMELINE

Create an illustrated timeline that shows efforts of the Soviet leadership to reform the Soviet Union. Begin with Krushchev's rise to power in 1955 and end with the breakup of the Soviet Union in December 1991. Be sure that you only include actions aimed at improving life under communism and that you illustrate each event appropriately.

ENRICHMENT AND EXPLORATION

1. Imagine that Khrushchev, Brezhnev, and Gorbachev met in a debate to argue that he had done the most for his country. Write five questions that you as the moderator would ask each leader. What responses would each leader have given? What evidence would each have given to support his answers? Write a dialogue for their imaginary debate. You may wish to use the school or public library for reference to make your "debate" more authentic.

2. Write a report that compares and contrasts Soviet foreign policy in the Middle East, Eastern Europe, Africa, and Latin America after the death of Stalin until the dissolution of the Soviet Union. Where was the Soviet Union most successful? Where were they least successful?

7 Transforming the Government and Economy

After the collapse of the Soviet Union in 1991, the newly independent nations of the region were faced with many decisions. The most critical were how to organize their governments and economies. The leaders of the new nations agreed that as a political and economic system, communism had failed. They now had to decide on an alternative system. Most people wanted to build democratic governments and free market economies. However, this would prove to be a major challenge since the leaders of the new nations had little experience with either democracy or free market economies.

The first part of this chapter discusses the political and economic systems of the former Soviet Union. Knowing why these systems failed will make clearer the issues the newly independent nations of the Commonwealth are attempting to resolve. The second part of the chapter explains the political structure of the Commonwealth of Independent States, a loose organization formed by 11 of the independent states. It also discusses the government and economy of Russia, the largest of the newly independent nations.

THE SOVIET STATE

When the Soviet Union existed, all real power was concentrated in one organization: the Communist Party of the Soviet Union, or **CPSU**. The party was in total control of the Soviet state. Each level of government had a parallel party organization, and top party officials held all the important governmental posts. In fact, there was such a close connection between the party and the state that it often was difficult to tell where one ended and the other began. When discussing the Soviet

168

Union's governing system, experts often referred to the Soviet "Party-State." To describe the almost total control the Party-State maintained over the Soviet people's lives, experts generally used the term "totalitarian society." (See Chapter 4.)

The Soviet state controlled all the productive resources of the country. In the Soviet Union, the state owned all natural resources, farmland, mines, department stores, and even most services, such as automobile repair shops. Other property was indirectly controlled by the state. In theory, a collective farm's machines and tools belonged to the farm. However, because the state controlled the collective farms, it controlled those tools and machines.

Soviet Education—Indoctrination of Marxist Theory.   The Soviet state controlled education throughout the country. One of the main aims of Soviet education was to produce outstanding scientists and engineers. Soviet schools stressed science and mathematics and Soviet students studied these subject far more intensively than do students in the United States. No less important was what Westerners would call indoctrination. The goal was to create a society of people who totally accepted the Soviet way of life. To this end, all Soviet students had to learn Karl Marx's views about history, why communism supposedly was superior to capitalism, and why capitalism eventually was doomed to collapse. (See Chapter 3.)

The Soviet Secret Police.   The Soviet state also operated what was the world's largest security network. Its main branch was the secret police, the Committee for State Security, known by its Russian initials, **KGB**. The KGB was the largest and most effective organization of its kind in the world. Because of this vast network of controls, Soviet citizens were forced to live under restrictions that they found increasingly intolerable.

The Soviet Party-State's far-reaching control of people's lives contradicted Marx's prediction that socialism would lead to communism and that the state would "wither away." Instead, in strengthening and expanding the powers of the state, the Soviet model of government followed the old Russian tradition of a powerful, highly centralized state that does everything it can to control the lives of its people.

The Soviet Constitution.   The Soviet Union had a constitution that in theory was the basis of its laws. The last of four Soviet constitutions was adopted in 1977. On paper, it guaranteed citizens a number of political rights, including freedom of speech, freedom of the press, and the right

The statue of V.I. Lenin, once revered as the father of the Russian Revolution, was one of the first symbols of the Soviet regime to be torn down when the Soviet state was overthrown in 1991.

to conduct public demonstrations. However, these rights could not be exercised in the Soviet Union without risking harsh punishment. The Soviet constitution also guaranteed certain economic and social rights, such as housing, health care, and social security. Although what the Soviet government provided was often of poor quality, Soviet citizens, far more than their U.S. counterparts, relied on their government to provide those services.

A central feature of the Soviet constitution was that it made all rights and benefits dependent on a citizen's performing certain "duties and obligations." These included doing "socially useful work," or work that was approved by the Soviet government. If, for example an artist created works that did not support the Communist party's point of view, the artist could lose his or her rights. Other duties included safeguarding the interests of the state, performing military service, and raising children to be "worthy members of a socialist society." Most significant, the 1977 constitution affirmed that the CPSU was the "leading and guiding force in Soviet society and the nucleus [center] of its political system." In other words, it was the Communist party that determined when and to what extent Soviet citizens could exercise their long list of constitutional rights.

The Structure of the Soviet State.   According to its constitution, the Soviet Union, like the United States, had several levels of government. At the top was the central government of the Soviet Union, or the "All-Union" government. The next level was made up of 15 union republics, which reflected the multiethnic character of the USSR. In theory, each republic had the right to secede from the USSR. In practice, each union republic was tightly controlled from Moscow by the CPSU. By far the largest of the union republics was the Russian Soviet Federated Socialist Republic (RSFSR). It alone accounted for more than three quarters of the Soviet Union's territory and about half its population.

Below the union republics were other subdivisions, each of which governed one of the larger minority groups living within the borders of the union republics. The most important subdivisions were called autonomous republics. Of the 20 autonomous republics in the Soviet Union, 16 were in the RSFSR. After that came 8 autonomous regions, 5 of which were in the RSFSR, and then 10 autonomous areas, all of which were within the RSFSR. The Soviet Union also had various local governmental units similar to those in other countries.

The All-Union government in theory exercised executive, legislative, and judicial authority for the Soviet Union as whole. It had a number of institutions and offices to carry out its tasks, including a two-house parliament. However, in reality decisions were made by the Communist party, not the All-Union government. The All-Union government's task was to administer the country according to decisions reached by the leaders of the CPSU, who also served at the top levels of the government apparatus.

The Supreme Soviet, with hundreds of members, was the legislature of the All-Union government. It had no real power and usually rubber-stamped decisions made by the Communist party.

THE COMMUNIST PARTY—THE REAL POLITICAL POWER

In the Soviet Union, there was only one **political party**—the Communist party of the Soviet Union. The USSR did hold elections for government offices. However, those elections usually had only one candidate for each office. All candidates had to be approved by the party. All the top positions in the government were held by party members. Although the people who held lower positions often were not CPSU members, they were people who actively supported the party's programs.

From shortly after the Bolshevik Revolution of 1917 until 1990, the Communist party was the only political organization permitted in the Soviet Union. It controlled the government and every significant organization in the country.

Organization of the Party. The Communist party was a strictly regulated hierarchy. Its broad base was formed at almost every institution in the country, including factories, farms, schools, and military units. By the 1980s, there were more than 400,000 primary party organizations in the Soviet Union. Each primary unit elected delegates to higher party organizations in towns and then to districts. Elections continued up the ladder through the provincial, union republic, and national levels. Party organizations from various levels elected delegates to an All-Union Party Congress. Beginning in 1961 and until the collapse of the Soviet Union in 1991, a new Party Congress met every five years.

By the 1960s, the Party Congress had grown into a huge meeting of about 5,000 delegates. The most important job of the Party Congress was to elect the **Central Committee**. The Central Committee in turn elected the **Politburo** and the **Secretariat**. The Politburo was the party's major policy-making body and its center of power. The Secretariat supervised operations of the various branches of the party. The Central Committee also elected the general secretary (sometimes called the president), the leader of the party.

Lenin's practice of **democratic centralism** was another element that determined the flow of power. According to democratic centralism, the minority on any issue had to accept the will of the majority. Because the party leadership from Lenin to Gorbachev always controlled the party machinery, it always controlled an overwhelming majority. Democratic centralism also required that lower party organizations carry out the orders of higher bodies. It thereby ensured the leadership's control over the party's rank and file.

172

The General Secretary. As the party leader, the general secretary, rather than the country's president or prime minister, was the real leader of the Soviet Union. Ironically, Lenin, the father of the Communist party, never held the post of general secretary, which was established in 1922. Lenin simply served as a member of the Politburo, but he was able to dominate that body and the party itself by virtue of his unbending will and enormous standing as the founder of Bolshevism. Stalin, on the other hand, used the position to accumulate so much power that he ruled as a dictator, with the Politburo subject to his will. After Stalin's death, the position of general secretary lost some of this power. To prevent the abuses that had taken place during Stalin's reign, the general secretary needed the Politburo's support to remain in power. Nevertheless, the general secretary remained by far the most powerful political person in the Soviet Union.

Membership in the CPSU—An Elite Organization. The Communist party was an elite organization. Out of a population of about 280 million in the 1980s, only about 18.5 million were allowed to belong to the party. This represented about 10 percent of the nation's adults. Real power, however, was in the hands of a much smaller number, much less than a million. After Stalin, the party drew its recruits from the privileged parts of Soviet society. The higher an individual's education or political standing, the more likely it was that he or she would be a party member. Giving preferential treatment in this manner angered many and led to the increasing unpopularity of the party.

Ethnic rivalries created another source of discontent with the CPSU. The party was dominated by Russians, Ukrainians, and Belorussians.Other minority groups were underrepresented, especially at higher levels of the party. The party also was dominated by men.

Duties, Privileges, and Party Discipline. By the 1980s, about 150,000 of the 18.5 million members of the CPSU worked full time running the party apparatus. But the party demanded obedience and devotion from all of its members, whether or not they were full-time party workers. Members had to give considerable amounts of time to party business and be prepared to move to distant regions if the party asked.

The party began its recruitment and political indoctrination of children at a young age through a network of youth organizations. Children between 7 and 9 enrolled in **Young Octobrist** groups. They then moved on to the **Pioneers** until age 14 or 15. The next step was the **Komsomol**

As members of the Pioneers, a Soviet-sponsored youth group, these girls were subject to political indoctrination.

(KUM-sah-mol), which by the 1980s enrolled over 30 million young people between the ages of 14 and 28. Komsomol members served the country in tasks ranging from local community projects to volunteering for heavy construction work in Siberia. The Komsomol also sponsored a full range of social and cultural activities for its members.

THE SOVIET ECONOMY

A country's **economic system**, or **economy**, is the way in which goods and services are manufactured and distributed. Although the Soviet Union's economy was one of the largest in the world, it did not succeed in fulfilling the needs of its people. It was a planned economy—very different from the free enterprise economies of the United States and other Western countries. The Soviet economy, like the government, was riddled with inequalities and inefficiencies. Perhaps more than the failure of the government to serve its people, the failure of the economy to provide a decent standard of living for most of its citizens led to the country's breakdown. This section will discuss how the Soviet economy worked and, equally important, why it failed to work.

In order to understand better how the Soviet economy functioned, it is helpful to review how other types of economies work. The United

174

States and other Western countries base their economies on the free enterprise system.

Free Enterprise and Planned Economies. In free enterprise systems, most economic decisions are made by people who base their actions on the marketplace. Individuals or companies first examine the **demand,** or quantity of a product or service customers may want. They will produce a good or service if they believe that demand is sufficient to make a profit, money earned over and above the costs of producing a good or service. This creates a supply of that product to meet the demand. The process involves tasks such as getting labor and raw materials and deciding what to charge for a product. In general, efficient producers make a profit and prosper, while those who are inefficient and unable to compete lose money and go out of business. While a great deal of planning is vital to produce anything in a **market economy,** that planning is done by millions of independent producers and enterprises scattered throughout society. Meanwhile, millions of consumers create the total demand for a society's goods and services.

This free enterprise system in the modern industrial world is called **capitalism.** Under capitalism, individuals or companies own the means of production such as factories, farms, and mines. Capitalism is based on the profit motive and freedom for individuals to make decisions. By contrast, the Soviet Union had what was called a **planned economy.** In a planned economy, government agencies decide what to produce, how much to produce, and what price to charge. Such planning is possible because the state owns and controls all the means of production. Individuals are not permitted to operate their own factories or farms. State enterprises that produce inferior goods do not go out of business, because they do not have to make a profit. There is no incentive to produce high-quality goods. Huge planning agencies employ thousands of people who make decisions according to an overall plan for the whole country.

How the Soviet Economy Worked. After 1929, the planned economy in the Soviet Union operated according to a series of Five Year Plans. (See Chapter 4.) The system was built around the State Planning Commission, or **Gosplan.** It worked up a Five Year Plan based on the economic goals set by the Politburo. An interlocking net of other state agencies such as the State Bank and State Committee for Material and Technical Supply helped Gosplan regulate the enormous Soviet economy. Instructions and orders based on these plans were passed out through a complex net of All-Union Ministries and various lower level agencies in each of the union republics.

Gosplan had to make many kinds of decisions. What crops should be grown and products manufactured and in what quantity? What factories should be built or expanded? What crops should be produced and in what part of the country? How many schools, hospitals, housing projects, railroads, and roads should be constructed, and where? What price should be charged for each product? How should wages be set, and how long should employees work? In short, Soviet planning was an enormously complex undertaking, one that eventually turned out to be too complex to manage efficiently.

Limited Success Under the Soviet Planned Economy.   The Soviet Union's planned economy had certain successes. As a result of the industrialization drive of the 1930s and Stalin's rebuilding programs after World War II, the Soviet Union became the world's second largest industrial power, trailing only the United States. The cost of this achievement, however, was inhumanly high. Millions of people died and tens of millions more lived in dire poverty and terror. Still, the Soviet Union's new industrial base enabled it to compete militarily with its noncommunist rivals. During World War II, the main rival was Germany. After the war, it became the United States.

After Stalin's death, the Soviet economy was able to produce a dramatic rise in the country's standard of living. From the 1970s to the 1980s, Soviet citizens doubled their food consumption, quadrupled their clothing consumption, and multiplied by 14 their consumption of durable goods (such as refrigerators, washing machines, and cars). In addition, housing conditions improved. However, the Soviet rate of economic growth fell with each passing decade. Nor was the Soviet Union able to match the standard of living in the West, where conditions also were improving.

Problems and Failures of the Soviet Planned Economy.   The planned Soviet economy was unable to match the West's standard of living for several reasons. One problem was that central planning was an extremely inefficient way to run a modern industrial economy. Such an economy, with its millions of products and advanced technology, was too complex to plan, manage, and coordinate from one central place. Factories or large construction projects often ground to a halt because they lacked vital materials. This wasted both resources and labor on a huge scale. Central planners might order a collective farm to plant a certain crop in

176

a region where the weather or soil was unsuited for that crop. The result was crop failure and hardship.

Factory managers, who were rewarded for fulfilling production quotas, tried to hide the capacity of their factories from the planners. This would get their factories a low production quota that the manager could meet. However, it wasted valuable resources invested in those enterprises. Nor did factory managers have any incentive to invest in new technologies. Introducing new technology might temporarily slow production and prevent a factory manager from meeting the production quota.

It was not just the quantity of goods that suffered. The quality of goods declined as well. Because the state guaranteed each factory its customers, there was no need to ensure high quality. As a result, many Soviet products, especially those sold to ordinary citizens, were notorious for their poor quality. For example, clothing generally was ill-fitting and unfashionable. Appliances were outdated, lagging years and sometimes decades behind what average people enjoyed in the West.

Perhaps the greatest failure in the Soviet economy was in agriculture. Prior to the Bolshevik Revolution, Russia was a major exporter of grain. By the 1960s, it was importing grain. Soon, it became the world's largest importer of grain. The problem was that the Soviet socialist farm system was extremely inefficient. Unlike the West, where farmers work for themselves, Soviet farmers worked for the state. The pay they received for working on collective or state farm fields was very low, and

The Soviet farmer in this cartoon is asking a bureaucrat, "What am I to do if all I get are instructions instead of fertilizers and machinery?" What weakness of Soviet agriculture does the cartoon address?

Because of the inefficiency of the Soviet agricultural system, the Soviet people relied on private markets like this one for a substantial portion of their supplies of fresh fruits and vegetables.

they responded by being inefficient and lazy workers. Furthermore, because the Soviet planners failed to provide adequate storage areas and improve rural roads for transportation, a large percentage of the annual Soviet harvest rotted in the fields. The only place Soviet farmers worked efficiently and diligently was on their small private plots. These plots, which accounted for about 3 percent of Soviet farmland, eventually produced about 25 percent of the country's farm output.

The Burden of Military Spending.   Another serious burden on the Soviet economy was military spending. During the Cold War years, the Soviets poured their resources into the military. As much as a quarter of the Soviet economy was devoted to the military. In the United States, military spending generally used about 6 or 7 percent of the economy. The Soviet military also claimed the talents of most of the country's best scientists and engineers. Massive spending allowed the Soviet Union to produce first-class weapons, such as fighter planes and rifles, and keep up with the United States in the nuclear arms race. However, the civilian economy suffered in the process.

The Soviet Economy in Crisis.   Squeezed by the failure to reform and the burden of military spending, the Soviet economy stagnated by the end of the 1970s. The standard of living in the Soviet Union stopped rising, while in the West it continued to improve. For example, in 1981, 20 percent of all urban families in the Soviet Union shared kitchens and bathrooms with other families. Health care, one of the areas in which the Soviets once had taken great pride, was deteriorating.

As Soviet citizens found the legal socialist economy unable to meet their needs, they increasingly turned to the illegal black market economy. The **black market**—or "second economy"—provided ordinary Soviet citizens with a vast range of goods and services. Illegal factories operating with stolen materials produced fashionable and high-quality clothing. Spare parts for machinery and automobiles, usually stolen from state stores and warehouses, were available in the second economy for the right price. Plumbers, electricians, engineers, and many others sold their services illegally to consumers who had no other means of getting their homes or cars repaired. By the 1970s, as much as 25 percent of all economic activity in the Soviet Union was illegal. This weakened the official economy and bred corruption and contempt for the authorities, who seemed increasingly unable to solve the country's economic problems.

By the early 1980s, the Soviet economy was nearing a crisis, and by the mid-1980s that crisis had arrived. Mikhail Gorbachev's inability to solve that crisis, despite his dramatic reform efforts, was one of the most important reasons the Soviet Union collapsed in 1991.

THE COMMONWEALTH OF INDEPENDENT STATES: POLITICAL STRUCTURE

On December 8, 1991, Boris Yeltsin of Russia, along with the leaders of Ukraine and Belarus, announced the end of the Soviet Union and the birth of the Commonwealth of Independent States (CIS). (See Chapter 6.) Nearly two weeks later, leaders from 11 of the 15 former Soviet republics met and formally became members of the new Commonwealth. The members of the Commonwealth were Russia, Ukraine, Belarus, Moldova, Armenia, Azerbaijan, Kazakhstan, Turkmenistan, Uzbekistan, Tajikistan, and Kyrgyzstan. Only Latvia, Lithuania, and Estonia, which had broken away from the Soviet Union in September, and Georgia, which was racked by bitter political violence, remained outside the Commonwealth. Together, the 11 republics accounted for more than 95 percent of the territory and population of the former Soviet Union.

Although the Commonwealth contained most of the physical assets of the former Soviet Union, the similarity stopped there. The Soviet Union, despite its official federal structure, was a highly centralized state dominated by the Communist party. The CIS was a loose association of independent states that had agreed to work together on certain issues, such as mutual defense. The Soviet Union was dominated by the communist Russian ruling class. The founding declaration of the CIS recognized all 11 members, each representing a different national group, as equal co-founders. It also recognized the independence of each member and guaranteed all the current borders. The main concession to Russian power was an agreement that Russia would take the former Soviet Union's seat in the United Nations Security Council.

An Uncertain Future. The joint declaration that established the CIS made it clear how far the new association had come from the old Russian Empire and the former Soviet Union. It declared the members intended to build "democratic states based on the rule of law." Relations between the member states would be based on recognition of "the inalienable right to self-determination, principles of equality . . . respect for human rights and freedoms . . . and other general principles and standards of international law." (See pages 162–163.)

However, the founding declaration was vague on almost everything else. For example, it said little that was specific about how the members would deal with the huge former Soviet military machine, which was supposed to provide for their common defense. Few observers dared to predict how long or even whether the CIS would survive. In short, the formation of the Commonwealth of Independent States posed at least as many questions as it answered. It was clear that what mattered was how each individual nation would organize itself.

The most important of these republics was Russia. With a territory of over 6 million square miles (17 million square kilometers), it dwarfed all the other republics put together. With about 150 million people, it had a larger population than the other CIS states combined. It had three times the population of Ukraine, the second most populous state.

The Government of Russia. The new Russian Republic began its existence with many problems to solve and little experience with democracy. Its president, Boris Yeltsin, had been chosen in a free election in mid 1991, when Russia still belonged to the Soviet Union. Its parliament, called the Congress of People's Deputies, had also been selected in a relatively free election in March 1990. A major problem was that the division of power between the president and the parliament was unclear. Many Russians believed in a powerful president who could rule with a "strong hand." This belief reflected continued faith in Russia's tradition of powerful one-person rule. It also reflected the fear that "too much democracy" in a divided parliament would lead to confusion and disorder. Other Russians wanted a strong parliament to limit the excessive growth of presidential power.

A second problem facing the new Russian government was the relationship between the central authorities in Moscow and the various

At the signing of the 1992 treaty between Russia and 18 of the nation's regional subdivisions, President Boris Yeltsin stressed the importance of Russian unity to the assembled delegates.

minority ethnic groups that lived in Russia. Although the overwhelming majority of the population of the new republic was Russian, the giant new state contained about 40 sizable **nationalities** and dozens of smaller ethnic groups. It was divided into 20 subdivisions. These corresponded to the autonomous republics and regions that dated from the Soviet era. However, during the Soviet era these subdivisions had little real power and took their orders from the Communist authorities in Moscow. Now these subdivisions were demanding some real local self-government. While President Boris Yeltsin was determined to keep Russia united, he had to face the growing demands of its minority ethnic groups.

This situation led to the treaty that was signed in the Kremlin in Moscow in March 1992. The signers included representatives from 18 of the 20 major regional subdivisions in Russia. Two autonomous republics did not sign, however. One, Checheno-Ingush (che-CHEN-oh-in-GOOSH), a troubled region near Georgia in the Caucasus, had already declared its independence in November 1991, a declaration the Russian government refused to recognize. The second nonsigning autonomous republic was Tatarstan, a small territory just east of the Volga River.

The treaty the 18 regions signed in March 1992 was a series of compromises. It made some concessions to national minorities, while keeping critical central powers concentrated in Moscow. Local regions were allowed considerable authority to make economic and social policies. The regions also gained control over their natural resources. At the same time, the central government kept control over defense, foreign policy and trade, the national budget, and the national money supply.

Other areas of responsibility—such as education and taxation—were shared. In short, the federation treaty attempted to keep Russia united, but not without recognition that its minority nationalities would have a significantly greater role in running their affairs than in the past.

Economic Problems of the Russian Republic.   One of the main reasons Boris Yeltsin led the effort to end the Soviet Union in December 1991 was to break the logjam preventing radical economic reform. While the Soviet Union continued to exist, President Mikhail Gorbachev had been unwilling to make a decisive break with the old planned socialist economy in favor of a market economy. While the old planned economy was slowly crumbling, a new free market economy was struggling to emerge. The results of this struggle were disastrous. During 1991, prices rose by 700 percent, while income lagged far behind. The grain harvest fell by a quarter, while oil and coal output dropped by 12 percent. Most industrial output fell between 5 and 10 percent, and production of most food products dropped 10 to 15 percent. By the end of the year, experts estimated that between 70 and 80 percent of the Russian population was living below the poverty line.

This cartoon appeared in a U.S. newspaper after the establishment of the Russian Federation. To sharpen your appreciation of the cartoon, answer the questions on page 187.

CASE STUDY:

Half-baked Reforms

In the early part of 1992, reporters from *U.S. News & World Report* interviewed Avedis Seferyan, who had recently decided to open a bakery. The article that resulted from the interview shows the difficulties of trying to make a profit in Russia's changing economy.

> The handmade sign on the front door of the new Yauza bread store in Northwest Moscow is nothing short of revolutionary. "Hot Bread," it announces in orange Cyrillic letters. In a country where customers are usually given the cold shoulder, Avedis Seferyan, the director of the Yauza bread factory, is trying to attract business by promising a nearly forgotten creature comfort.
>
> Seferyan spends much of his day on the phone fighting a system that still prefers [a planned economy] to competition. "Our working day starts with the telephone," he says. "We make noise. . . . [If] we don't call, send faxes, write cables, send letters, we get nothing."
>
> In Moscow, the bread king is MosKhleb (Moscow Bread Amalgamated), the state-run association. Seferyan cannot deal with MosKhleb's four mills directly or bargain with them for better prices or services. Instead, he leans on the flour czar at MosKhleb-Snab (Moscow Bread Supplies) to call up the mill director to press for another load of flour or dry milk or sugar. . . .
>
> Although Seferyan can squeeze enough flour out of MosKhleb's mills, he has set up a commodity exchange in Krasnodar in southern Russia, where he can purchase emergency supplies—at twice the state price. . . .
>
> Bypassing the official delivery system has let [Seferyan] cut the price of a loaf from 1.25 rubles to 1.10. By opening his own shops, he can turn over his inventory more quickly, test-market new products, stay open late and accumulate capital for expansion and salaries. . . . Next, he plans to expand to five shops and to begin selling hot bread right off the vans at the subway stops.

U.S. News & World Report, February 3, 1992.

1. Why is it difficult for Avedis Seferyan to obtain supplies?

2. What problems do you think Seferyan might encounter when he expands and sells bread at the subway stops?

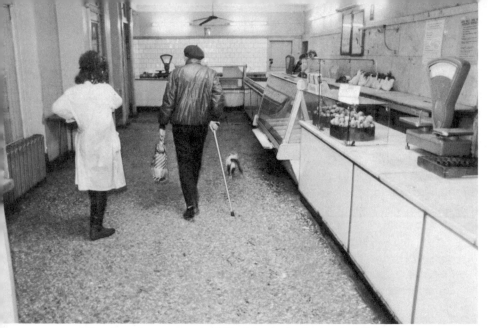

The first winter after the fall of the Soviet Union in 1991
brought severe food shortages in Moscow and other cities.
Food shops like this one had little to sell.

Yeltsin waited less than a month after the collapse of the Soviet Union to bring radical economic reform to Russia. On January 2, 1992, he took the dramatic step of ending price controls, a step economists said was essential to establishing a market economy. Instead of being set by the government, prices would rise and fall according to the laws of supply and demand. The only exceptions were certain foods, such as milk and bread, and essential items such as medicine and heating fuel. As expected, prices shot up, causing great hardship across Russia. In one day, the price of chicken in Moscow jumped from 22 rubles a kilo to 36 rubles, making chicken an unaffordable luxury to the average Russian. That same day, sugar tripled in price. A 67-year-old Moscow shopper summed up the problem that millions suddenly faced:

> The same bread I bought yesterday for 56 kopecks [there are 100 kopeks to a ruble] is now 1.65 rubles. White bread is very expensive. It costs 2.10 rubles. We have to buy less. If we bought one loaf, now we'll buy half. We'll live more modestly and humbly.

The other key part of Yeltsin's program was **privatization**, or turning over state enterprises to private ownership. This obviously would lead to many business failures and unemployment. It remained to be seen how long and difficult the transition from a planned socialist economy to a free enterprise market economy would be.

REVIEWING THE CHAPTER

I. Building Your Vocabulary

In your notebook, write the numbers 1 to 6. After each number, write the word that matches the definition.

CPSU   democratic centralism   capitalism
KGB   Politburo   economy

1. Communist party's major policy-making body

2. free enterprise system

3. Communist Party of the Soviet Union

4. way in which a nation manufactures and distributes its goods and services

5. Committee for State Security—the Soviet Union's secret police

6. practice stating that the minority must accept the will of the majority

II. Understanding the Facts

In your notebook, write the numbers 1 to 5. Write the letter of the correct answer next to its number.

1. Young Soviets between the ages of 14 and 28 could serve their country through the
   a. autonomous areas.   b. Pioneers.   c. Komsomol.

2. In the Soviet Union, which of the following elected the general secretary?
   a. Politburo   b. Central Committee   c. Secretariat

3. The greatest failure in the Soviet economy was in
   a. agriculture.   b. industry.   c. housing.

4. Because the Soviet economy was unable to meet its citizens' needs, people bought goods and services on the
   a. black market.   b. autonomous regions.   c. CPSU.

5. Which of the following Soviet Republics did not join the CIS?
   a. Ukraine   b. Uzbekistan   c. Georgia

III. Thinking It Through

In your notebook, write the numbers 1 to 5. Write the letter of the correct answer next to its number.

1. The idea that the minority on any issue must accept the will of the majority is
   a. democratic centralism.
   b. *the Communist Manifesto.*
   c. Gosplan.
   d. Marxism.

2. Which of the following leaders of the Soviet Union did *not* serve as general secretary?
   a. Lenin   c. Andropov
   b. Khrushchev   d. Gorbachev

3. Which of the following was not a cause of discontent among average Soviet citizens with the Communist party?
   a. The majority of members came from the privileged class.
   b. Russian and Slavic ethnic groups were over represented.
   c. Most children were illiterate.
   d. Few women were allowed to hold positions of power.

4. The CIS can best be described as
   a. a highly centralized state.
   b. the last domain of communism.
   c. a loose association of independent states.
   d. another term for the Soviet Union.

5. A problem that most nations in the CIS face is
   a. too much presidential power.
   b. an oversupply of wheat but not enough bakeries.
   c. ethnic unrest.
   d. illiteracy.

DEVELOPING CRITICAL THINKING SKILLS

1. Why was it said that the Communist party of the Soviet Union had total control of the state?

2. Explain the difference between a market economy and a planned economy.

3. In what ways were Stalin's economic programs successful? In what ways were they unsuccessful?

4. Explain the following parts of Boris Yeltsin's economic program: a. ending of price controls and b. privatization.

5. Evaluate life for the average citizen in the Soviet Union and in the CIS. Under which system will a private individual have more personal freedom?

USING VISUAL EVIDENCE

Study the cartoon on page 182. Then answer the questions.

1. What is the subject of the cartoon?

2. What is the cartoonist saying about the situation in the Commonwealth of Independent States?

3. What title would you give this cartoon?

ENRICHMENT AND EXPLORATION

1. Write a speech that explains to the people of the Commonwealth what they must do to create a free enterprise system. Give them a step-by-step program for establishing a market economy.

2. In a small group, analyze the social, economic, and political problems facing Russia and the newly independent republics. Decide which are the most serious. Then create solutions. Present your analyses and solutions to the class.

8 Russian Society and Culture

The Russian people are the most numerous of three Eastern Slav ethnic groups. The East Slavs first settled in eastern Europe about 14 centuries ago. (See Chapter 2.) Today, more than 145 million Russians live in the lands that once made up the Soviet Union. They account for about 82 percent of the population of Russia itself. However, Russians also make up a significant part of the populations of other independent republics. Approximately 22 percent of Ukraine's people, 13 percent of Belarus's, and 13 percent of Moldova's are Russian. In Kazakhstan, there are nearly as many Russians as Kazakhs. Russians make up 21 percent of the population of Kyrgyzstan, 10 percent of the population of Turkmenistan, and over 5 percent of the population of Tajikistan and Azerbaijan. (See map on pages 224–225.) Outside the CIS, Russians account for over 30 percent of Latvia's and Estonia's populations and about 8 percent of Lithuania's.

While we speak of "the Russians" as one people, they are really a mixture of many peoples whose paths crossed over centuries of migration and conquest. Over many generations, the East Slavs living in the forests of northeastern Europe gradually absorbed large numbers of Finnish peoples. Smaller numbers of Turkic and Baltic peoples also were absorbed into the Russians.

Two important factors that contributed to the process of assimilation were religious conversion and expansion of the Russian state. After the Russians converted to Orthodox Christianity in the 900s, they began to convert other peoples. Russian territorial expansion began with the rise of Muscovy after the Mongol conquest and continued during the days of the Russian Empire. (See Chapter 2.) Meanwhile, as Russian settlers moved into regions beyond their nation's borders, they intermarried with local peoples and gradually Russified many of them.

RUSSIAN TRADITIONS AND THE MODERN WORLD

Two institutions that played a critical role in shaping Russian life were the church and the **mir.** The Russian Orthodox Church had a great influence on Russian culture and society. Even with the suppression of religion during the Soviet regime, a large number of people continued to practice their faith. The *mir* was a village organization that structured peasant life. Some of the traditions of the mir continue to influence Russian society today.

The Russian Orthodox Church.   For centuries, one of the central features of Russian national identity was the Russian Orthodox religion. The Russians were converted to Orthodoxy in A.D. 988 by missionaries from Byzantium. Thereafter, the church played a major role in their lives. Russian peasants, the overwhelming majority of the population until the 1900s, arranged their lives according to church holidays. Religious holidays marked important points in the year, such as the beginning of the planting season and the start of the harvest. Every Russian peasant cottage had what was called an icon corner, where small pictures of saints or religious scenes provided a little decoration in an otherwise dreary home. Important events such as birth, marriage, and death also brought Russian peasants to their church.

The Cathedral of the Epiphany in Moscow, with its golden onion-shaped dome, is the seat of the patriarch of the Russian Orthodox Church.

While some Russians followed other religions, most were Orthodox believers until the Soviet era. Then for three generations, Soviet antireligious propaganda and discrimination discouraged all religious practice. Though some religions, especially Judaism, were attacked more harshly than others, all religious groups suffered, including the Russian Orthodox Church. At times, especially under Stalin, those who practiced religion risked severe punishment. Stalin and, later, Nikita Khrushchev closed or destroyed thousands of Orthodox churches as well as the houses of worship of other religions. Despite this discrimination, by the last decade of the Soviet regime, there still were about 50 million Orthodox believers in the Soviet Union. One of them was Maria Pantelevna Gorbacheva, Mikhail Gorbachev's mother.

During the Gorbachev era, when many restrictions on its activities were removed, the church opened over 6,000 houses of worship across Russia. Monasteries reopened after decades of having been used as factories or for other nonreligious purposes. In April 1992, bells rang in the towers of the Kremlin to announce the coming of Easter, renewing a 400-year-old tradition broken by the Bolsheviks in 1918.

Other religious groups in Russia also experienced a renewal after communism's collapse. For example, many Russians responded enthusiastically to visits from Protestant evangelical missionaries from abroad. While Russian Christians celebrated Easter, increasing numbers of Jews were marking Passover.

Peasant Traditions and the *Mir*.   The peasant way of life was another traditional feature of Russia's national identity. Russia remained a largely peasant society until Stalin's industrialization campaign of the 1930s. The most important organization in a Russian village was called the *mir*, or commune. Its modern form can be traced to the 1500s and 1600s, when autocracy and serfdom developed in Russia.

The *mir* served two main purposes. Under the czars, the state used it to control the peasants—to tax them and to recruit soldiers. The Russian peasants used the *mir* to protect themselves against a harsh outside world, by banding together to share burdens and risks. Heads of member households made decisions at the meetings of the *mir*. The *mir* controlled the land the peasants farmed. It distributed land among member families, according to the number of workers in each family. The *mir* set the times for planting, harvesting, and other important tasks. It paid the taxes for all its members and decided who might work outside the village. The *mir* also looked after maintenance of village roads and other public facilities.

Both the czarist government and the Russian peasant subjects valued the *mir*. The czarist government kept the *mir* when it abolished serfdom in 1861. After czarism fell in 1917, the Russian peasants clung to their *mirs* until Stalin destroyed them in the collectivization campaign after 1929. (See Chapter 4.)

Today Russia is an urban society, far removed in most ways from its peasant traditions. But certain attitudes that evolved over centuries in the *mir* can still be found in many Russian city dwellers today. Specifically, the *mir* placed the community above the individual. As a result, Russian peasants generally mistrusted anyone who acted as an individual—anyone who did things differently or wanted to get ahead. The peasants brought these attitudes with them when they migrated to the cities. The Communist government encouraged these attitudes because Soviet society stressed socialist cooperative ideals over capitalist individualistic ones. As a result, millions of Russians still tend to mistrust individual initiative. They suspect that anyone who has achieved success by starting a business has been corrupt. These suspicions and fears may explain some of the resistance to Mikhail Gorbachev's economic reforms. They reflect an attitude formed not only by 70 years of communism, but by centuries of peasant life. As such, this attitude is one of many obstacles to the economic reforms that many Russian leaders see as vital to a better future.

RUSSIAN CULTURAL, ARTISTIC, AND SCIENTIFIC ACHIEVEMENTS

Throughout their history, the Russian people have demonstrated great creativity in many fields, from literature, art, and music to architecture and science. Russian works of literature and music, particularly, enjoy worldwide popularity, and their creators are world famous.

Early Russian Literature. Early Russian literature developed from two sources. The oral tradition grew for centuries before being written down. The written literature developed after Russia's conversion to Christianity. Russia's oral folklore gave the country its earliest literary heritage. It included poems, songs, and tales. The most important creations in Russia's oral literary tradition were the epic songs or poems called *byliny* (bee-LEE-nee). Recited for generations by traveling **bards**, or poets, before being written down, these epics recorded the adventures of Russian heroes who battled enemies on the vast and dangerous steppe. These heroes, like Ilya of Murom, a huge, straightforward peasant, and Churlino Plenkovich led adventurous lives, in which they were always saving people or wooing beautiful maidens. Russia's *byliny* have been compared to the epic poems of Greek literature, which also evolved as part of an oral tradition.

Russia's first written literature developed as a result of the country's conversion to Christianity and therefore followed religious themes. It included sermons, hymns, instructional works, and tales that depicted the lives of the saints. Ironically, the best-known work by a Russian church official deals largely with secular themes. Known as *The Primary Russian Chronicle*, it is a blend of songs, biographies, and historical and legendary events. *The Primary Chronicle*, while far from being entirely reliable, is the best available source on Russian history between the mid-800s and early 1100s.

Another work, *The Tale of the Host of Igor*, dates from the early 1200s and is the most famous of Russia's early literary creations. This tale tells about a disastrous Russian campaign led by Prince Igor in 1185 against steppe nomads. A beautiful and moving epic poem, *The Tale of the Host of Igor* is a patriotic plea for Russian unity in the face of a growing foreign threat. The story of Prince Igor is a masterpiece that is cherished by the Russians to this day.

Russia's tiny educated class produced a variety of works during the two centuries of Mongol control. These works drew on the old Kievan heritage. With the rise of Moscow, new styles of writing developed. Church officials discussed and debated religious issues, while secular writers often focused on the growth of the new Russian autocracy. The 1600s and 1700s marked a transition period, during which the modern Russian literary tradition gradually emerged. When it finally flowered in the 1800s, it had transformed Russian literature into one of the richest in the world.

Modern Russian Literature.   Literacy and the reading public expanded rapidly during the 1800s. Some of the world's greatest poets, novelists, and playwrights wrote for that growing audience. Among them are Russia's greatest poet Alexander Pushkin (POOSH-kihn; 1799–1837), whose *Bronze Horseman, Eugene Onegin*, and *Boris Godunov* are classics of world literature. The appearance of Pushkin's works began what is called the golden age of Russian literature. Another outstanding poet of that era was Mikhail Lermontov (LAYR-mun-tawf; 1814–1841). Lermontov probably is best known for his short novel *A Hero of Our Time*, which was one of the first of Russia's great tradition of realistic

Alexander Pushkin is considered to be Russia's greatest writer. His poems, stories, and dramas are a cornerstone of the Russian literary heritage and are beloved by Russians of all ages.

novels. However, Lermontov's greatest poem, A *Demon*, was not published in Russia during his lifetime because of government censorship, a situation not uncommon for Russian writers.

Another outstanding writer of this era, Nikolai Gogol (GOH-guhl; 1809-1852), criticized Russia's social and moral shortcomings in the novel *Dead Souls* and the play *The Inspector General*. He also provided an unforgettable picture of bitter struggle between Ukrainians and Poles for control of the steppe in his epic work *Taras Bulba*.

Gogol was succeeded by two giants of Russian literature, Fyodor Dostoyevsky (dohs-tuh-YEHV-skee; 1821–1881) and Leo Tolstoy (tohl-STOI; 1828–1910). Both men wrote several novels that rank among the greatest in the world. Dostoyevsky's brilliant *Crime and Punishment* gave literature one of its classic tormented criminals in a young student named Raskolnikov. *The Brothers Karamazov* is a monumental exploration of themes such as sin and redemption, power and principle, and faith and immorality. Tolstoy's *War and Peace* is an epic about Russia's struggle against Napoleon in 1812. It ranks among literature's most acclaimed novels.

Two other outstanding Russian writers of the 1800s were Anton Chekhov (1860–1904), Russia's most distinguished playwright and master of the short story, and Maxim Gorky (GAWR-kee; 1868–1936). Among Chekhov's best-known plays are *The Seagull, The Cherry Orchard,* and *Uncle Vanya.* Novelist and playwright Gorky bridged the czarist and Soviet regimes. Gorky wrote about the poor and downcast in prerevolutionary Russia in his moving novel *Mother* and his play *The Lower Depths.* Gorky was a friend of Lenin and an active supporter of the Bolshevik cause.

CASE STUDY:

The Tale of the Host of Igor

Written in the late 1200s, *The Tale of the Host of Igor* tells of Prince Igor's battle to defend his lands against invaders from the Asian steppe. Not long after Prince Igor's battle, Russia was overrun by the Mongols. The following excerpt describes Igor's defeat.

They fought one day,
They fought another,
And on the third day around noon
Igor's banners [flags] fell!
Here the brothers parted on the banks of the swift Kaiala
Here too the bloody wine ran out
And here the brave Russians finished the feast.
(They got their guests drunk)
And themselves fell in defense of the Russian land!
The grass wilts because of the sorrow
And the tree bends down because of grief!
Brothers, a sad time has descended!
A wilderness has covered our strength.
Forces of Dazhbog's [the Kievan sun god's] grandsons have been
    wounded!
Misfortune has descended on the land of Troian like a maiden
Who flapped her swan wings
Over the blue sea and by the Don.
Gone are the days of abundance,
Over are princely wars against the infidel [non-Christian]!
Now brother said to brother:
This is mine and that is mine also!
And the Princes began to argue about trifles [small things]
As if they were great things.
And they began to create discord [arguments] among themselves!
And from all sides the pagans invaded the Russian land victoriously.
Oh, falcon, you have gone too far to the sea in slaying birds!
Igor's brave troops cannot be resurrected [restored]!
The mourners began to weep
And sorrow spread throughout the Russian land
Spreading among the Russian people embers in a glowing horn!
Russian women wept, saying:
"We shall never be able to visualize our dear husbands
Nor to think of them nor even to see them!

194

Much gold and silver has been lost!"
Brothers, Kiev groaned from sorrow,
Chernigov from disaster,
Anguish engulfed the Russian land.
Deep sorrow spread over Russian lands.
Princes brought the discord upon themselves
While pagans [nonbelievers] made victorious inroads into the Russian
 land
Collecting from each household a tribute [payment] of one squirrel's
 skin.

The Tale of the Host of Igor. In *Medieval Russia: A Source Book, 900–1700,* edited by Basil Dmytryshyn (Hinsdale, Illinois: Dryden Press, 1973.)

1. What kind of payment did the invaders demand of the Russians?

2. Why do you think the princes began to fight over trifles after the nomads defeated them?

3. How might the princes' arguments with each other have helped the invaders?

The story of Prince Igor was the basis of an opera written by Alexander Borodin. This is a scene from a production by the famed Bolshoi Opera of Moscow.

Anna Akhmatova (ahk-MAH-tuh-vuh; 1889–1966), is considered one of 20th-century Russia's most important poets. Her later work, which was written during the Soviet era, took on a special depth of meaning. It told about her suffering and the suffering of the Russian people under Stalin and during World War II. Her most famous poem, which dealt with this theme, is called "Requiem." Ossip Mandelstam (MAHN-duhl-shtahm; 1891–1938) was perhaps Russia's greatest 20th-century poet. He also wrote about the suffering of the Russian people in fresh and forceful language. Like millions of his fellow Russians, Mandelstam was arrested under Stalin and died in a forced labor camp. Vladimir Mayakovsky (mah-yuh-KAWF-skee; 1893–1930) was an important poet who supported communism. He wrote propaganda as well as excellent lyrical poetry and plays that made fun of official abuses during the early years of the Soviet regime. Although an officially approved poet of the revolution, Mayakovsky became disillusioned and committed suicide. Another important postrevolutionary writer was Isaac Babel (BAH-buhl; 1894–1941). He wrote short stories and novels that told about the suffering of the Russian people during the civil war. Although he was praised by Soviet critics, Babel fell out of favor and eventually was arrested and died in a prison camp.

Russian Literature in the Soviet Era.   As the fates of Mandelstam and Babel testify, Russian literature suffered enormously during the Soviet regime. Writers who did not conform to the political demands of the Soviet state could not get their work published. Under Stalin, many writers went to prison and lost their lives. One of the few genuinely outstanding novels to be published during the Stalin era was Mikhail Sholokhov's (SHAWL-uh-kawf) *And Quiet Flows the Don*. After Stalin's death, things improved, but writers still were harassed by Soviet authorities. Many were prevented from publishing their best works.

The fate of poet and novelist Boris Pasternak serves to illustrate the Soviet Union's repressive policy. As you read in Chapter 6, Pasternak was denied the right to publish *Doctor Zhivago*, his epic novel about the Bolshevik Revolution, in the Soviet Union. In 1957, Pasternak smuggled his manuscript abroad for publication. The following year, he won the Nobel Prize for Literature, in large part for *Doctor Zhivago*. Pasternak was denounced in the Soviet press and was forbidden to leave the country to accept his award.

During the post-Stalin decades, Soviet policy swung back and forth between periods of greater freedom and harsh crackdowns. One period of relaxation occurred under Khrushchev. In 1961, the young poet Yevgeny Yevtushenko (yef-tuh-SHENG-koh) published "Babi Yar," a bold attack on Soviet anti-Semitism. The next year, Alexander Solzhenitsyn was allowed to publish *One Day in the Life of Ivan Denisovich*, a gripping exposé of Stalin's labor camps. During Brezhnev's regime, the pendulum again swung toward repression. Solzhenitsyn, considered by many to be Russia's outstanding 20th-century novelist, had to publish his masterpieces—*The Cancer Ward, The First Circle*, and *The Gulag Archipelago*—in the West. Eventually, Solzhenitsyn himself was deported for publishing abroad.

Yet Russian literature survived and in some cases even thrived. Solzhenitsyn influenced a new group of younger writers called the "village writers." They focused on the lives and problems of ordinary Russian peasants and advocated a return to traditional prerevolutionary Russian values. Outstanding among them were Valentin Rasputin (rahs-POO-tihn) and Vasily Shukshin (SHOOK-shin). Rasputin is a talented writer of novels and stories. Vasily Shukshin's talents extended from fiction to theater and film during a career cut short by his death at 45.

After Mikhail Gorbachev came to power and the era of *glasnost* began, the old Soviet restrictions on literature crumbled. Thousands of once-forbidden works were published. For the first time in over 70 years, Russian writers were free to create as they saw fit.

Music. Russia's early music was folk and church music. From the 1800s through the early part of the 1900s, Russian music was graced by many distinguished names. Mikhail Glinka (GLING-kuh; 1803–1857), who often based his works on traditional Russian melodies, has been called the "father" of Russian music. The giant of 19th-century Russian music is Peter Ilich Tchaikovsky (cheye-KAWF-skee; 1840–1893), whose operas, ballets, and symphonies are known, loved, and played the world over. An influential composer of the late 1800s and early 1900s was Alexander Scriabin (SKRYAH-been; 1871–1915), a man who hoped his music could transform evil in the world into beauty. The careers of Sergei Rachmaninoff (rahk-MAHN-uh-nawf; 1873–1943) and Igor Stravinsky (struh-VIHN-skee; 1882–1971) also began in the late 1800s and extended into the 1900s. Both men left Russia for Western Europe and the United States after the collapse of czarism.

The best-known Russian composers of the Soviet era are Sergei Prokofiev (pruh-KAWF-yef; 1891–1953), and Dmitri Shostakovich (shahs-tuh-KOH-vich; 1906–1975). Both of these distinguished composers had to endure interference from the Soviet state. They were criticized because their experiments with musical forms strayed beyond limits set by the Communist party. Despite government interference during the Soviet era, the talent of many Russian composers and musicians won them world recognition. Among them was the distinguished cellist Mstislav Rostropovich (rahs-truh-POH-vich). However, Rostropovich paid the price for not toeing the Communist party line. Because he supported dissidents, Rostropovich was stripped of his Soviet citizenship in 1978 and now lives in the United States.

Ballet.   Russian ballet has a history dating back over 200 years. In the late 1800s, classic ballets such as *Swan Lake* and *The Sleeping Beauty* were created to Tchaikovsky's music. Today, they still are popular. By the early 1900s, Russian ballet was the equal of any in the world. Brilliant dancers and choreographers like Vaslav Nijinsky (nuh-ZHIHN-skee; 1890–1950), Anna Pavlova (PAV-luh-vuh; 1881–1931), and Mikhail Fokine (FAW-keen; 1880–1942) were renowned in Russia and the West. One of the great promoters of Russian ballet was Sergei Diaghilev (dee-AHG-uh-lef; 1872–1929), who introduced several classic Russian ballets to the world. Among them were *Petrouchka*, *The Firebird*, and *The Rite of Spring*, for which Igor Stravinsky wrote the music.

The Soviet regime supported dance to a considerable degree. Dancers were trained at state expense, and outstanding ones had celebrity status. The Soviets supported many ballet companies, including the world-famous Bolshoi and Kirov ballets. However, the state made sure that the ballets did not conflict with official state ideology. Young choreographers and dancers felt stifled by party-imposed restrictions. They wanted to experiment with new styles, new music, and

198

more individualistic interpretations. In frustration, several outstanding Russian dancers defected, or escaped, to the West. Rudolf Nureyev's (nuh-RAY-yef) defection in 1961 shocked his fellow Russians. He was followed to the West by others, including Natalia Makarova (mah-KAH-roh-vuh) and Mikhail Baryshnikov (bah-RIHSH-nih-kawf). During the Gorbachev era in the late 1980s, Nureyev returned to his native land to visit his family. He noted the increased freedom of expression that Gorbachev's reforms had brought about.

Theater and Film.   Russian theater flourished before the Bolshevik Revolution. During the 1800s and early 1900s, many large theaters offered plays by Chekhov, Gogol, and others. The great actor and director Konstantin Stanislavsky (stan-ih-SLAHF-skee; 1863–1938) developed a form of method acting that has greatly influenced acting in many countries. His Moscow Art Theater was one of the most innovative and famous theaters of its day.

The Bolshevik Revolution had a dual effect on Russian theater. Many talented people emigrated, but many of those who stayed produced creative new works during the early 1920s. Vsevolod Meyerhold (MEYE-er-hohld; 1874–1942) ranks among the most creative theatrical directors in the world. He pioneered techniques to bring the actors and the audience closer together. Although Meyerhold was dedicated to the goals of the communist revolution, he too fell victim to Stalin's purges.

Sergei Eisenstein's film Ten Days That Shook the World, *from which this is a scene, was made to celebrate the tenth anniversary of the Communist Revolution of 1917.*

The 1920s also saw extraordinary creativity in Russian film making. Sergei Eisenstein (EYE-zuhn-steyn) directed *Potemkin* and *Ten Days That Shook the World*—two films that brilliantly conveyed the idealism that inspired supporters of the Bolshevik Revolution. Both films have become classics and are still shown today. However, although Eisenstein escaped Meyerhold's fate, he was forced to denounce one of his greatest films, *Ivan the Terrible,* as "worthless and vicious." Eisenstein was brutally criticized in the Soviet press and died a broken man.

After Stalin's death, Russian theater and film artists were able to exercise more creativity and even focus on some controversial issues. Yuri Liubimov (lee-OO-bihm-awf) was probably the most creative Russian director of the post-Stalin era. Liubimov staged a great variety of plays at the Taganka Theater in Moscow. They ranged from Shakespeare's *Hamlet* to a new and controversial interpretation of Chekov's *The Three Sisters.* In 1977, Liubimov dramatized a book called *The Master and Margarita.* Banned for three decades, the book, which was not published in the Soviet Union until 1966, poked fun at Soviet life. Liubimov continued to shock Soviet audiences and officials until he traveled abroad in 1984 and was not permitted to return home.

After Gorbachev introduced *glasnost,* the public began to learn that many Soviet films had been completely censored or shown only to carefully selected audiences. Between 1985 and 1988, over 100 previously banned films were released. New documentary films explored once forbidden subjects like Stalin's labor camps and the Soviet Union's long war in Afghanistan. Any Communist party interference that remained in Russian film-making finally was swept away when the Soviet Union collapsed in 1991.

Painting and Sculpture. The earliest Russian art dates from Kievan times. Russian artists created religious frescoes and mosaics to decorate the country's Orthodox churches. Their techniques were learned from the Byzantines, who had converted Russia to Christianity. Gradually, the Russians developed their own styles, especially with icons. A distinctly Russian style of icon painting developed after the collapse of the Kievan state. Russia's outstanding icon painter was Andrei Rublev (ROO-blef), who lived in the late 1300s and early 1400s. His icon of the Holy Trinity is considered a masterpiece that firmly established a genuine Russian artistic style. Not until the 1600s did Russian art turn to secular subjects, mainly portraits and landscapes. By then, Western European styles were influencing Russian artists—a tendency that increased with the Westernizing reforms of Peter the Great.

This icon, called "Our Lady of Jerusalem," dates from the second half of the 1500s. It is typical of the religious paintings that dominated Russian art at that time. From which culture did the Russians adopt icon painting?

During the 1800s, Russian art was dominated by what was called the realist school. The most famous realist painter was Ilya Repin (RYAY-pyihn). Repin's paintings like those of other realists often were a protest against the social injustices. His painting "The Easter Procession" contrasts the haughtiness of czarist officials, Orthodox priests, and wealthy people with the misery of poor Russians. By the end of the century, Russian painters like Wassily Kandinsky (kan-DIHN-skee) were exploring the techniques of modern art.

After the 1920s, Russian painting, along with the rest of the arts, suffered from Stalin's efforts to repress creativity. During the Stalin era, artists were expected to follow the rules of a style called socialist realism. Socialist realism meant that artists had to produce works that glorified Stalin and socialism. Art became lifeless and lacked individuality. After Stalin's death, Russian artists were freer to experiment, but often were harassed by the state. Modern artists still found it impossible to get support or even to exhibit their work. Many painters chose to join other artists and emigrate to the West. Not until the 1980s and 1990s could Russian painting emerge completely from the shadow of political interference.

This music box in the form of the Kremlin in Moscow was but one of the many exquisite works of the Russian jeweler and goldsmith Peter Carl Fabergé.

Architecture.   Russia has many beautiful old churches with distinctive onion-shaped domes. Originally, Russian churches were built according to Byzantine models. Over time, the domes of the churches took on the characteristic onion shape that is now considered typically Russian. Russian churches and other public buildings built in later years reflected Italian and French influences. Postrevolutionary Russian architecture had far less style than its old churches and public buildings. Under the Soviet regime architects built huge, dreary blocks of buildings that were marked by their massiveness, poor quality, and lack of character.

Science and Technology.   Russia's distinguished scientific tradition dates back well over 200 years. Mikhail Lomonosov (loh-moh-NAW-sawf; 1711–1765) did pioneering work in chemistry and physics. The chemist Dmitry Mendeleyev (men-duh-LAY-uhf; 1834–1907) formulated the periodic table of elements. Physiologist Ivan Pavlov (PAV-lawf; 1849–1936), who studied the effects of behavioral conditioning on dogs, won the 1903 Nobel prize for physiology and medicine. Biologist Élie Metchnikov (mech-nee-KAWF; 1845–1916) won a Nobel prize in 1908 for his work in physiology and medicine.

During the Soviet era, Russia had many outstanding scientists. The Russian physicist Andrei Sakharov, who is known as the father of the Soviet hydrogen bomb, won a Nobel prize in 1975. However, the prize came not for his scientific work, but for his efforts on behalf of world peace.

Russians played a central role in the success the Soviet Union enjoyed in their space program. Soviet achievements in space exploration included the first artificial satellite to orbit the earth (Sputnik I, 1957), the first satellite to carry an animal (1957), the first man in space (1961), and the first woman in space (1963). Soviet scientists were responsible for the first instrument landing on the moon (1966) and pioneered in the exploration of the planets Venus and Mars.

RUSSIAN SOCIETY

The Soviet era had an immense impact on Russian family life. The two greatest influences on Soviet policy were the enormous demand for labor during the industrialization drive and the Marxist belief in equality between men and women. This led the Soviet government to recruit millions of women to do work previously done only by men, especially after the industrialization drive began.

Women. The effects of Stalin's purges and World War II increased the demand for women in the workforce. At least 80 percent of the victims of Stalin's purges were men. During World War II millions of Soviet men fought and died in the Red Army's bloody battles against the Germans. By the end of the Soviet era, the overwhelming majority of Russian women worked outside the home. This work included highly skilled jobs in fields such as engineering and medicine, and also more physically demanding jobs in construction and general labor. A greater percentage of Russian women held nontraditional jobs than did women in any other industrial society. By the 1980s, women made up 52 percent of the workforce in the Russian republic.

These new opportunities for Russian women came at a very high price. Despite Marxist promises about equality, Russian women during the Soviet era rarely rose to the top ranks of their professions. Occupations such as medicine, where women were well represented, lost status and paid less than occupations dominated by men. When women returned home after a hard day's work, their husbands were not very helpful with the housework, shopping, or childcare. In addition,

The world's first woman cosmonaut, Valentina Tereshkova, is greeted by the first human to travel in space, Yuri Gagarin in June 1963. She had just completed a space trip of 45 revolutions around the earth.

Russian women lacked many of the conveniences available in the West, such as private automobiles, dishwashers, or well-stocked supermarkets. In effect, Russian women were forced to work a double shift—the first in the workplace and the second at home.

Young People and the Family. Like young people everywhere, Russian youths express their own tastes and interests. Even during the Soviet era, Russian young people were attracted to Western styles such as blue jeans, rock music, and slang. No force in the Soviet Union could stop this trend. For example, in 1981 a major Soviet newspaper complained about students who wear "T-shirts emblazoned with the stars and stripes, portraits of rock-music idols, dollar bills, and inscriptions in English that the owners don't even attempt to translate before putting on." Another newspaper worried that students in large cities sounded as though they came from "some sort of Michigan, Texas, or California with their endless strings of distorted English words like *liebl* (label), *batton* (button), *voch* (watch), and *beg* (bag)." By the mid-1980s the Soviet regime, which long had opposed rock music as a decadent Western intrusion, was forced to permit thousands of rock bands to exist across the country. In 1985, a rock recording studio was opened in Moscow. With the collapse of the Soviet regime, Western influences are likely to grow among young Russians.

The Russian family, like the family in other modern societies, has undergone change during the 1900s. As in other industrialized societies, the Russian family is smaller than it was before industrialization and urbanization took hold. Cramped living quarters in the cities, women working outside the home, and the desire to have more money for other purposes led Russian couples to have fewer children. The pressures of modern society contributed to an increase in the divorce rate. Still, the Russian family has survived and recent surveys showed that families prefer to spend their free time at home doing activities together.

SPORTS AND RECREATION

During the Soviet era, the government placed great importance on participation in sports. With the collapse of the Soviet Union, no longer will such tremendous resources continue to be devoted to sports.

Sports. Many Russian athletes achieved great success in international competition. Among the favorite sports in Russia are soccer, hockey, gymnastics, and basketball. The Russian people are enthusiastic about sports of all kinds. During the Soviet period, athletes were supported by government organizations that trained, fed, and housed them. A national program that attempted to involve all Soviet citizens created a high level of national fitness. The success of the Soviet sports program resulted in consistent victories in the Olympic games in a wide range of

Russian gymnast Svetlana Boginskaya performs on the parallel bars. Without the financial support of the Soviet government, many Russian athletes worry about the future of sports.

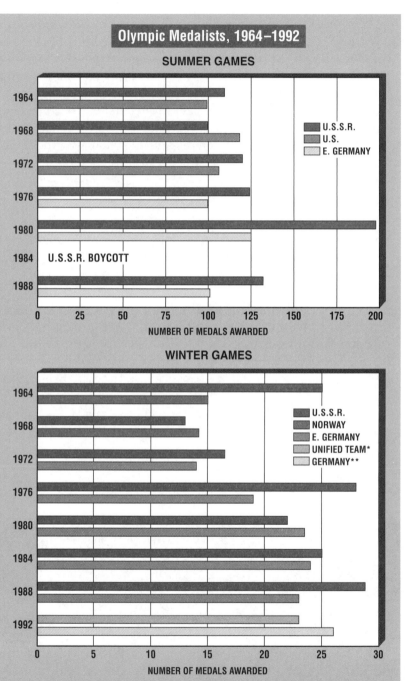

Olympic Medalists, 1964–1992

SUMMER GAMES

NUMBER OF MEDALS AWARDED

1984 U.S.S.R. BOYCOTT

Legend:
- U.S.S.R.
- U.S.
- E. GERMANY

WINTER GAMES

NUMBER OF MEDALS AWARDED

Legend:
- U.S.S.R.
- NORWAY
- E. GERMANY
- UNIFIED TEAM*
- GERMANY**

* The Unified Team represented the former Soviet republics of Russia, Ukraine, Belarus, Kazakhstan, and Uzebekistan.
** The German team represented the newly unified Germany.

sports, including track and field, weight lifting, wrestling, hockey, and even basketball. (See the chart on page 206.)

Pastime and Playtime. Russians engage in many leisure activities. Millions of Russians enjoy reading. They spend far more time reading books and newspapers than Americans do. Russian citizens also spend considerable time visiting museums. One of the more unusual activities Russians enjoy is mushroom picking. A mushroom hunt is a perfect way to escape the city and enjoy the countryside.

Other favorite pastimes from the prerevolutionary era that did not disappear under communism are eating and drinking with family and friends. Any occasion, especially a holiday, will do to enjoy a feast. Many different kinds of food are served.

The downside of this tradition is alcohol dependence. Abuse of alcohol has caused a serious problem in Russia for many years. The Russians have long been the world's largest consumers of vodka. Alcoholism and drunkenness are among Russia's most grave social problems. Between the 1960s and 1980s, the consumption of alcoholic beverages in Russia doubled. Antidrinking campaigns, including one under Mikhail Gorbachev, have failed to reduce alcoholism. Alcoholism is one of the reasons the average life expectancy fell in Russia during the latter part of the Soviet era. Frightening statistics on alcoholism illustrate the trends over the past 80 years. In 1913, 2 percent of all Russians 15 years or older were classified as alcoholics. By 1985, the figure had soared to 17 percent. During that time, the per capita consumption of alcohol among Russians increased eightfold.

RUSSIAN NATIONALISM

Modern Russian nationalism emerged in the 1960s as a reaction to the failures of communism and its impact on Russian life. Russian nationalists focused on a variety of themes and ideas. They wanted to revive interest in their nation's prerevolutionary culture and religious heritage. However, many of them tended to glorify what they called the Slavic race and were hostile to non-Russians. The best known Russian nationalist is Alexander Solzhenitsyn, the famous writer. In 1974, his "Letter to Soviet Leaders" suggested that the non-Slavic nations of the USSR be allowed to secede. This letter, which clearly was suggesting the end of the Soviet Union as it then existed, was one of the main reasons Solzhenitsyn was sent into exile.

Supporters of Boris Yeltsin and his spirit of Russian nationalism demonstrate in Moscow's Red Square in May 1990.

Russian nationalism grew and spread during the Gorbachev era. Two factors fed nationalist sentiments among Russians: the increased freedom of expression possible under *glasnost* and the Russian reaction to nationalist movements among non-Russian ethnic groups. This growing movement was sharply divided. Most Russian nationalists were strongly anticommunist. At the same time, many continued to be anti-Western and often anti-Semitic. One of the most outspoken nationalist organizations was called *Pamyat*, which means "memory" in Russian. With its angry rejection of democracy and bitter anti-Semitism, Pamyat reminded many people of the fascist movements of the 1930s.

A more tolerant tendency in Russian nationalism is best symbolized by Boris Yeltsin. After becoming president of Russia, Yeltsin spoke out strongly for Russian national interests. At the same time, he tried to reach out to minority ethnic and religious groups living within Russia. He also worked hard to introduce economic reforms and establish good relations with the United States and other Western nations. However, although Yeltsin and his allies were in powerful positions after the breakup of the Soviet Union, there was no guarantee that moderate Russian nationalism would prevail.

REVIEWING THE CHAPTER

I. Building Your Vocabulary

In your notebook, write the numbers from 1 to 6. After each number, write the word that matches the definition.

mir	bards	*byliny*
Sputnik I	village writers	socialist realism

1. a style of art that glorified Stalin and socialism

2. traveling poets who recited Russian epics

3. the first artificial satellite to orbit the earth

4. the most important organization in a Russian village

5. epic songs or poems

6. writers who wrote about peasant life and called for a return to prerevolutionary Russian values

II. Understanding the Facts

In your notebook, write the numbers 1 to 5. Write the letter of the correct answer to each question next to its number.

1. The period when Alexander Pushkin and Mikhail Lermontov wrote is known as the
   a. golden age of Russian literature.
   b. Great Purges.
   c. age of socialist realism.

2. During the 1930s, creativity in the Russian film industry was limited because of the policies of
   a. Sergei Eisenstein.
   b. Joseph Stalin.
   c. Konstantin Stanislavsky.

3. After the collapse of the Kievan state, Russians developed a distinct style in which of the following types of painting?
   a. fresco painting   b. portrait painting   c. icon painting

209

4. Russian physicist Andrei Sakharov won a Nobel prize for his work in

a. behavioral conditioning.

b. developing the hydrogen bomb.

c. promoting world peace.

5. Many Russians are concerned about the extreme nationalism, anti-Semitism, and antidemocratic sentiments of

a. Boris Yeltsin. b. *Pamyat.* c. *glasnost.*

III. Thinking It Through

In your notebook, write the numbers 1 to 5. Write the letter of the correct answer to each question next to its number.

1. Many people were absorbed into the group known as Russians because of

a. *glasnost* and *perestroika.*

b. Marxism and communism.

c. the Bolshevik revolution.

d. religious conversion and territorial expansion.

2. Which of the following institutions have played an important role in Russian life from the A.D. 900s until today?

a. the *mir*

b. the Russian Orthodox Church

c. the Communist party

d. the czar and the royal family

3. Which of the following statements is *not* true about Russian architecture after the Revolution of 1917?

a. It lacks character.

b. The buildings are of poor quality.

c. It is massive, but dreary.

d. The buildings have onion-shaped domes.

4. Which of the following statements is a true generalization about Russian women in the workforce?

a. The career fields women entered lost prestige and women were paid less than men.

b. Women were not successful in medicine.

c. Few Soviet women chose to work outside the home.

d. Women were able to work outside the home because men took over many of the domestic responsibilities.

5. All of the following are examples of how family life in Russia has changed during the 1900s *except*

    a. the family is smaller.

    b. the divorce rate has increased.

    c. people prefer to spend their free time away from their families.

    d. more women work outside the home.

DEVELOPING CRITICAL THINKING SKILLS

1. Russian nationalism arose in the 1960s as a reaction to the failure of communism. What were some of the positive results of nationalism? What were some of the negative results?

2. Evaluate the role of the Russian Orthodox Church in the history of Russia. How has it benefited the people? Why has it survived?

3. Based on what you have read in Chapter 8, what can you conclude about the status of women in Russia? What extra responsibilities and pressures did economic opportunity bring to individual women?

4. In which field of the arts or science do you think the Russians have made the greatest contribution to the world? Explain your answer.

ANALYZING LITERATURE

Alexander Solzhenitsyn vividly described the savage conditions in a slave-labor camp in *The Gulag Archipelago*. The word archipelago, which means a group of islands, refers to the dozens of slave-labor camps scattered across the Soviet Union isolated like "islands" from the rest of the country. He also described how the victims were arrested during the Great Purge.

> They take you aside in a factory corridor after they have had your pass checked—and you're arrested. They take you from a military hospital with a temperature of 102°F, as they did with Ans Bershtein, and the doctor will not raise a peep about your arrest—just let him try! They take you right off the operating table—as they took N. M. Vorobyev, a school inspector, in 1936, in the middle of an operation for a stomach ulcer—and drag you off to a cell, as they did him, half-alive and all bloody. . . . Or, like Nadya Levitskaya, you try to get information about your mother's sentence, and they give it to you,

but it turns out to be a confrontation—and your own arrest! In the Gastronome—the fancy food store—you are invited to the special-order department and arrested there. You are arrested by a religious pilgrim whom you have put up for the night "for the sake of Christ." You are arrested by a meterman who has come to read your electric meter. You are arrested by a bicyclist who has run into you on the street, by a railway conductor, a taxi driver, a savings bank teller, the manager of a movie theater. Any one of them can arrest you, and you notice the concealed maroon-colored identification card only when it is too late.

Alexander Solzhenitsyn, *The Gulag Archipelago 1918–1956: An Experiment in Literary Investigation*. New York: Harper and Row, 1975.

1. Why do you think the situation described here was so effective in controlling the daily lives of those Soviet citizens who were not arrested? Compare this "terror"—a situation where there are no rules that a person can count on for protection and where one can be struck down at any time—with the rule of law as it exists in the United States.

2. Many important things have changed in Russia since Stalin's time. Discuss some of the important changes in personal security, freedoms in daily life, and freedom of expression. Use information in this chapter and previous chapters to help make the comparison.

ENRICHMENT AND EXPLORATION

1. Choose one of the scientists or scientific research projects described in this chapter. Use the library to investigate the person or the particular project. Prepare a short report describing the scientific or medical finding and the impact it had.

2. Russia has produced many outstanding artists, writers, dancers, and musicians. Choose one individual who is outstanding in his or her field and prepare a short "autobiography" of that person. Writing in the first person, tell about how that person achieved greatness in his or her chosen field. Discuss the obstacles that had to be overcome. Explain the person's feelings as he or she worked and grew.

9 The Non-Russian People of the Commonwealth

The non-Russian countries of the Commonwealth of Independent States differ greatly from each other in many ways. They range in size from gigantic Kazakhstan to tiny Armenia. Ukraine, with over 50 million people, has over 15 times the population of Turkmenistan, which has over 3 million people. Ukraine and Belarus are relatively modern, urban and industrial European societies, while Kyrgyzstan and Tajikistan are largely traditional, rural Central Asian societies. (See table on page 2.) Some of the CIS states such as Armenia are almost entirely Christian, while others such as Uzbekistan are largely Muslim.

At the same time, these countries have important things in common. All of them must cope with the challenges associated with becoming independent. For example, none of them have direct experience with democracy. Their lack of experience will make it difficult to create stable, democratic governments. In addition, the nations of the CIS need to formulate economic programs, plans for national defense, and social policies. They must deal with ethnic disputes that already have led to violence in Moldova, Tajikistan, and other countries. They must also develop relationships with each other, Russia, and the rest of the world.

COUNTRIES OF THE WEST

Ukraine, Belarus and Moldova border central European countries and have important cultural ties with the West. Ukraine and Belarus are Slavic countries. Like Russia, their populations descended from the Eastern Slavs. (See Chapter 2.) The majority of the people of Moldova are Romanians who live in territory that had been taken during the rule of the czars.

Ukrainian History.   Ukraine, with an area of more than 230,000 miles (595,700 square kilometers), is the second largest country in all of Europe. Only Russia is larger. Yet for most of its history, Ukraine has been under foreign control. Foreign domination began with the Mongol invasion and the destruction of the Kievan state in the 1200s. By the 1300s, the majority of what today is Ukraine was controlled by Lithuania and the Mongol state called the Golden Horde. Later Poland became the dominant power in the region. During the 1600s, Russia began to challenge Polish control of Ukraine. After a long and bitter struggle during the 1600s and 1700s, Russia gradually conquered most of Ukraine. During the last part of the 1700s, Russia seized the southern and eastern parts of Ukraine, which had been under the control of the Ottoman Empire. Overall, Russia controlled most of Ukraine for a period lasting over 300 years, from the mid-1600s to the late 1900s.

Between the Mongol invasions and the collapse of the Soviet Union, Ukraine enjoyed two brief periods of independence. The first resulted from a rebellion that began in 1648 against Polish rule. Ukrainian peasants fought against their Polish landlords and Polish attempts to force them to become Roman Catholic. The rebellion was led by a group known as the Cossacks—descendents of runaway peasants who had established their own communities on the steppe beyond the reach of either Polish or Russian authorities. The rebellion of Cossacks and Ukrainian peasants was an explosion of uncontrolled hatred and merciless violence. Along with taking vengeance on their Polish overlords, the Cossacks unleashed a reign of terror against the Jewish inhabitants of the region. At least 100,000 Jews were massacred.

Despite defeating the Poles, the Cossacks were unable to maintain Ukrainian independence. In 1654, the Ukrainians were again threatened by Poland and the Ottoman Empire. They sought the protection of the czar and swore allegiance to Russia. But their loss of independence did not bring peace to Ukraine. For the next three decades, Ukraine was a battleground for its powerful neighbors during a series of wars and invasions Ukrainians call "The Ruin." When peace finally did come, it brought Russian domination with it.

The second period of Ukrainian independence came after the collapse of czarism in 1917. Once again Ukrainians set up an independent state, and once again the region was overwhelmed by invasion and war. Germans, Bolsheviks, anti-Bolsheviks, and others fought for control of Ukraine. As in the 1600s, the country was left in ruin and under Russian control. However this time, the Russian-dominated state that controlled Ukraine was called the Soviet Union.

214

Ukrainian Nationalism. The relationship between Russia and Ukraine from the 1600s to the 1900s revolved around one fundamental question: were the Russians and Ukrainians one nationality with a few minor variations, or were they two distinct nationalities? Most Russians considered the Ukrainians to be part of the broad Russian nation. Russians insisted that while foreign conquest had resulted in some differences between Russians and Ukrainians, these were minor compared to what united them. As for the Ukrainian language, Russian leaders considered it a dialect of Russian. Under both czarist and Soviet rule, there were attempts to suppress the Ukrainian language and national identity. During the Stalin era, the brutality of the collectivization campaign in Ukraine resulted in the famine of 1932–33 and at least 5 million deaths. (See Chapter 4.) The policy was designed to crush Ukrainian separatism and national identity. Stalin also purged Ukrainian Communist leaders who encouraged or permitted Ukrainian cultural expression. An independent Ukrainian Orthodox Church, which had been organized after the collapse of czarism, was forced to merge with the Russian Orthodox Church. In 1938, all Ukrainian schoolchildren were forced to study Russian as part of their regular schoolwork (as were schoolchildren of other nationalities throughout the Soviet Union).

After Stalin's death, the Soviet government continued to harass Ukrainian cultural leaders. During the 1970s, when a cultural revival swept the Ukraine, the Soviet government imprisoned many Ukrainian dissidents. Several escaped imprisonment only by leaving the Soviet

During the Stalin era, collectivism was forced on Ukrainian farmers. In addition, the Ukrainians were made to give up their national identity.

Union. During the early 1980s, a number of Ukrainian dissidents died in Soviet labor camps. Not even powerful Ukrainian Communist officials were safe if they were sympathetic to their national culture. In 1972, the head of the Ukrainian Communist party was removed from office because he failed to crack down hard enough on local cultural and nationalist dissidents.

While Russians have considered them a subgroup, Ukrainians have emphasized their distinct culture and national identity. They point to non-Russian characteristics that developed as a result of Ukraine's ties with the nations of western Europe prior to Russia's conquest of the region in the 1700s. For example, as a result of several centuries of Polish rule, educated Ukrainians were more exposed to Western ideas than were Russians. Many Ukrainians in the western part of the country belong to the Uniate Church, a branch of Catholicism. Ukrainians point out that small parts of the region were under Austrian rule until the 1900s. Ukrainian cultural leaders also believe that Ukrainians are more individualistic than the Russians. As proof, they stress that while Russian peasants traditionally belonged to communes that divided land equally among their members, Ukrainian peasants rarely engaged in that practice.

Ukrainian Literature. Ukrainian people have a significant literary tradition that sets them apart from the Russians. In the 1500s and 1600s, Ukrainian Orthodox clergy wrote religious works that often advocated freedom from Polish rule. During the 1600s and 1700s, Ukrainian writers often were influenced by Western literary movements. Ukraine's first great national writer was the poet Taras Shevchenko (SHEHF-chayn-koh; 1814–1861). Shevchenko's most important work was a collection of poems called *Kobzar*, which pictured life in Ukrainian peasant villages. Because of his activities promoting Ukrainian independence, Shevchenko spent 10 years in exile in Siberia.

After Shevchenko's death, the czarist regime tried to suppress the development of Ukrainian literature, but it did not succeed. Shevchenko's work was continued by writers, poets, historians, and playwrights. Some, such as Ivan Franko (1856–1916), were arrested because of their revolutionary activity. Along with writing original works in his native language, Franko translated into Ukrainian the works of Shakespeare, Goethe, Dante and other great Western European literary figures. One of the most revered Ukrainian literary figures of the Soviet era was poet Vassyl' Stus, who died while on a hunger strike in prison during the Brezhnev era.

Taras Shevchenko, Ukraine's leading poet, was born a serf. In 1838, a benefactor bought his freedom. Shevchenko's poetry reveals a deep love of his homeland.

The Effect of *Glasnost* on Ukrainians. With the rise to power of Mikhail Gorbachev and the beginning of his policy of *glasnost*, Ukrainian dissidents and cultural leaders increased their activities to promote their native culture. Their efforts resulted in the publication of previously banned literary works. Ukrainian intellectuals pressed for increased study of the Ukrainian language in local schools.

Gorbachev's reforms sparked Ukrainian national hope. Although nobody yet dared publicly to use the word independence, the idea clearly was on people's minds. Ukrainians were encouraged when, in 1989, the Baltic states of Lithuania, Latvia, and Estonia openly demanded independence. That year, a Ukrainian nationalist movement called Rukh was founded. Although it made a variety of demands on the Soviet government, it still did not openly talk about independence.

The Ukrainians did not hesitate when their chance for independence finally came. On December 1, 1991, Ukrainians voted overwhelmingly for independence in a national referendum. That vote was one of the final blows to the Soviet Union, which collapsed that same month. One election worker summed up the mood of millions of Ukrainians when she said, "This is a great day—it is the flowering of our soul." A more realistic prediction about the effects of independence came from one of the voters who said, "Hard times are coming, no doubt, but we'll get through it better this way."

217

CASE STUDY:

In The Fortress

Taras Shevchenko was among Ukraine's greatest poets. In this excerpt from "In the Fortress," Shevchenko expresses his love for his homeland.

> It makes no difference to me,
> If I shall live or not in Ukraine
> Or whether any one shall think
> Of me 'mid foreign snow and rain.
> It makes no difference to me,
> In slavery I grew 'mid strangers,
> Unwept by any kin of mine;
> In slavery I now will die
> And vanish without any sign.
> I shall not leave the slightest trace
> Upon our glorious Ukraine,
> Our land, but not as ours known
> No father will remind his son
> Or say to him, "Repeat one prayer,
> One prayer for him; for our Ukraine
> They tortured him in their foul lair."
> It makes no difference to me,
> If that son says a prayer or not.
> It makes great difference to me
> That evil folk lull now to sleep
> Our mother Ukraine, and will rouse
> Her, when she's plundered in the flames.
> That makes great difference to me.

Taras Shevchenko. "In The Fortress," in *Selected Poems of Taras Shevchenko*, Translation by Clarance A. Marwins (Jersey City, New Jersey: Ukrainian National Association, 1945), pp. 181-182.

1. Why does Shevchenko write that it does not matter if he lives in Ukraine?

2. What is it that makes a difference to Shevchenko?

218

On the same day the people of Ukraine voted for independence, they chose their first freely elected president, Leonid M. Kravchuk. A long-time Communist party official, Kravchuk had scrambled to present himself as a Ukrainian nationalist as the Soviet Union started disintegrating during 1991. He now faced the far more difficult job of turning Ukraine from a republic of the Soviet Union into an independent country. Kravchuk has many resources available to help him. Ukraine is a modern industrial state that also has many natural resources. About one fifth of all the industry of the former Soviet Union is located in Ukraine. Its factories produced about 18 percent of all Soviet consumer goods. Ukraine produces heavy machines, metals, cement, chemicals, railway vehicles, food processing equipment, and many other commercial goods. Its natural resources include iron, coal, some oil, and the belt of *chernozem*, the rich black earth that for centuries made Ukraine the breadbasket of both Russia and the Soviet Union. Its fertile soil yields wheat, potatoes, sugar beets, barley, cotton, fruits, tobacco, and other crops.

However, Ukraine will have to settle the differences among the various ethnic groups that make up its population. While about 73 percent of its population is Ukrainian, over 20 percent of its population is ethnic Russian. Some areas with large concentrations of Russians, such as the Crimean Peninsula, did not fully support Ukrainian independence. A number of Russians in the Crimea have spoken of seceding from Ukraine. (See Chapter 10.) Although Ukraine has the best opportunity in its history to establish a prosperous and independent life, it also faces enormous challenges in turning that opportunity into reality.

Belorussian History. The Belorussians, who number more than 10 million, are the smallest of the three East Slav peoples. Prior to 1991, except for a brief period in 1918, the Belorussians had never been independent. After the Mongol invasions and the fall of Kievan Rus (see Chapter 2), Belarus fell first to Lithuania and then to Poland. Belarus became part of Russia after the partition of Poland in the late 1700s. When Poland regained its independence after the collapse of czarism in Russia, Belarus had a short period of independence. After a fierce Russo-Polish war, Belarus was divided between its two larger neighbors. At the end of World War II, the Soviet Union claimed all of Belarus.

Belarus often has been a battleground because of its location on the routes leading between eastern and western Europe. It lay on Napoleon's invasion route into Russia in 1812, and was on one of the paths the German army took when it struck against the Soviet Union in 1941. (See page 125.)

Although the Belorussians maintained their distinct ethnic identity throughout their difficult history, Belorussian nationalism did not develop until the late 1800s for several reasons. Because of the tug-of-war between Catholic Poland and Orthodox Russia, Belorussians are divided by religion. The majority of Belorussians in the country's western regions are Catholic, while the majority of those living in the east are Orthodox. The foreign powers that occupied the country did all they could to suppress the Belorussian language. In 1697, Poland banned the use of the Belorussian language. From 1859 to 1906, Russia prohibited Belorussian publications and the use of Belorussian in the schools. In addition, most Belorussians were denied education. That slowed the development of Belorussian as a written language.

Belorussia Under Soviet Control. Not until 1902 did the Belorussians form their first political organization. It advocated Belorussian autonomy within the Russian Empire. In 1918, Belorussian nationalists proclaimed the Belorussian Democratic Republic. But in 1919, the Bolsheviks took control and the name was changed to the Belorussian Soviet Socialist Republic. A few years later it was incorporated into the Soviet Union. Belorussian identity developed much more fully during the Soviet era. This is ironic, since the leadership of the Soviet Union tried to promote a Soviet identity based largely on the Russian language and culture. However, certain Soviet policies worked in the opposite direction. Belorussia was one of the 15 republics in the union. This gave the Belorussians a political unit, even if it was controlled by the Soviet leadership in Moscow. In addition, under the Soviets education spread and more Belorussians learned to read and write their native language.

At the same time, Soviet policies encouraged industrialization and urbanization in Belorussia. Among the more important industries developed in Belorussia are machine tools, high technology metals, petrochemicals, plastics, engineering, and wool manufacturing. During the first half of the 1980s, Belorussia had one of the most successful economic records among the Soviet republics. Its industrial and agricultural production grew at the second fastest rate among the Soviet Union's 15 republics. Urbanization brought growing numbers of Belorussians together, which tended to increase their national awareness. Several small organizations formed to promote Belorussian language and culture. However, on balance the process of adopting Russian culture and language was growing faster than the movement to promote Belorussian identity. For example, by the 1970s more than half of Belorussian schoolchildren were being taught in Russian, rather than Belorussian. By 1989, over 77 percent of the students were being taught in Russian. The tendency toward the Russification of Belorussia continued during the era of *perestroika*, despite the efforts of Belorussian intellectuals. After the collapse of the Soviet Union, Belorussians suddenly gained independence and a chance to assert their national identity.

Moldova. Moldova is a region of lowlands squeezed between the Dneister and Pruth rivers and between Ukraine and Romania. It is the least urbanized of the western CIS states. About 64 percent of its population is Moldovan, about 14 percent Ukrainian, and 13 percent Russian. The region produces crops such as wine grapes, fruit, and tobacco. Most of its industries process the foods grown in the region.

The Moldovans are actually Romanians. Their language, while showing some Ukrainian influences, is very similar to Romanian. Their

The village of Gorodishche (goh-ROHD-ish-cheh) is nestled in the woodlands of Moldova. Gorodishche, which means "townsite," is supported by surrounding orchards and vineyards.

history, culture, and religion link them to Romania. What separated them from Romania was Russian expansion in the 1800s.

Moldova is located on territory that traditionally has been called Bessarabia. It was united with Romania after World War I when Russia was greatly weakened. The Soviet Union took the region back during World War II. During the Soviet era, the region was called the Moldavian Soviet Socialist Republic.

In order to justify its control over Moldova, the Stalin regime made up the fiction that the Moldovans were a nationality distinct from the Romanians. To make the case that Moldovans spoke their own language, the Soviets forced them to write it in the Cyrillic script used to write Russian, rather than in the Latin script used to write Romanian. The Soviets also encouraged the use of Russian wherever possible, including in schools and government offices. The situation was so extreme that in many local libraries it was impossible to find a single book in Moldovan. Like the czarist government before it, the Soviet regime encouraged non-Moldovans to move into the region to balance the local population. None of this turned out to be very convincing to the Moldovans. During the Gorbachev era, Moldovans began to throw off the fake identity imposed on them by outsiders. Protesters began to display the once-forbidden Romanian flag and intellectuals openly called the language of their region Romanian. However, the seeds of future problems already were sprouting. Moldovans are only 64 percent of the republic's population. Ethnic Russians, Ukrainians, and a number of small minorities feared that the upsurge of Moldovan ethnic pride would lead to discrimination against them. In 1989, Russians living in Moldova demanded their own autonomous republics to protect themselves from the majority Moldovans. These ethnic tensions erupted into open conflict after the collapse of the Soviet Union and the establishment of the independent state of Moldova.

COUNTRIES OF THE CAUCASUS

The Caucasus Mountains stand like giant white-capped guards at the frontier where Europe and Asia meet. Since ancient times, these mountains have been the site of countless invasions. The waves of invasions have left hostile ethnic groups living next to one another in the valleys and hills of the Caucasus. Today, the three largest nationalities living in the Caucasus Mountains and the region just south of it called

Transcaucasia are the Armenians, Azerbaijanis, and Georgians. The homelands of all three groups were annexed by the Russian Empire during the 1800s. The Armenians, Georgians, and Azerbaijanis all briefly established independent states after Russia's collapse in 1917, and they immediately became locked in territorial disputes with one another. During the Soviet era, each nationality had its own republic in the union. After the collapse of the Soviet Union, Georgia, which was torn by political violence, did not join the CIS. However, Armenia and Azerbaijan, despite a long history of mutual hostility, became part of the new Commonwealth.

Armenia. The Armenians are an ancient people who trace their origins as far back as 900 B.C. They converted to Christianity about A.D. 300. The Armenian Apostolic religion has been one of the central features of their national identity. The Armenians were the first people in the world to adopt Christianity as a state religion. The origins of a written Armenian language and literature date from the A.D. 400s. The first books in Armenian were printed in the 1500s, while modern Armenian literature dates from the late 1800s. While they occasionally have enjoyed periods of independence, for most of their history the Armenians have been under the control of more powerful neighbors. Romans, Persians, Byzantines, Arabs, Turks, and Russians all have fought to rule Armenia.

While the Armenians have known many conflicts, it is the Turks who have been their most bitter enemies. Much of historic Armenia lies in the Anatolia (now the part of Turkey located in Asia), which was conquered by the Ottoman Turks during the 1300s and 1400s. After centuries of oppression under the Turks, most Armenians welcomed the Russian conquest of the eastern part of their homeland in the late 1800s. The long struggle between the Muslim Turks and the Christian Armenians culminated in the part of Armenia still under Turkish control in 1915. At the height of World War I, the Turkish government was worried that its long-time rival, the Armenians, would aid enemy Russia. To prevent that, the Turks launched a campaign of deportation, imprisonment in concentration camps, and murder that eventually claimed more than 1.5 million Armenian lives. The refusal of the nations of the world to stop the genocide is central to Armenia's history. Armenians saw themselves as an outpost of Western and Christian civilization in Central Asia. Fear of genocide also explains why Armenia, desperate for protection from the Turks, voluntarily accepted Soviet control of their country in 1920.

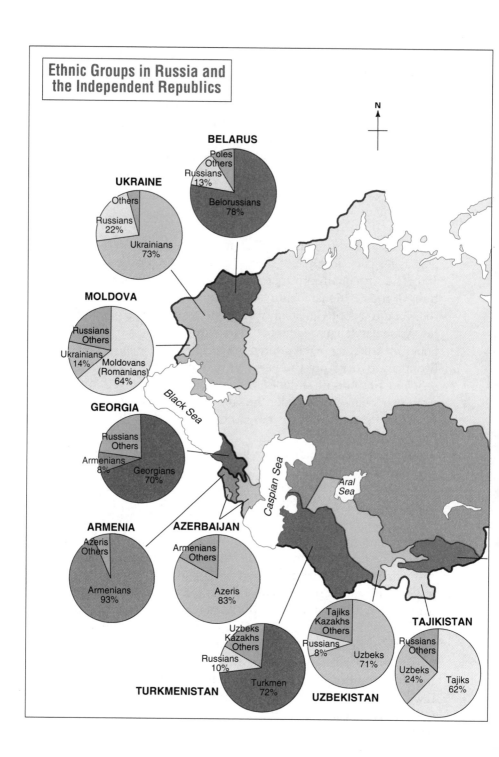

Ethnic Groups in Russia and the Independent Republics

N

BELARUS
Poles
Others
Russians 13%
Belorussians 78%

UKRAINE
Others
Russians 22%
Ukrainians 73%

MOLDOVA
Russians
Others
Ukrainians 14%
Moldovans (Romanians) 64%

Black Sea

Caspian Sea

Aral Sea

GEORGIA
Russians
Others
Armenians 8%
Georgians 70%

ARMENIA
Azeris
Others
Armenians 93%

AZERBAIJAN
Armenians
Others
Azeris 83%

TAJIKISTAN
Russians
Others
Uzbeks 24%
Tajiks 62%

Tajiks
Kazakhs
Others
Russians 8%
Uzbeks 71%

UZBEKISTAN

Uzbeks
Kazakhs
Others
Russians 10%
Turkmen 72%

TURKMENISTAN

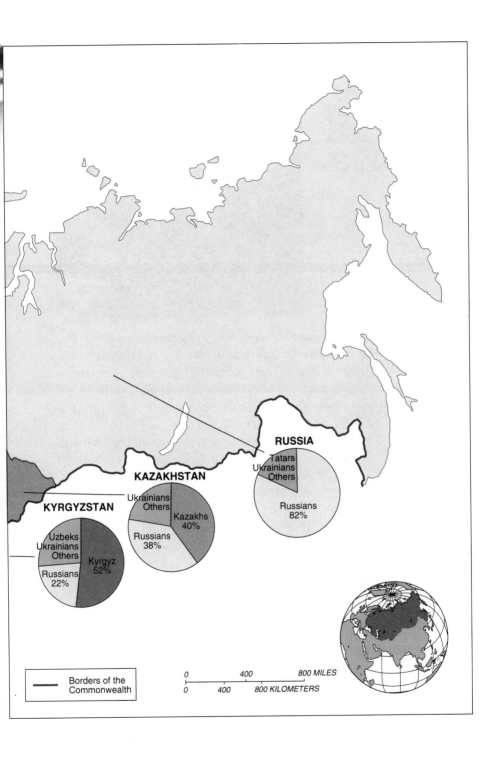

RUSSIA

Tatars
Ukrainians
Others

Russians
82%

KAZAKHSTAN

Ukrainians
Others

Kazakhs
40%

Russians
38%

KYRGYZSTAN

Uzbeks
Ukrainians
Others

Kyrgyz
52%

Russians
22%

Borders of the
Commonwealth

0   400   800 MILES

0   400   800 KILOMETERS

Because of the conflict between Armenia and Azerbaijan over the region of Nagorno-Karabakh, many people have lost their homes and businesses. How do ethnic tensions threaten the stability of the CIS?

Armenia's first decade under Soviet rule was generally positive. The country recovered from the destruction of World War I, and the relatively lenient policies of those years permitted Armenian culture to flourish. This changed drastically beginning with Stalin's collectivization and industrialization drives. Armenians along with the rest of the Soviet people suffered terribly as a result. Conditions improved after Stalin's death. The standard of living rose and the possibilities for cultural expression expanded. Under Soviet rule Armenia was transformed from a society that was 80 percent rural and agricultural to a society in which two thirds of the population lived in towns and cities.

The openness of the Gorbachev era benefited Armenia as it did the rest of the Soviet Union. But the relaxation of Soviet controls also allowed old ethnic quarrels to surface. In the Caucasus, the old tensions flared between the Armenians and their Azerbaijani neighbors, who are a Muslim people. The focus of the dispute was a region inside Azerbaijan called Nagorno-Karabakh in which most of the people were Armenian. In 1988, Nagorno-Karabakh demanded that it be transferred to Armenian control. The dispute soon led to violence and many deaths. Soviet troops were sent to the Caucasus to try to stop what was turning into civil war. Soviet authorities refused the Armenians' demands regarding Nagorno-Karabakh, despite demonstrations in Armenia of as many as 700,000 people. When the Soviet Union collapsed in 1991, the issue of Nagorno-Karabakh became even more urgent because Azerbaijan also became a fully independent state. Fighting intensified in Nagorno-Karabakh, in what was an undeclared war between Armenia and Azerbaijan. By the spring of 1992, over 1,500 people had been killed in the fighting. At least 200,000 people on both sides became refugees. For Armenia, independence did not mean freedom from problems that had plagued its people for centuries.

Azerbaijan. Azerbaijan is divided into two parts. Northern Azerbaijan was annexed by Russia in the 1800s. It became part of the Soviet Union in 1922, and today is an independent state within the CIS. Southern Azerbaijan is part of Iran. Like Armenia, Azerbaijan has been visited by many conquerors. Thus, today's Azerbaijanis are a mixture of Turkic, Iranian, and Caucasian people. Arab conquerors of the A.D. 600s brought Islam to Azerbaijan, and it remains the religion of the Azerbaijani people today. Although the Azerbaijanis speak a Turkic language, their culture has been heavily influenced by the Iranians who live directly south of them. The Azerbaijanis have a long literary tradition dating back 1,000 years.

Azerbaijan fared much like its neighbors during the Soviet era. The 1920s were a relatively relaxed period that was followed by terror and upheaval during the 1930s. Collectivization brought misery to many Azerbaijani peasants. Industrialization brought large numbers of rural Azerbaijanis into the cities, where they worked in new factories or the enormous oil industry around the city of Baku on the Caspian Sea. Urbanization, however, proceeded at a slower pace in Azerbaijan than in Armenia. It was not until the late 1980s that the urban population in Azerbaijan exceeded the rural population. Despite its oil industry, Azerbaijan remained one of the poorest republics of the Soviet Union.

During the Gorbachev era, Azerbaijani attention was focused on the struggle with Armenia over Nagorno-Karabakh. Azerbaijan also was concerned about the fate of a territory called Nakhichevan, a part of Azerbaijan that was separated by Armenia, where violence occurred during 1992.

COUNTRIES OF CENTRAL ASIA

Central Asia was the last area to fall under the control of the Russian Empire. Most of Kazakhstan was annexed during the first half of the 1800s, while the territory of the other Central Asian republics was annexed between 1853 and 1885. The five largest native ethnic groups living in the region—Kazakhs, Uzbeks, Turkmen, Kyrgyz, and Tajiks— are united by their common Islamic heritage. Some of them speak very similar languages, and people in some groups have intermarried. However, there is also a great deal that divides them. The Kazakhs and Kyrgyz, while speaking similar languages, have different social and political structures. The Turkmen speak a language that is more similar to Azerbaijani than to that of their Central Asian neighbors. Unlike the traditionally nomadic Kazakhs, Kyrgyz, and Turkmen, the Uzbeks became farmers several centuries ago. The Tajiks speak an Iranian language, which is distinct from the Turkic languages of the other nationalities of the region.

When the Russians took over the region, they encouraged the development of differences between the Central Asians as part of a "divide-and-rule" policy. That policy was continued under the Soviet regime. Ethnic tensions exist within all the Central Asian states, each of which has a substantial minority population. These tensions have been increased by language laws that have made the language of the majority the country's official language in all of the states except Turkmenistan. In Kazakhstan, where Russians are almost as numerous as Kazakhs and no group has a majority of the population, the Russian language is still used for communication between ethnic groups.

Kazakhstan. The Kazakhs trace their origins to nomads who lived in the region around the 1200s. By the 1700s, the Kazakhs' most feared enemy was Mongols from the east. The Kazakhs therefore looked to Russia for protection. However, after Russian control was firmly established during the first half of the 1800s, the Kazakhs faced a new threat: the immigration of large numbers of Russian and Ukrainian peasants. An even greater threat came with Soviet rule and Stalin's policy of collectivization. Collectivization devastated Kazakh nomads and farmers. At least 1 million people out of a total population of about 4 million died from starvation during the 1930s.

After Stalin's death, Soviet policy became less murderous, but it remained harsh. Under Nikita Khrushchev's Virgin Lands Policy, millions of acres of Kazakhstan steppe were plowed up for raising wheat. (See Chapter 6.) More Russian farmers came to work the land. As a result of Russian migration and the slaughter of Kazakhs during the collectivization period, the Kazakhs became a minority in their own land. Because of their high birth rate, the Kazakh population increased relative to that of the Russians and finally surpassed it at the end of the 1980s. However, because of the presence of Ukrainians and other ethnic groups, the Kazakhs are only about 40 percent of the population of Kazakhstan. (See map on pages 224–225.)

Because snow covered the ground during an unusually harsh winter, these Kazakh horse breeders had to bring fodder to their herd.

Like other newly independent republics, Kazakhstan faced many challenges. As with other ethnic groups across the Soviet Union, Kazakh national feeling grew rapidly during the Gorbachev era. In 1989, Gorbachev appointed Nursultan Nazarbaev head of the Kazakhstan Communist party as part of the reform program. Nazarbaev proved himself to be an outstanding leader. He opposed the conservative coup against Gorbachev in August 1991, and he played a leading role in the formation of the Commonwealth of Independent States. He was a voice for moderation and common sense during an unstable and dangerous time. However, he faced enormous problems in creating stability in his country. Kazakhstan's rapidly growing population caused a severe unemployment problem, especially among its youth. Many young people are turning to drugs and crime at a frightening rate. The region's environment has been polluted by industries built during the Soviet era and by radioactivity from nuclear test sites. (See Chapter 10.) Kazakhstan also has been the site of outbreaks of ethnic violence.

Uzbekistan.   The Uzbeks, who number about 16.5 million people, are the largest Muslim nationality in the CIS and the third largest nationality behind the Russians and Ukrainians. While most live in Uzbekistan, over 2 million Uzbeks live in neighboring Central Asian states. They trace their ancestry to the Golden Horde, which ruled much of Russia after the Mongol invasion. The Uzbeks also are a mixture of other groups that have inhabited the Central Asian steppe over the centuries.

Uzbekistan is a predominantly Muslim country. Here, a young couple take their wedding vows in a traditional Islamic ceremony.

Uzbek national feeling is in large part a creation of Soviet-era policies. Beginning in the 1920s, the Soviet regime encouraged Uzbek ethnic identity to separate them from other Central Asian peoples. This allowed the Soviets to control Central Asia without the worry that its Muslim peoples would unite to challenge rule from Moscow. Soviet rule in Uzbekistan brought literacy to a largely illiterate people, but at a price. The Soviets required the Uzbek language to be written in Cyrillic instead of its traditional Arabic script. This was done in all the Central Asian regions to integrate them into the new Soviet order. However, this left modern Uzbeks unable to read their traditional literature that includes works by the great poet Nismaddin Alisher.

Effects of Soviet Rule on Uzbekistan. As elsewhere in the Soviet Union, the Uzbeks suffered terribly during the 1930s as a result of collectivization. Although Stalin's worst policies were abandoned after 1953, Soviet economic policies continued to damage Uzbekistan. The Soviet policy of growing cotton in Uzbekistan proved to be an environmental catastrophe. Cotton demands a great deal of water and the two main rivers that feed the Aral Sea have been drained of their water to feed the cotton irrigation canals. The result was good for cotton. Production in the 1980s almost equaled that of the United States. However, the Aral Sea, once the world's fourth largest inland body of water, began to dry up. By the 1980s, the Aral Sea had lost one third of its water. As its waters retreated, salt beds at the bottom of the sea were exposed. Windstorms released a combination of salt and dust into the air, which ruined farmland. Climate changes, including ever-stronger storms, have taken place. The poisonous salts and the chemicals sprayed on the cotton to combat pests have caused health problems, especially in young children. Uzbekistan has suffered an environmental and health disaster as bad or worse than Chernobyl in Ukraine.

The country faces other problems as it begins its independence. Like Kazakhstan, population growth has led to severe unemployment among Uzbekistan's youth. Ethnic clashes between the majority Uzbeks and a small ethnic group called the Meskhetians has led to deadly violence. There is a large gap between a small educated, secular urban elite and a larger traditional group in the villages. Uzbekistan is one of the poorest countries in the CIS, and may lack the resources and leadership necessary to make an easy transition to independence.

Turkmenistan. Although they were divided into feuding groups, the Turkmen were the last people in Central Asia to be brought fully under Russian control. The Turkmen vigorously opposed Russian expansion into Central Asia. In one of their last battles against the Russian invaders in 1881, over 14,000 Turkmen died defending a fortress called Geok-Tepe. Even after that battle, Turkmenistan was not completely occupied until 1885. After World War I, the Turkmen participated in the Basmachi Revolt against the Soviet authorities. The revolt began in 1918, spread across Central Asia, and involved guerrilla units from several Central Asian nationalities. The Basmachi Revolt was not defeated until 1926. Turkmen guerrillas also fought the Soviet authorities for several years during the 1930s.

The Turkmen trace their roots in Central Asia to groups that migrated there between the 900s and 1100s. Their language is Turkic and has a written tradition dating to the 1200s. Modern Turkmenian literature dates from the 1800s. As with the other languages of Central Asia, Turkmen originally was written in Arabic script. However, the Soviet regime forced a change first to Latin script and then to Cyrillic script in order to bring the Turkmen closer to Russian culture. Like other Central Asia peoples, the Turkmen are Muslims and have remained so despite decades of Soviet campaigns against religion.

Turkmen history under Soviet rule parallels that of the other major Central Asian peoples. The Soviets encouraged a Turkmen national identity in order to prevent any unity among the Muslim Turkic people of Central Asia that might threaten Soviet rule. The ways of life of Turkmen farmers and nomads were destroyed by Stalin's collectivization policies in the 1930s.

Turkmenistan must cope with many problems as it faces independence. The same Soviet economic policies that did so much damage to Uzbekistan damaged Turkmenistan. As a result of environmental damage caused by the drying of the Aral Sea and pollution from cotton production, Turkmenistan has the lowest life expectancy of all the former Soviet republics. (See the table on page 2.) It also has the highest infant mortality rate. Turkmenistan has severe unemployment because of high population growth and the Soviet failure to build enough industry in the region. The standard of living in the country is low and declined during the late 1980s.

Turkmenistan's main resources are its large oil and gas deposits. There is tension between ethnic groups in the country. Relations between Turkmen and Russians, who are about 10 percent of the population, are not good. Other minority groups living in Turkmenistan include Uzbeks, Kazakhs, Armenians, Azerbaijanis, and Baluchis.

Kyrgyzstan. The Kyrgyz people emerged as a distinct ethnic group in the 1500s. They are a mixture of Turkic, Mongol, and other groups of the Central Asian steppe. In the second half of the 1600s, the Kyrgyz converted to Islam. Islam has since become an important part of their national identity. Although the first alphabet for the Kyrgyz language was created in the 1920s, the Kyrgyz have a oral tradition of poetry and song that dates from their earlier history as nomads. A poem called "Manas" is considered the national epic of the Kyrgyz people.

Kyrgyzstan has a variety of natural mineral resources and produces electric power from hydroelectric stations on its mountain rivers. A number of important industries were built in the country during the Soviet period, including machine tool building and metal working. The country suffered gravely during the 1930s collectivization and industrialization campaigns.

Like other central Asian republics, Kyrgyzstan faces some serious challenges. Despite the growth of towns and cities, Kyrgyzstan still remains over 60 percent rural, in part because of rapid population growth among its village inhabitants. A large percentage of the urban population of the country is non-Kyrgyz, while the great majority of Kyrgyz continue to live in their traditional villages. Kyrgyzstan, like the other Central Asian republics, has experienced ethnic conflict since Soviet controls loosened after 1985. This is an especially serious problem because the country is truly multinational. Only 52 percent of the population is Kyrgyz. Of the rest, 22 percent is Russian and 26 percent is made up of Uzbeks and other groups.

Tajikistan. The Tajiks are descendents of Iranian groups that migrated to Central Asia at least 1,000 years before the Turkic peoples. Most of the territory that today is Tajikistan came under Russian control during the 1860s. The Russians brought large-scale cotton farming to the region and began to mine its deposits of coal. They often seized the lands of the local people to further their economic and settlement goals.

Many Tajiks participated in the Basmachi Revolt of the 1920s. They also resisted collectivization. As a result, it took longer to collectivize Tajikistan than it did other parts of the Soviet Union. While Soviet policies brought some industry to Tajikistan, the emphasis both during Stalin's lifetime and under his successors was on producing cotton. Soviet policies also brought many Russians into the country. In 1926, Russians were less than 1 percent of the population. Today, Russians make up about 8 percent of the country's population. The percentage of Russians had been higher until recent years, as the Tajiks have the fastest growing population of any nationality in the former Soviet Union. Between 1979 and 1989, the Tajik population grew by 34 percent, which was almost four times higher than for the Soviet Union as a whole. Most of that increase is in rural areas where most Tajiks live. Other ethnic groups, especially Russians, are concentrated in the towns. For example, the population of the Tajik capital Dushanbe is 30 percent Russian.

These Tajiks Muslims are gathered outside their mosque.
What effect did Soviet rule have on Tajik culture?

Although Tajikistan has not suffered the severe environmental damage that occurred in other Central Asian countries, it shares other problems of its neighbors. Rapid population growth has produced rising unemployment, especially among young people. The country remains poor, with one of the lowest per capita incomes in the CIS.

Tajikistan has no experience with democracy, and political disputes have led to violence. The present government is controlled by former Communist party officials. In 1990, riots in Dushanbe caused several deaths. Since the collapse of the Soviet Union, there has been additional political violence. During the spring of 1992, over 100 people were killed during two months of protests against the government. Making matters more complicated, the opposition to the former communists is far from united. One group of opponents favors democracy, while another favors an Islamic republic. In short, Tajikistan's future is likely to be unstable, raising doubts whether its serious problems will be addressed.

Horses cross rough, but beautiful terrain in Tajikistan.
Tajikistan faces many of the same problems the other
Central Asian republics face. What are some of the prob-
lems the non-Russian republics must solve?

REVIEWING THE CHAPTER

I. Building Your Vocabulary

In your notebook, write the numbers from 1 to 6. After each number, write the country that matches the description.

Kazakhstan   Armenia   Ukraine

Uzbekistan   Turkmenistan   Moldova

1. unique because its people are Romanian

2. largest non-Russian country of the Commonwealth

3. most populous country after Russia

4. people of this country are the largest Muslim nationality

5. the last people in Central Asia to be brought under Russian control

6. the smallest country in the Commonwealth

II. Understanding the Facts

In your notebook, write the numbers 1 to 5. Write the letter of the correct answer to each question next to its number.

1. Which of the following is *not* located in Europe?
   a. Belarus   b. Tajikistan   c. Moldova

2. Which of the following is *not* located in Central Asia?
   a. Kazakhstan   b. Kyrgyzstan   c. Ukraine

3. Which of the following states is mostly Christian?
   a. Azerbaijan   b. Armenia   c. Tajikistan

4. What do Uzbekistan and Tajikistan have in common?
   a. They are mostly Christian.
   b. Their populations are Slavic.
   c. They are rural societies.

5. Which country from Transcaucasia did *not* join the Commonwealth in 1991?
   a. Georgia   b. Armenia   c. Azerbaijan

III. Thinking It Through

In your notebook, write the numbers 1 to 4. Write the letter of the correct answer to each question next to its number.

1. In order to suppress national identity in many of the republics the czars and, later, the Soviet Union
   a. suppressed the national language.
   b. encouraged membership in the Russian Orthodox Church.
   c. gave Communist party members special privileges.
   d. gave everyone Russian citizenship.

2. The Armenian and Azerbaijani dispute over Nagorno-Karabakh was a problem caused by
   a. Russification.
   b. *perestroika.*
   c. ethnic tensions.
   d. collectivization.

3. Which of the following is *not* a major problem for most of the central Asian republics?
   a. pollution and environmental damage
   b. high birth rates
   c. unemployment
   d. flooding

4. From 1918 to 1926, Central Asian nationalities rebelled against Soviet power in
   a. the Basmachi Revolt.
   b. the Communist revolution.
   c. the Kyrgyz Riots.
   d. Bloody Sunday.

DEVELOPING CRITICAL THINKING SKILLS

1. Compare and contrast the three non-Russian regions of the Commonwealth of Independent States. What historical experiences do they share with one another? What problems do they have in common? How are they different?

2. Agree or disagree with the following statement: Nationalism in the republics of the former Soviet Union is solely due to intervention by the Russian Empire and the Soviet Union through the years. Give reasons for your position.

3. How did Soviet control benefit the non-Russian republics? Do you think the Soviets did more harm than good or did they bring improvements that compensated for the damage they caused?

4. Analyze the conflict over Nagorno-Karabakh. How did the conflict begin? Why did the issue become more urgent after the breakup of the Soviet Union? What do you think should be done to resolve this conflict in the Caucasus region?

INTERPRETING GRAPHS AND A MAP

Study the graphs and map on pages 224–225 and answer the following questions in your notebook.

1. What national groups live in Tajikistan? What is the percentage of each?

2. Which country has the highest percentage of its own nationality living in it?

3. In which country does the national group make up less than half the population? What other groups live in that republic? What are the percentages of each?

4. In what republics do Russians make up less than half the population?

5. Based on what you have read in Chapter 9, why do Russians make up a significant part of the population in many of the independent republics?

ENRICHMENT AND EXPLORATION

1. Imagine that you were the leader of one of the non-Russian republics. What would you do to strengthen your nation? Choose one of the independent countries and develop a program to improve its economic, environmental, and social problems.

2. Form groups of two or three students and research the culture of one of the major national or ethnic groups that live in the non-Russian republics. Use your school or public library to discover what the people eat, how they dress, and what they do in their leisure time. Investigate what type of homes they live in, how most of the people make their living, and what religion they practice. Present what you have learned to the class in an oral report.

10 The Independent Republics and the World

The collapse of communism in the Soviet Union and the countries of Eastern Europe in the late 1980s and early 1990s led to events of momentous importance. In Germany, the Berlin Wall was torn down and East Germany and West Germany were reunited. As Communist governments were toppled, independence was restored to the countries of Eastern Europe. The most astonishing event, however, was the breakup of the Soviet Union itself. The breakup signaled the end of an empire—originally called the Russian Empire and then the Soviet Union—that had imposed its control over millions of people in Europe and Asia. The collapse of communism meant the end of the Cold War. The threat of nuclear war was reduced and the arms race was slowed.

The collapse of communism in the Soviet Union exposed numerous problems that the newly independent republics now have to solve. Many of these problems were related to the deficiencies and failures of the Communist system. (See Chapter 3.) Because of Communist mismanagement, all the newly independent countries had inefficient economies and low standards of living. Each of them faced the difficult task of changing from a centrally planned economy to a free-market economy. In addition, these countries had little or no experience with democracy. The countries of the region also had to cope with environmental catastrophes that had seriously undermined the health of many of their people.

Some of the region's other problems had been suppressed by the Soviet government. As you have read, over 100 different ethnic groups lived in the Soviet Union. Now that Soviet authority had broken down, long-simmering ethnic tensions quickly boiled over into open conflicts. Some conflicts were between nations, while others took place within individual nations.

RELATIONS BETWEEN THE REPUBLICS OF THE CIS

One of the most urgent problems Russia and the independent republics faced was how to deal with one another. Within the Commonwealth, there were 11 independent nations. For more than 100 years they had been part of a single nation. Many of the new nations resented Russia as a colonial power. Other nations had long-standing arguments with one another. Some nations, such as Russia, wanted the Commonwealth to provide strong links between its members. Others, including Ukraine, wanted to keep ties among the member nations minimal. The result was a series of disputes and conflicts that plagued the Commonwealth from its start.

Nuclear Weapons. One dispute that immediately concerned people all over the world was about nuclear weapons. The republics of the former Soviet Union had to decide what to do with the thousands of nuclear weapons scattered across the Commonwealth. The weapons were divid-

After the breakup of the Soviet Union, the newly independent republics began to make decisions about the huge nuclear stockpile they inherited. Here, two soldiers are removing a nuclear warhead from Ukraine.

ed into two categories: about 12,000 strategic, or long-range weapons, and about 18,000 tactical, or short-range weapons. The long-range weapons were based in four republics: Russia, Ukraine, Belarus, and Kazakhstan. The short-range weapons were in most of the CIS states. (See map below.) The dangerous possibility existed that without Soviet control some of these weapons could fall into the hands of unfriendly groups, including terrorists.

By the end of February 1992, the short-range missles in all but Ukraine, Belarus, and Kazakhstan had been moved to Russia. Ukraine, Belarus, and Kazakhstan were not eager to give up their nuclear weapons. Pressed by the United States and its NATO allies, the three republics agreed to ship their short-range weapons to Russia by July 1992. They also agreed to give up their long-range weapons by the end of the 1990s. None of this was accomplished very easily.

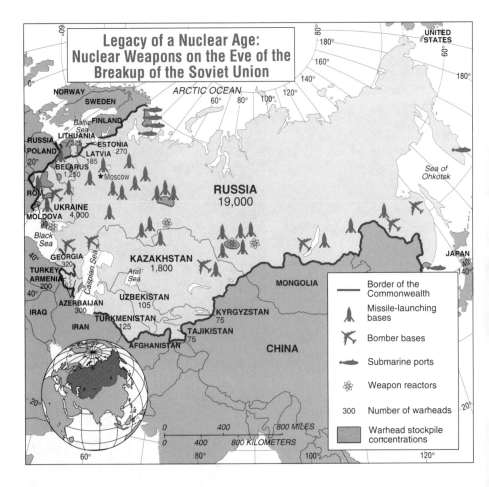

Legacy of a Nuclear Age: Nuclear Weapons on the Eve of the Breakup of the Soviet Union

——	Border of the Commonwealth
🙼	Missile-launching bases
🗡	Bomber bases
⊶	Submarine ports
✲	Weapon reactors
300	Number of warheads
▨	Warhead stockpile concentrations

Russia versus Ukraine. Russia and Ukraine, the two most powerful members of the CIS, clashed over several issues. Ukraine, which borders the Black Sea, claimed control of part of the Black Sea fleet of the former Soviet Union. Russia insisted that the 300-ship fleet be under Commonwealth command. In 1992, the two countries agreed to divide the ships and share the naval bases located on the Black Sea.

The territorial dispute over the Crimean Peninsula, which juts into the Black Sea from the southern tip of Ukraine, proved harder to resolve. Over 60 percent of Crimea's population is ethnic Russian. The Crimea had never been part of Ukraine until Soviet authorities shifted it to Ukrainian authority in 1954. Soon after the breakup of the Soviet Union, the Crimea's Russian majority began pushing for independence from Ukraine. In May 1992, the Crimean parliament voted overwhelmingly for "independence." The Ukrainians viewed this as an attempt by Russia to take over part of Ukraine's territory. Ukrainians worried that other large Russian populations in the southern and eastern parts of the country would follow Crimea's lead. If this happened, Ukrainian leaders feared the unity of their country could be threatened.

These soldiers were once part of the Soviet Union's army—the world's largest military machine. After the breakup of the country, these soldiers pledged an oath of loyalty to Ukraine's military.

Conflicts Among the Nations of the Commonwealth. In addition to the tensions between Russia and Ukraine, there were pressing issues to settle between other countries. One of them was the dispute between Armenia and Azerbaijan over Nagorno-Karabakh. (See pages 223–226.) By 1992, this dispute had turned into a virtual state of war. The fighting not only led to casualties on both sides, but also threatened the stability of the Commonwealth.

During the Commonwealth's first months of existence the member nations could not reach agreement regarding military defense and economic policy for the Commonwealth as a whole. Nor was there progress in finding a formula for dividing the state property of the former Soviet Union among the members of the CIS. This lack of progress amid so many disputes was discouraging and dangerous for the future of the Commonwealth. Ukraine's President Kravchuk, for one, warned that if the situation did not improve "the entire existence of the CIS is questionable." Russia's President Yeltsin, on the other hand, argued that building the Commonwealth was a "dynamic process," not something that could be completed in a short period.

Ethnic violence has been wreaking havoc in many of the newly independent republics. This tank rolls down a street in Nagorno-Karabakh, a region over which Armenia and Azerbaijan have been fighting.

One sign of the weakness of the Commonwealth was a so-called "summit meeting" in May 1992, where only six of the eleven Commonwealth presidents attended. However, all eleven republics sent delegations. Despite the absence of five presidents, those present did reach several agreements. They created a collective security pact under which member states agreed to come to one another's aid in the event of outside aggression. They also formulated a plan for a Commonwealth peacekeeping force. But these agreements did not have the clear support of Ukraine and several other CIS states. The division between its members continued to cloud the Commonwealth's future.

ETHNIC PROBLEMS WITHIN THE STATES OF THE CIS

Ethnic tension caused problems that plagued most of the CIS states. When the Soviet Union split apart, most of the newly independent states were faced with internal ethnic conflicts that had been suppressed for years. These problems caused strains within the new states, and in some cases, led to violence. Fears arose that minority groups within some CIS states would not be guaranteed basic human rights. In some cases, ethnic problems were a potential threat to the unity of the new states.

Problems in Moldova.   In December 1991, Russian and Ukrainian inhabitants of a region in eastern Moldova called Trans-Dniester voted to secede. The ethnic Russians and ethnic Ukrainians feared that if Moldova decided to unite with Romania, they would face discrimination as a small minority in a large Romanian country. Weeks of violence early in 1992 led the Moldovan government to impose emergency rule on Trans-Dniester. However, fighting continued.

Ukraine and the Crimean Tatars.   Ukraine, aside from its problem with ethnic Russians, had to worry about a smaller group called the Crimean Tatars. They had been driven from their homes in the Crimea by Stalin's regime after World War II. By the 1980s, large numbers of them were returning to the Crimea illegally, and they demanded the right to reclaim their homes.

Difficulties in Uzbekistan.   Even before it gained independence, the Asian republic of Uzbekistan was torn by ethnic violence. In summer

1990, Uzbeks fought bloody battles with a small ethnic group called the Meskhetians. The following summer, Uzbeks fought Kyrgyz in a dispute over border lands. Uzbekistan also had a large minority population of Tajiks, while neighboring Tajikistan had a minority Uzbek population.

Unrest in Russia.   Russia, the country with the largest number of minority ethnic groups, also faced ethnic problems. Russians made up about 82 percent of the population of their state. Still, they had difficulties with several minority groups. The most active were the Tatars, a group that declared its independence from Russia in March 1992. Other groups did not seek independence but demanded greater autonomy. The many minority ethnic groups living in Russia add yet another complication to the task of building a new nation out of the ruins of the Soviet Union.

AN ENVIRONMENT IN RUINS

Soviet economic policy called for rapid industrialization at all costs. This policy caused extensive damage to the natural environment and a condition called ecocide. The word ecocide refers to the destruction of the natural environment. It is a word that applies to many disastrous practices such as pollution of the water supply, destruction of the rain forests, and pollution of the air. The level of environmental damage in the countries of Eastern Europe and the former Soviet Union is among the worst in the world. Environmental damage has undermined the health of millions of people, especially the young. It is one of the major reasons that life expectancy has dropped in the countries of the CIS in recent years. In addition, through water and weather systems the environmental damage inside the CIS has spilled over to other parts of the world, especially central and western Europe.

It will cost enormous amounts of money to begin the environmental cleanup in the CIS. Despite all efforts, there is little doubt that some environmental damage can never be repaired.

Nuclear Radiation and Fallout.   The 1986 explosion at the Chernobyl nuclear power plant in Ukraine was the worst nuclear disaster yet in the world. While the explosion and the resulting spread of nuclear fallout shocked the world, the long-term damage of the explosion is not as well known. At first, the Soviet Union claimed that 31 people had died from the blast and the resulting radiation sickness. By the early 1990s, few scientists believed these figures. An independent group of Soviet citizens said that at least 300 people had died. Since then, some Russian and Ukrainian scientists have estimated that at least 4,000 of the workers who were brought in for cleanup work have died. Total fatalities, including local residents exposed to radiation, has pushed that figure to more than 5,000. In Ukraine, at least 1 million people continue to live in areas contaminated by radiation. The situation was even more serious in neighboring Belarus, where winds had carried much of the radioactive fallout from the explosion. Two million people, including 800,000 children, live in contaminated areas. In addition, there has been extensive land damage. Tens of thousands of square miles of farmland had been contaminated by radioactive elements. Yet much of that farmland continues to be used, producing food that poisons the people it feeds. Meanwhile, farm animals raised on the land are given feed contaminated with radioactive elements. As much as 20 percent of the entire territory of Belarus has been polluted by Chernobyl.

The disastrous effects of radiation poisoning in the countries of the former Soviet Union are not limited to the aftermath of Chernobyl. Most of the nuclear power industry in the Soviet Union was considered unsafe. One of the most unsafe plants is located in Armenia, where a generator exploded in 1982. In the Ural mountain region of

Pollution in the former Soviet Union has devastated much of the landscape. The air and water of the Russian city of Kemerovo is fouled by smokestacks and industrial debris.

Russia, a plutonium plant has contaminated the surrounding area with 20 times the fallout of the Chernobyl disaster. Extremely high rates of cancer have been found among inhabitants of northern Russia, where above-ground nuclear tests had been conducted on Arctic islands. One small ethnic group living near the Arctic Circle has a liver cancer rate ten times the average for the rest of the country. A similar situation exists in Kazakhstan, another region where above-ground nuclear tests took place. Kazakhstan is also plagued by nuclear waste storage sites.

Nuclear contamination from the former Soviet Union has affected other countries in Europe. In 1991, Russian officials revealed that for years the Soviet navy had dumped radioactive wastes into the shallow waters of the Arctic Sea. This has put some of the world's richest fishing grounds at risk.

Industrial and Agricultural Pollution. As a result of economic development policies followed by the Soviet regime, the states of the CIS suffer from some of the worst industrial pollution on earth. One of the showplaces of Soviet industrialization was Magnitogorsk in Russia's Ural Mountains. Magnitogorsk was the world's largest steel complex. Today it is an economic dinosaur, burdened by out-of-date machinery and mismanagement. It is also an environmental disaster. As a result of pollution from the steel mills, 34 percent of all adults and over 60 percent of all children in Magnitogorsk have respiratory illnesses. Forty percent of all babies born in the city are sick or have developmental problems. Air pollution in the southeastern Ukraine region of Krivoy Rog is even worse than at Magnitogorsk. In Kazakhstan, enormous factories producing lead, zinc, cement, and phosphate have blackened the countryside and undermined the health of the people. In a typical lead factory, workers in the 1990s labored with nothing more than flimsy cotton masks to protect them from the poisonous fumes around them. According to one estimate, pollution has lowered the life expectancy of the inhabitants of every major industrial region of the former Soviet Union.

Agricultural pollution has also taken a terrible toll. Pesticides, herbicides, and defoliants used to grow cotton have poisoned both the land and the people who live in the areas where they are used. The poisonous chemicals used in the cotton fields in Kazakhstan and Turkmenistan have seeped into the water supply. Both regions have high levels of disease. Although the Soviet Union officially banned the pesticide DDT in 1970, its use continued through most of the 1980s. Among its many victims were Armenians who suffered from abnormal amounts of cardiovascular disease, allergies, and other serious diseases.

Many of the lakes and rivers of the CIS also have been damaged by industrial and agricultural pollution. The Volga, the symbol of Russia, is its longest river. Once its blue waters flowed freely into the Caspian Sea. Today, the river is blocked by dams and polluted by industrial wastes. Its fish die in massive numbers. Those that are caught by fishers often are swarming with worms. The waters of the Volga are polluting the Caspian Sea, the world's largest inland body of water. The Dnieper, which flows through Kiev and the heart of Ukraine, also is badly polluted by industrial and radioactive wastes.

The Russian campaign to save Lake Baikal has been partially successful. Lake Baikal in southern Siberia is the oldest and deepest freshwater lake in the world. Over a mile deep, Lake Baikal is the world's single largest source of fresh water. Beginning in the mid-1950s, industrial development along Lake Baikal's shores started to pollute its waters. Protests from Soviet scientists and local residents pressured the Soviet regime to take some substantial antipollution measures. However, pollutants still pour into the lake.

Industrial complexes, like the one shown here, pour pollutants into the Caspian Sea. Why is pollution in the independent republics a world-wide concern?

The pollution originating in Russia and the other CIS states affects countries outside the Commonwealth. One of the most graphic examples of pollution crossing international boundaries is a gigantic nickel smelter in northern Russia near the Norwegian border. The smelter's three stacks belch out more polluting sulfur dioxide than is produced in all of Norway. Pollutants from the plant have destroyed thousands of acres of forests on both sides of the border.

The people of the CIS face a future polluted by decades of neglect. A desperate question from a Belorussian peasant woman expressed the concerns of millions:

> Tell me, please, how are we supposed to live? We are afraid of the
> water; we are afraid of the sun; we are afraid of the grass; we are
> afraid of the soil. . . . How can we go on living?

RUSSIA: KEY TO THE COMMONWEALTH

Russia is the key to the CIS because it is so much larger and more powerful than any other member country. By most measures it is larger than all of them put together. Aside from containing about three quarters of the territory of the CIS, Russia has about 52 percent of its population and 62 percent of its gross domestic product. It produces about 90 percent of its oil, 77 percent of its natural gas, 55 percent of its coal, 54 percent of its grain, 53 percent of its total food, and 55 percent of its nonfood consumer goods. If the Commonwealth of Independent States is to succeed, Russia must succeed. It must overhaul its economy and improve the standard of living of its people, make democracy work, and firmly establish normal and friendly relations with Western nations.

Economic and Political Problems.   In recent years, Russia has had a declining economy. Production of most food and industrial product has declined, and inflation has risen. To change over from a centrally planned to a free-market economy Boris Yeltsin took some bold and painful measures. In 1991, he signed an executive order to encourage private farming. The law gave collective farm workers greater opportunity to buy and sell individual plots of land. In 1992, Yeltsin took a difficult step that Mikhail Gorbachev had been unwilling to take—he ended price controls on most products. Only milk, bread, baby food, fuel, and a few other commodities were exempted. The result was rapidly rising prices. Within a month, prices had risen by 350 percent. Many people, especially the elderly and those on fixed incomes, experienced great hardship. By March, unemployment stood at 3 million, and there were fears it would jump to 11 million.

Although praised by Western economists, Yeltsin was heavily criticized by conservatives in Russia. When the Russian Congress of People's Deputies met in April 1992, Yeltsin's government barely survived a no-confidence vote that would have resulted in the government's collapse.

Yeltsin still managed to push ahead, despite the opposition in the Congress of People's Deputies and the hardships facing millions of ordinary Russians. His reforms brought help from the West. In 1992, several Western countries announced a $6 billion fund to help Russia stabilize its currency. Russia and the other members of the CIS, except Azerbaijan, were admitted to the **International Monetary Fund (IMF)**, an international organization that provides economic assistance to countries in need. IMF membership was very important because it helped clear the way for $18 billion in loans.

Yeltsin took another major step toward economic reform in May 1992, when he partially decontrolled fuel prices. However, decontrol caused those prices to skyrocket. This created another burden for the already hard-pressed Soviet consumer.

Economic Reform Brings Change. There were some bright spots in Russia's economic situation. By the beginning of spring 1992, predictions of starvation in Russia's cities had been proven inaccurate. Supplies of some foods were increasing, and through private trading and work Russians were somehow making enough money to survive. Foreign investment from abroad was slowly making a difference. There were 2,600 joint ventures between Russia and foreign firms. They employed about 120,000 Russians and were starting to have an impact on the economy. In 1991, foreign firms based in Russia produced 10 percent of the country's telephone equipment and 17 percent of its computers. They represented a small but significant start in bringing Western capital and expertise into Russia.

In 1992, Yeltsin announced a plan for a new Russian army. Yeltsin's plan had important political and economic implications. The major part called for a significant decrease in the size of Russia's armed forces. A smaller Russian army would save the country a great deal of money that could be used for economic rebuilding. A smaller army would help to improve relations with the West still further.

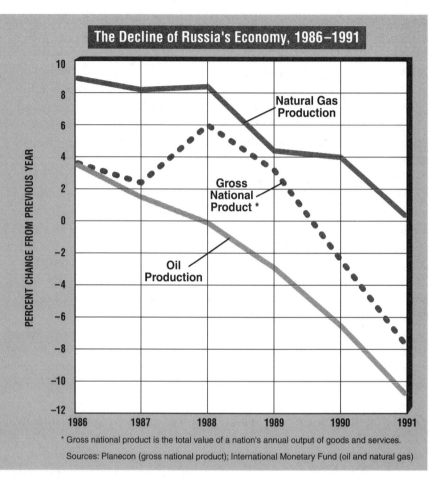

The Decline of Russia's Economy, 1986–1991

Natural Gas Production

Gross National Product *

Oil Production

PERCENT CHANGE FROM PREVIOUS YEAR

10
8
6
4
2
0
-2
-4
-6
-8
-10
-12

1986   1987   1988   1989   1990   1991

* Gross national product is the total value of a nation's annual output of goods and services.

Sources: Planecon (gross national product); International Monetary Fund (oil and natural gas)

THE COMMONWEALTH OF INDEPENDENT STATES AND THE WORLD

For seven decades, the countries that were part of the former Soviet Union were locked in an often hostile relationship with much of the world. As part of the Soviet Union, they had few economic ties with nations outside the Soviet bloc. Soviet censorship virtually cut them off from the culture and ideas of the outside world. Soviet citizens could not travel freely to other countries because of travel restrictions. Those barriers began to fall during the Gorbachev era. Gorbachev did a great deal to normalize the Soviet Union's relationship with foreign countries, especially the United States and Western Europe. But with the collapse of the Soviet Union, a far greater change took place. Each newly independent CIS state has needed to establish political and economic ties with the outside world and develop a foreign policy that fit its interests and capabilities.

Forging New Relationships with the West.   Russia has taken the lead in forging new ties with the outside world. Barely a month after the Soviet Union was abolished, Russian President Yeltsin met with U.S. President George Bush. The goal was to continue the trend of cooperation begun during the Gorbachev era. Presidents Bush and Yeltsin proclaimed a new era of "friendship and partnership" and declared that 70 years of rivalry between their two nations was over. The two presidents also announced a program for a joint center where U.S. and Soviet nuclear scientists could work together to stop the spread of nuclear weapons. By providing work for unemployed Russian scientists, the center would hopefully prevent Russian scientists from selling their services to nonnuclear powers who want to develop nuclear weapons.

In May 1992, a conference involving the United States, Russia, Ukraine, Belarus, and Kazakhstan also discussed measures to stop the spread of nuclear weapons. The following month, presidents Yeltsin and Bush met in Washington, D.C., and agreed to reduce drastically their countries' nuclear stockpiles.

Another sign that Russia's relations with the West were improving was agreement by the U.S. government to allow U.S. companies to buy high technology products from the former Soviet states. This was a reversal of U.S. policy dating from the Cold War. It broke down yet another barrier in U.S.-Russian relations. At the same time, the U.S. government promised to increase the number of high technology goods that may be sold to Russia, changing another Cold War policy. Not all Russian sales met with U.S. approval, however. The United States imposed trade sanctions against a Russian arms agency when it announced the sale of rocket engines to India. The United States feared that India, which had exploded a nuclear device, would use the engine to build a missile that can carry a nuclear warhead.

Ties to the Islamic World.   Most of the people of the Central Asian republics of the CIS are Muslim. After the breakup of the Soviet Union, Islamic nations outside the CIS, such as Iran, began to establish relationships with Tajikistan, Kyrgyzstan, Uzbekistan, Kazakhstan, and Turkmenistan.

Some Western nations are concerned that the newly independent nations of Central Asia will establish governments controlled by Islamic

CASE STUDY:

Boris Yeltsin Calls for Democracy

In June 1992, Russian President Boris Yeltsin met with U.S. President George Bush to discuss arms control, the Russian economy, and other issues. On the last day of the summit, Yeltsin addressed the U.S. Congress. Following are excerpts from his speech.

> It is indeed a great honor for me to address the Congress of the great land of freedom as the first . . . popularly elected President [of Russia], as a citizen of the great country which has made its choice in favor of liberty and democracy.
>
> For many years, our two nations were the two poles, the two opposites. . . . The world was shaken by the storms of confrontation. It was close to exploding, close to perishing beyond salvation. . . .
>
> That evil scenario is becoming a thing of the past. . . . We have left behind the period when America and Russia looked at each other through gunsights, ready to pull the trigger at any time.
>
> . . . it can be said today, tomorrow will be a day of peace, less of fear and more of hope for the happiness of our children. The world can sigh in relief. The idol of Communism, which spread everywhere social strife, animosity, and unparalleled brutality, which instilled fear in humanity, has collapsed. . . . I am here to assure you, we will not let it rise again in our land. . . .
>
> We must carry through unprecedented reforms in the economy, . . . lay the foundations for democracy; and restore the rule of law in the country that for . . . years was poisoned with political strife and political oppression.
>
> We have no right to fail in this most difficult endeavor, for there will be no second try, as in sports. Our predecessors have used them all up. The reforms must succeed. . . .

The New York Times, June 18, 1992, p. A18.

1. According to Yeltsin, what political system has Russia chosen?

2. How did communism affect Russia? How will the fall of communism affect relations between the United States and Russia?

fundamentalists, or extremely strict orthodox Muslims. Many Islamic fundamentalists reject Western ideas and values. Western governments are concerned that Iran, whose fundamentalist Islamic regime is hostile to the West, will be able to influence the newly independent Central Asian Republics. The West is concerned that instead of democratic governments, these republics will establish fundamentalist Islamic dictatorships similar to the one in Iran.

New Regional Organizations.   After the demise of the Soviet Union, the newly independent republics worked to form new ties with nations around the world. In 1992, the leaders of Russia, Ukraine, Georgia, Moldova, Azerbaijan, and Armenia joined with the leaders of Turkey, Greece, Romania, Albania, and Bulgaria to form a Black Sea regional economic organization. The economic group hoped to establish a forum under which the nations of the region could coordinate economic plans.

In a mass public rally, the people of Moscow demonstrate for democratic government. Why will establishing democracy be a difficult task for the newly independent republics?

Kazakhstan's Oil Deal. Kazakhstan took a major step of its own toward building economic ties with the West and helping its own economy. In 1992, it announced a deal with the Chevron Corporation, a U.S. company. Chevron would invest $10 billion over the next 40 years to develop the huge Tengiz oil field on the eastern shore of the Caspian Sea. Chevron hoped to build a pipeline to the Black Sea to export some of the oil to countries outside the CIS. Kazakhstan would receive 80 percent of the income from the project. The Chevron deal was expected to bring vital Western technology and money into Kazakhstan and boost oil production in the CIS.

Breaking Old Ties. As you have read in Chapters 5 and 6, in addition to controlling its Eastern European satellite nations, the Soviet Union supported Communist governments in Latin America, Africa, and Asia. The Soviet Union had abandoned some of these causes even before its breakup. For example, the Soviet Union had withdrawn support from the Communist regime in Afghanistan, which fell in 1992. The Soviet Union had also begun to withdraw its support from Fidel Castro's communist government in Cuba.

An Uncertain Future. The breakup of the Soviet Union has dramatically altered world affairs. At this turning point in history, the rest of the world is anxious about the choices the newly independent nations of the CIS might make. Russia, because of its size and its resources is likely to be the leading nation of the region. However, each nation of the Commonwealth is likely to have the chance and responsibility to be the master of its own fate.

REVIEWING THE CHAPTER

I. Building Your Vocabulary

In your notebook, write the numbers from 1 to 5. After each number, write the word that matches the definition.

ecocide   Chernobyl   Crimea
International Monetary Fund   Nagorno-Karabakh

1. an international organization that provides economic aid

2. destruction of the natural environment

3. region in Ukraine that is over 60 percent ethnic Russian

4. region over which Armenia and Azerbaijan are fighting

5. site of an explosion at a nuclear power plant in 1986

II. Understanding the Facts

In your notebook, write the numbers 1 to 5. Write the letter of the correct answer to each question next to its number.

1. Which of the following republics did NOT have strategic, or long-range nuclear weapons?
   a. Belarus   **b.** Kazakhstan   **c.** Armenia

2. In the Crimea, Russia and Ukraine disagreed over control of the
   a. navy.   **b.** army.   **c.** air force.

3. The site of one of the worst nuclear disasters in history was
   a. Lake Baikal.   **b.** Chernobyl.   **c.** Aral Sea.

4. What Russian leader ended price controls in 1992?
   a. Boris Yeltsin   **b.** Mikhail Gorbachev   **c.** Leonid Kravchuk

5. Even before the breakup of the Soviet Union, the Communist government had withdrawn its support from
   a. India.   **b.** China.   **c.** Afghanistan.

III. Thinking It Through

In your notebook, write the numbers 1 to 5. Write the letter of the correct answer to each question next to its number.

1. Which of the following is *not* a problem of the republics of the CIS?
   a. inefficient economies
   b. inexperience with self-government
   c. overpopulation
   d. damaged environments

2. The dispute about nuclear weapons caused world-wide concern because
   a. the weapons might fall into the hands of terrorists.
   b. the republics had decided to give all their weapons to the United States.
   c. NATO might take advantage of the disorganization and attack.
   d. neighboring Islamic republics threatened to take the weapons.

3. Russia is involved in a territorial dispute with which Eurasian country?
   a. Armenia
   b. Tajikistan
   c. Ukraine
   d. Azerbaijan

4. Magnitogorsk today is an environmental disaster for all but one of the reasons below. Which one does *not* apply to Magnitogorsk?
   a. Pollution from steel mills has caused respiratory illnesses for a large portion of the population of the area.
   b. Forty percent of the babies have developmental problems.
   c. Pollution is caused by antiquated machinery.
   d. Nuclear fallout has polluted the ground water.

5. One problem that the republics of the CIS must face is
   a. overproduction of consumer goods.
   b. oversupply of minerals.
   c. ethnic conflict.
   d. too much aid from the IMF.

DEVELOPING CRITICAL THINKING SKILLS

1. What problems did the people of the former Soviet Union face when the Communist government failed?

2. Analyze the measures Boris Yeltsin took to improve the economy when he took office. How effective were his efforts to promote economic change and develop a free-market economy?

3. What have the nations of the West done to help the CIS establish a stable free-market economy and a democratic government? Do you think that Western countries have done enough? Explain.

4. The republics of the Commonwealth face serious environmental problems. Describe the problem that you think is the most serious. What do you think should be done to improve the situation?

INTERPRETING A MAP

Study the map on page 240 and answer the following questions.

1. Which republics had missile-launching bases in 1990?

2. Where are submarine ports located?

3. What republic had the most nuclear weapons and support systems? How can you account for that?

ENRICHMENT AND EXPLORATION

1. Use your school or local library to research the environmental problems that exist at Lake Baikal and the Aral Sea. Prepare a poster, booklet, or illustrated article that presents the problems and possible solutions.

2. The economy of the Commonwealth is in need of dynamic new businesses and industries if it is to become a strong market economy. In a small group, develop a business or industry that you think would be successful in the CIS. Create a marketing plan and a pamphlet for your venture. Present your business plan to the class. Be prepared to answer questions and defend your proposal.

Glossary

anarchism: an ideology advocating abolition of the state *(p. 79)*

arable: land suitable for farming *(p. 13)*

arms race: the continued buildup of nuclear weapons in the United States and the Soviet Union *(p. 153)*

autocratic state: a state with unlimited power over its subjects *(p. 46)*

bard: a composer, singer, or writer of epic verse *(p. 191)*

Berlin Blockade: Soviet siege of Berlin in an effort to starve the Western powers out of Berlin *(p. 132)*

black market: illegal economic system that provided ordinary Soviet citizens with goods and services difficult to obtain elsewhere *(p. 178)*

Bolsheviks: a Marxist faction that staged the revolution of 1917; they called for a strongly centralized party and later became the Communist party *(p. 69)*

boyars: noble class under the czars; abolished by Peter the Great *(p. 45)*

byliny: epic songs or poems from Russia's oral literary tradition *(p. 191)*

capitalism: economic system with private or corporate ownership of capital goods, with prices, production, and distribution of goods determined by competition in a free market *(p. 175)*

Central Committee: Communist party committee elected by the party congress; responsibilities included electing the Politburo, the Secretariat, and the general secretary *(p. 172)*

Cheka: Bolshevik secret police, organized in 1917 *(p. 98)*

chernozem: dark fertile soil in the steppe *(p. 13)*

climate: pattern of weather over a period of time *(p. 9)*

Cold War: the state of tension and hostility between the Soviet Union and the United States from the mid-1940s to 1990 *(p. 133)*

collective security: Stalin's foreign policy during the 1930s based on forming alliances with other countries to guard against German and Japanese aggression *(p. 122)*

collectivization: agricultural program of the 1930s combining small farms into large collective farms *(p. 104)*

COMECON (the Council for Mutual Economic Assistance): economic organization of communist countries *(p. 132)*

Cominform (Communist Information Bureau): communist organization founded in 1947 to promote communist ideas and communist parties outside the Soviet Union; replaced Comintern *(p. 130)*

Comintern (Communist International): government-controlled organization founded in 1919 to promote communist revolutions in Europe *(p. 121)*

communism: a theory advocating elimination of private property; a final stage of society in Marxist theory replacing socialism; totalitarian system of government in which a single party controls state-owned means of production with the professed aim of establishing a stateless society (*p. 84*)

containment: U.S. policy of actively opposing any attempt by the Soviet Union to extend its influence (*p. 130*)

Cossack: member of a group who descended from runaway peasants and established their own communities on the steppe (*p. 51*)

Council of People's Commissars: government that Lenin installed in 1917 after the czarist regime was overthrown (*p. 97*)

counterrevolution: Bolshevik term for any dissent or criticism of the government (*p. 98*)

coup d'état: forcible overthrow of the government (*p. 55*)

CPSU: Communist Party of the Soviet Union (*p. 68*)

cultural diffusion: the movement and borrowing of ideas, beliefs, objects, and customs among regions or peoples (*p. 41*)

Cyrillic alphabet: alphabet developed in the 800s by two missionary monks, Cyril and Methodius (*p. 42*)

dekulakization: the massacre and deportation to labor camps of kulaks to assure collectivization in the 1930s (*p. 105*)

demand: the quantity of a product or service that customers may want (*p. 175*)

democratic centralism: principle of the Communist party in which the minority on any issue had to accept the will of the majority, and that lower party organizations had to carry out the orders of higher bodies (*p. 172*)

demokratizatsia: democratization; Gorbachev's attempt to introduce limited democracy to the Soviet Union (*p. 155*)

de-Stalinization: Khrushchev's attempt to reverse some of Stalin's repressive policies (*p. 139*)

détente: relaxing of tensions between the United States and the Soviet Union in the 1970s and 1980s (*p. 153*)

dialectical: concept of Marxism that describes how changes occur beginning with thesis, which leads to antithesis, and then to synthesis, before beginning the process again (*p. 81*)

dialectical materialism: Marxist theory stating that there is only a materialist reality and that this changes in a dialectical process (*p. 81*)

dictatorship of the proletariat: Marxist concept that called for giving complete and unlimited power to the revolutionary proletariat-led government (*p. 84*)

dissident movement: Soviet citizens who risked openly criticizing the Communist government (*p. 144*)

Duma: Russian parliament established by Czar Nicholas in 1905 (*p. 72*)

economic system: the way in which goods and services are manufactured and distributed within a country (*p. 174*)

European Economic Community (ECC): economic alliance among European countries founded in 1957; also known as the Common Market (*p. 151*)

Fertile Triangle: richest farming area in the Commonwealth of Independent States; extends north from the Black Sea to St. Petersburg and east to the Ural Mountains (*p. 18*)

Five Year Plan: a plan that set five-year goals for the Soviet Union's economic development (*p. 104*)

foreign policy: official policy clarifying the way one nation relates to other nations (*p. 119*)

glasnost: openness; Gorbachev's policy of opening up the flow of information in the censored Soviet world (*p. 155*)

Golden Horde: Tatar (Mongol) state from the 1200s to the 1400s (*p. 44*)

Gosplan: State Planning Commission; in charge of economic planning in the Soviet Union (*p. 175*)

Grand Alliance: the alliance of the United States, France, Great Britain, and the Soviet Union during World War II (*p. 125*)

Great Patriotic War: Soviet term for World War II (*p. 126*)

Great Purge: the killing and deportation to labor camps of millions of people, in the 1930s (*p. 109*)

Great Reforms: series of reforms under Alexander II that freed the serfs, and that affected the judicial and educational systems, the military, and local governments (*p. 64*)

humid-continental climate: climate with long, cold winters and short, warm summers (*p. 12*)

iron curtain: term coined by Winston Churchill, used to denote the Soviet-controlled countries of Eastern Europe (*p. 128*)

KGB: Committee for State Security; the Soviet secret police (*p. 169*)

khan: ruler of Mongol lands (*p. 44*)

khanate: land ruled by a khan (*p. 49*)

kolkhoz: collective farm owned and operated by its members (*p. 106*)

Komsomol: Communist organization for people between the ages of 14 and 28 (*p. 174*)

kulaks: prosperous peasants of the early 1900s (*p. 101*)

lend-lease: U.S. wartime program that provided the Allies with food, machines, and other material during World War II (*p. 125*)

Leninism: Lenin's interpretation of Marxist theory; stressed the importance of a centralized political party that would lead the workers to revolution (*p. 86*)

market economy: *See* **capitalism.**

Marshall Plan: U.S. European Recovery Act; provided aid to rebuild Europe after World War II (*p. 130*)

Marxism: political, economic, and social philosophy developed by Karl Marx based on socialism (*p. 69*)

materialism: the idea that all human history, from everyday events to major historical developments, depends completely on what people do, rather than on any spiritual forces (*p. 81*)

means of production: the equipment and facilities necessary to run an economy, for example, factories, railroads, mines, and farms (*p. 84*)

Mensheviks: a Marxist faction of the Social Democrats that split from the Bolsheviks; advocated a democratic party organization (*p. 69*)

metropolitan: chief bishop of the Orthodox Church (*p. 42*)

mir: commune; a village organization in czarist Russia that had joint ownership of land and farming by individual families (*p. 63*)

mode of production: how people work and use technology at a given time to produce what they need to live (*p. 81*)

multicultural: made up of many cultures (*p. 50*)

mutually assured destruction (MAD): theory that nuclear attack and counterattack would destroy both sides (*p. 153*)

nationality: a group of people sharing a common origin, language, and traditions (*p. 28*)

NEPmen: private merchants and small manufacturers of the early 1900s who used capitalist business methods (*p. 101*)

New Economic Policy (NEP): Lenin's program, which included some capitalistic measures; formulated to deal with the post-civil war economic crisis (*p. 101*)

Nihilism: movement of the 1860s that held that people were responsible only to their own moral code and that real change could come only when all existing institutions were destroyed (*p. 67*)

North Atlantic Treaty Organization (NATO): defensive military alliance formed in 1949 to defend Western Europe against the Soviet military threat (*p. 132*)

oprichnina: first political police, formed by Ivan the Terrible (*p. 47*)

peaceful coexistence: term used to refer to the Soviet Union's and the United States's living peaceably together and competing only in the economic sphere (*p. 146*)

perestroika: restructuring; Gorbachev's program of reforming the Soviet system, particularly the economy (*p. 155*)

permafrost: frozen ground that thaws only about two feet below the surface briefly in summer (*p. 9*)

Pioneers: Communist youth organization for children between the ages of 9 and 14 (*p. 173*)

planned economy: economic system wherein government agencies decide what to produce, how much to produce, and what prices to charge (*p. 175*)

pogroms: riots of murder and pillage directed against Jews (*p. 65*)

polar climate: climate with temperatures averaging below freezing for eight months or more each year (*p. 9*)

Politburo: the Communist party's top decision-making body and center of power (p. 143)

political party: organization of voters and politicians who voluntarily support a particular public program (*p. 172*)

political purge: the expulsion from a political party or government of members whose conduct has become unacceptable (*p. 109*)

populists: socialists of the 1800s, who believed that peasants and *mirs* were the key to establishing socialism in Russia (*p. 67*)

privatization: the process of turning over state enterprises to private ownership (*p. 184*)

proletariat: the working class (*p. 69*)

Provisional Government: temporary committee of the *Duma* that succeeded the monarchy in 1917 (*p. 96*)

Reds: Bolsheviks (*p. 99*)

Red Guards: armed Bolshevik units of soldiers (*p. 97*)

Russification: campaign to force Russian culture and language on Poland after 1830; similar policies were carried out toward other national groups during the Soviet era (*p. 61*)

SALT I: agreement reached during the strategic arms limitation talks between the United States and the Soviet Union to limit strategic nuclear weapons (*p. 153*)

satellite system: countries whose political and economic systems are controlled by a more powerful country (*p. 128*)

scorched-earth policy: strategy used by the Soviets during World War II under which they destroyed everything in the path of Nazi invaders (*p. 125*)

Secretariat: Communist party organization that supervised operation of various branches of the party (*p. 172*)

self-determination: principle of allowing a country to decide its own political future (*p. 113*)

serfs: peasants who were bound to their owner's estates, could be bought and sold, could not move, marry, or learn to read without their owner's permission, and were subject to taxes (*p. 48*)

Social Democrats: Russian Marxists of the late 1800s (*p. 69*)

socialism: economic system in which there is group or government ownership of the means of production and distribution of goods (*p. 67*)

Solidarity: Polish labor union; first trade union in the Soviet bloc that was not controlled by the Communist party (*p. 150*)

soviet: council (*p. 72*)

sovkhoz: state farm, larger than a collective farm, on which the peasants were employees (*p. 106*)

steppe: Russian word for *plains*; grasslands that contain about two-thirds of the CIS's arable lands (*p. 13*)

Strategic Arms Limitations Talks (SALT): discussions between the United States and the Soviet Union that led to an agreement to limit Soviet and U.S. strategic weapons *(p. 153)*

subarctic climate: severe climate with winter temperatures sometimes reaching 40° below zero *(p. 12)*

substructure: economic organization of a society; the mode of production *(p. 81)*

superstructure: a society's laws, customs, political principles, and religious beliefs *(p. 81)*

surplus value: the difference between the value of the goods a worker produces and the wages of that worker *(p. 84)*

taiga: thick forest that stretches across almost all of Russia *(p. 12)*

Third Section: secret police formed by Nicholas I *(p. 61)*

Third World: term used to refer to developing countries that did not side with either the Soviet Union or the United States *(p. 147)*

totalitarian state: single party state in which almost every aspect of human life is tightly controlled *(p. 110)*

tribute: a forced payment from one nation or group to another *(p. 45)*

Truman Doctrine: U.S. statement made in 1947 proclaiming that the U.S. would provide aid to Greece and Turkey to prevent communist takeovers in those countries *(p. 130)*

tundra: treeless land around the Arctic Circle; located in the polar climate zone *(p. 9)*

union republics: the 15 largest political units of the Soviet Union; after the breakup of the Soviet Union each union republic became an independent nation *(p. 28)*

united front: movement that joined local Communist parties with socialists and other left-wing parties throughout Europe in the late 1930s to establish antifascist governments *(p. 122)*

veche: citizen council of self-government of the 1000s *(p. 43)*

war communism: Bolshevik policy during the civil war; forcibly directed economic resources to support the Bolshevik cause *(p. 99)*

weather: the temperature and rainfall of a particular location at a given time *(p. 9)*

Whites: opponents of the Reds; included a variety of factions *(p. 99)*

Young Octobrists: Communist youth organization for children between seven and nine years old *(p. 173)*

zemstvos: institutions of rural government created by edict in 1864 *(p. 63)*

Bibliography

Chapter 1

Andrews, William B. *The Land and People of the Soviet Union.* New York: Harper-Collins, 1991.

Cole, J.P. *Geography of the Soviet Union.* Cambridge: Cambridge University Press, 1984.

Editors of Time-Life Books. *The Soviet Union.* Revised. Amsterdam: Time-Life Books, 1990.

Milner-Gulland, Robin. *Cultural Atlas of Russia and the Soviet Union.* New York: Facts on File, 1989.

Chapter 2

Alexander, John T. *Catherine the Great: Life and Legend.* New York: Oxford University Press, 1989.

Bonnell, Vitoria E., ed. *The Russian Worker: Life and Labor under the Tsarist Regime.* Berkeley, CA: University of California Press, 1983.

Kort, Michael. *The Soviet Colossus: A History of the USSR.* Boston: Hyman, 1990.

Pipes, Richard. *The Russian Revolution.* New York: Alfred A. Knopf, 1990.

Chapter 3

Lane, David. *The Roots of Russian Communism: A Social and Historical Study of Russian Social Democracy, 1898-1907.* University Park: Pennsylvania State University Press, 1975.

Wren, Christopher S. *The End of the Line: The Failure of Communism in the Soviet Union and China.* New York: Simon and Schuster, 1990.

Chapters 4–5

Commager, Henry Steele. *The Story of the Second World War.* New York: Brassey's (US), Inc., 1991.

Conquest, Robert. *The Great Terror: A Reassessment.* Oxford: Oxford University Press, 1990.

Kennan, George F. *The Fateful Alliance: France, Russia, and the Coming of the First World War.* New York: Pantheon, 1984.

McNeal, Robert H. *Stalin: Man and Ruler.* New York: New York University Press, 1988.

Pipes, Richard. *The Russian Revolution.* New York: Knopf, 1990.

Reed, John. *Ten Days that Shook the World.* New York: Vintage, 1960.

Tucker, Robert C. *Stalin in Power: The Revolution From Above, 1928-1941.* New York: Norton, 1990.

Chapters 6-7

Beschloss, Michael R. *The Crisis Years: Kennedy and Khrushchev, 1960-1963.* New York: Harper-Collins, 1991.

Blight, James and Welch, David A. *On the Brink: Americans and Soviets Examine the Cuban Missile Crisis.* New York: Hill and Wang, 1989.

Burcatsky, Fedor. *Khrushchev and the First Russian Spring.* New York: Scribner's, 1991.

Conquest, Robert. *The Harvest of Sorrow: Soviet Collectivization and the Terror Famine.* Oxford: Oxford University Press, 1986.

Dawisha, Karen. *Eastern Europe, Gorbachev, and Reform.* 2nd ed. Cambridge: Cambridge University Press, 1990.

Goldman, Marshall. *What Went Wrong with Perestroika.* New York: Norton, 1991.

Gorbachev, Mikhail. *The August Coup.* New York: Harper Collins, 1991.

Gorbachev, Mikhail. *Perestroika: New Thinking for Our Country and the World.* New York: Harper and Row, 1987.

Kaiser, Robert G. *Why Gorbachev Happened.* New York: Simon and Schuster, 1991, 1992.

Kort, Michael. *Mikhail Gorbachev.* New York: Watts, 1990.

Rapaport, Yakov. *The Doctors' Plot of 1953.* Cambridge: Harvard University Press, 1991.

Yeltsin, Boris. *Against the Grain: An Autobiography.* New York: Summit Books, 1990.

Chapters 8-10

Akiner, Shirin. *Islamic Peoples of the Soviet Union.* London: KPI, 1986.

Feshbach, Murray and Friendly, Alfred, Jr. *Ecocide in the USSR.* New York: Basic Books, 1992.

Hasking, Geoffry. *The Awakening of the Soviet Union.* Cambridge: Harvard University Press, 1991.

Lourie, Richard. *Russia Speaks: An Oral History from the Revolution to the Present.* New York: Edward Burlingame, 1991.

Sakharov, Andrei. *Memoirs.* New York: Alfred A. Knopf, 1990.

Smith, Hedrich. *The New Russians.* New York: Random House, 1990.

Solzhenitsyn, Alexander. *Rebuilding Russia: Reflections and Tentative Proposals.* New York: Farrar, Straus and Giroux, 1991.

Subtelny, Orest. *Ukraine: A History.* Toronto: University of Toronto Press, 1988.

Zickel, Raymond E., ed. *Soviet Union: A Country Study.* Washington DC: Federal Research Div., 1991.

Index

Bulgaria, 113, 128, 132-133, 149, 150, 159, 253
Bush, George, 161, 251, 252
byliny, 191-192
Byzantine Empire, 39, 41, 44, 47, 189, 200, 223

Canada, 159
canals, 8-9, 23, 53, 107
Capital, 80
capitalism, 80, 83-84, 85, 87-88, 101, 120, 140, 146, 169, 191
Carpathian Mountains, 6
Carter, James (Jimmy) E., 154
Caspian Sea, 1, 6, 8, 9, 15, 19, 23, 227, 247, 254
Castro, Fidel, 148, 152, 254
Cathedral of St. Sophia, 43
Catherine II (the Great), 55-57
Caucasus mountain region, 29-30, 32, 50, 105, 181, 222-227
Caucasus Mountains, 1, 6, 19, 160, 222
censorship, 141, 144, 149, 155-156, 157, 193, 196-197, 200, 250
Central Asia, 1, 2, 3, 6, 9, 18
   countries of, 102, 227-234
   during Soviet era, 119, 141, 147, 160, 228
   peoples of, 30-31, 32, 34, 223
Central Committee, 109, 157, 172
Central Powers, 99
Checheno-Ingush, 181
Chechens, 32
Cheka, 98
Chekhov, Anton, 13, 193, 199
Chernenko, Konstantin, 110, 145, 154
Chernobyl, 18, 155, 244-245
Cherry Orchard, The, 193
Chersky Mountains, 6
Chile, 148
China, 6, 122, 133
Christians, 30, 32, 33, 62, 213
   Armenian, 29, 34, 222, 223
   Russian, 45, 190, 191, 192, 200
Churchill, Winston, 128
Circassians, 32
civil rights, 57, 64, 96, 149, 151, 169-170, 180, 208, 243
civil war (Russian), 99-100, 110, 121, 141, 196
class struggle, 81, 83
Cold War, 133, 151-153, 159, 178, 238, 251
collapse of the Soviet Union, 89, 161, 164, 184, 238
   causes of, 164, 179, 218
   effects of, 7, 16, 32, 180, 204, 220, 222, 226, 234, 243, 250-251, 254
collective farms, 106, 145, 155, 176-178
collective ownership, 63, 79

collectivization, 104-106, 139, 191, 215, 223, 226-227, 228, 230, 231, 233
Common Market, *See* European Economic Community.
Commonwealth of Independent States (CIS), 162-163, 164, 213
   cities of, 26-27
   climate of, 9-16
   defense of, 242-243
   economic aid to, 249
   economy of, 16-26, 242, 253, 254
   ethnic problems in, 243-244
   foreign relations of, 250-254
   formation of, 229
   geography of, 1-9
   peoples of, 28-34, 213-234
   political structure of, 179-182
   pollution in, 244-248
   relations within, 239-243
   trade with U.S., 251
communes, 63, 215 *See also mir.*
communism, 78-90, 120, 122, 140, 144, 146, 147, 196, 207
   collapse of, 89, 159, 164, 190, 207, 238
   spread of, 113, 127-128, 130, 148
   See also Marxism.
Communist Information Bureau (Cominform), 130
Communist International (Comintern), 121, 130
Communist Manifesto, The, 79-80, 82, 83
Communist party, 33, 86, 109, 110, 139, 140, 142, 156, 158, 159, 161, 164, 168, 171, 172-174, 179, 198, 234
   leadership of, 103, 113, 137, 143, 157, 171, 173
   membership in, 102, 173
   organization of, 121, 172-173
   outside Soviet Union, 149
   privileges in, 142, 145, 174
Communist Party of the Soviet Union (CPSU), *See* Communist party.
Congress of People's Deputies, 157-158, 159, 180, 249
Congress of Vienna, 59
Constantine, 60
Constantinople, 39, 41-43, 47, 61
Constituent Assembly, 98
constitution, Soviet, 169-170
constitutional monarchy, 60
containment, 130-132
Cossacks, 51, 56, 59, 214
Council for Mutual Economic Assistance (COMECON), 132-133
Council of People's Commissars, 97
Crime and Punishment, 193
Crimean Peninsula, 15, 32, 61-62, 219, 241
Crimean Tatars, 243
Crimean War, 61-62

267

269

Photo Acknowledgments: Cover Photo: © Andy Hernandez/SIPA Press; 7, 12, Tass from Sovfoto; 15, Yevgeni Shulepov/Sovfoto; 22, Anatoly Kuzyarin/Tass from Sovfoto; 31, Tass/Sovfoto; 33, S. Metelitsa/Tass from Sovfoto; 43, Tass from Sovfoto; 46, 48, Sovfoto; 49, V. Cheredintsev/Tass from Sovfoto; 51, from *Boris Godounov*, illus. by Boris Zvorykin, copyright © 1982, by Viking Penguin Inc; 52, Historical Pictures Service, Chicago; 54, M. Blokhin/Tass from Sovfoto; 56, Tass from Sovfoto; 62, Novosti from Sovfoto; 64, Tass from Sovfoto; 66, Bettmann Archive; 68, (top) Soviet Life from Sovfoto; (bottom) Sovfoto; 72, © G.D. Hackett, N.Y.; 74, Historical Picture Service, Chicago; 80, Sovfoto; 83, Brown Brothers; 85, Soviet Life from Sovfoto; 86, Sovfoto; 92, © G.D. Hackett, N.Y.; 96, Novosti from Sovfoto; 98, Novosti from Sovfoto; 100, Tass from Sovfoto; 104, Sovfoto; 106, Sovfoto; 111, © G.D. Hackett, N.J.; 112, Novosti from Sovfoto; 120, Alain Nogues/Sygma; 124, Sovfoto; 127, Tass from Sovfoto; 132, Bettmann Archive; 140, Sovfoto; 141, Sovfoto; 142, Sovfoto; 144, Tass from Sovfoto; 150, Bettmann Archive; 152, Wide World Photos; 156, 158, Tass from Sovfoto; 161, Tass from Sovfoto; 164, Shone/Gamma Liaison; 170, Tass from Sovfoto; 171, Y. Yegorov/Tass from Sovfoto; 174, Sovfoto; 178, Sovfoto; 182, Itar-Tass from Sovfoto; 184, Tass from Sovfoto; 189, RIA Novosti/Sovfoto; 193, Novosti from Sovfoto; 195, Sovfoto; 196, Novosti/Sovfoto; 199, 201, Sovfoto; 202, Novosti/Sovfoto; 204, Tass from Sovfoto; 205, Novosti from Sovfoto; 208, 216, Sovfoto; 221, Tass from Sovfoto; 226, Itar-Tass/Sovfoto; 227, 229, 230, 233, Sovfoto; 234, Tass from Sovfoto; 239, Sygma; 241, Andy Hernandez/Sipa Press; 242, Sovfoto; 246, Novosti from Sovfoto; 247, Sovfoto; 253, Tass from Sovfoto.

274